Dream Cruises
of the World

Dream Cruises
of the World

Contents

The snow-white houses of Thira on the Greek island of Santorini look out over the sea below. The climb up to the top of the town from where the cruise ships dock in the port below is long and steep. You may prefer to make one of the patient mules waiting at the waterside do the work instead.

Pages 2–3: Midsummer is a good time to take a Hurtigruten line cruise to Kirknese, in the land of the midnight sun. However, the cruise can be equally spectacular in winter, when the jagged coastline and landscape inland are covered in a thick blanket of snow and ice.

Pages 4–5: The sea around the Canary Islands is very popular for sailing craft. The *Anna Kristina*, an historic sailing ship built in 1889 and her sister ship, Amundsen's *Gjøa*, steer a course through the waters off the coast of Tenerife.

Pages 6–7: A cruise through the Polynesian islands is like sailing through paradise. This liner is cruising past Bora-Bora, one of the Society Islands.

Pages 8–9: The Caribbean is one of the most popular cruise destinations. Modern cruise ships are like floating leisure parks with everything that passengers could possibly require, from stores and boutiques to swimming pools, such as the one here on the MV *Galaxy* in Montego Bay in Jamaica.

Pages 10–11: All the romance of the south as the Mississippi paddle steamer *Delta Queen* passes a riverboat casino in Natchez.

Pages 12–13 Top: Arctic waters are no barrier to strong ships. Here the Russian icebreaker *Kapitan Khlebnikov* anchors between the ice floes in the Beaufort Sea.

Pages 12–13 Bottom: A cruise ship leaves the Balearic island of Ibiza: Phoenician seafarers believed it to be an island of the gods.

Passengers cruising on a ship belonging to the Hurtigruten line will experience the full beauty of the Norwegian fjord coastline. The MS *Nordkapp* (seen here is the ship's bridge) was built in 1996 and boasts impressive lounges offering panoramic views out over the sea and coastline.

Introduction

"Twenty years from now you will be more disappointed by the things that you didn't do than by the ones you did do. So throw off the bowlines. ... Catch the trade winds in your sails. Explore. Dream. Discover".
Mark Twain

Everyone who takes to the water will agree that it is a very special experience, whether on a luxurious cruise ship, a river boat or island-hopping by ferry.
In this book we present eighteen well-researched travel routes. The journeys range from classic cruise routes such as the Northwest Passage, to cruises in the Caribbean and Antarctic, river cruises on the Danube, Nile, and Mississippi, island-hopping in the Aegean Sea or around the islands of the Galápagos.

The routes
Each route begins with an introduction outlining the itinerary, and introducing the region and its scenic, historical, and cultural characteristics. Significant places and landmarks along the route are described, accompanied by ravishing photographs. Each stop along the way is numbered, helping you to trace the route on the map at the end of the chapter. Important information about the journey length, time required, weather and the best time of year to travel, as well as useful addresses, is supplied in the "Travel Information" panel for each route. Interesting aspects of local culture and nature are explained in the separate information panels at the sides of some pages. Highlighted panels also suggest worthwhile short additional excursions that can be taken at certain points during the cruise, should time allow.

Town plans
Major towns along the routes are presented on special spreads, showing a map of the town and giving details of their places of interest.

Tour maps
Specially drawn tour maps at the end of each chapter show the travel route and indicate major places and sights. The main route is always clearly marked and supplemented with a variety of suggestions for interesting short trips and excursions along the way.
The location and type of key sights en route are indicated by symbols, while colour photographs and captions around the edge of the map highlight outstanding places of interest.

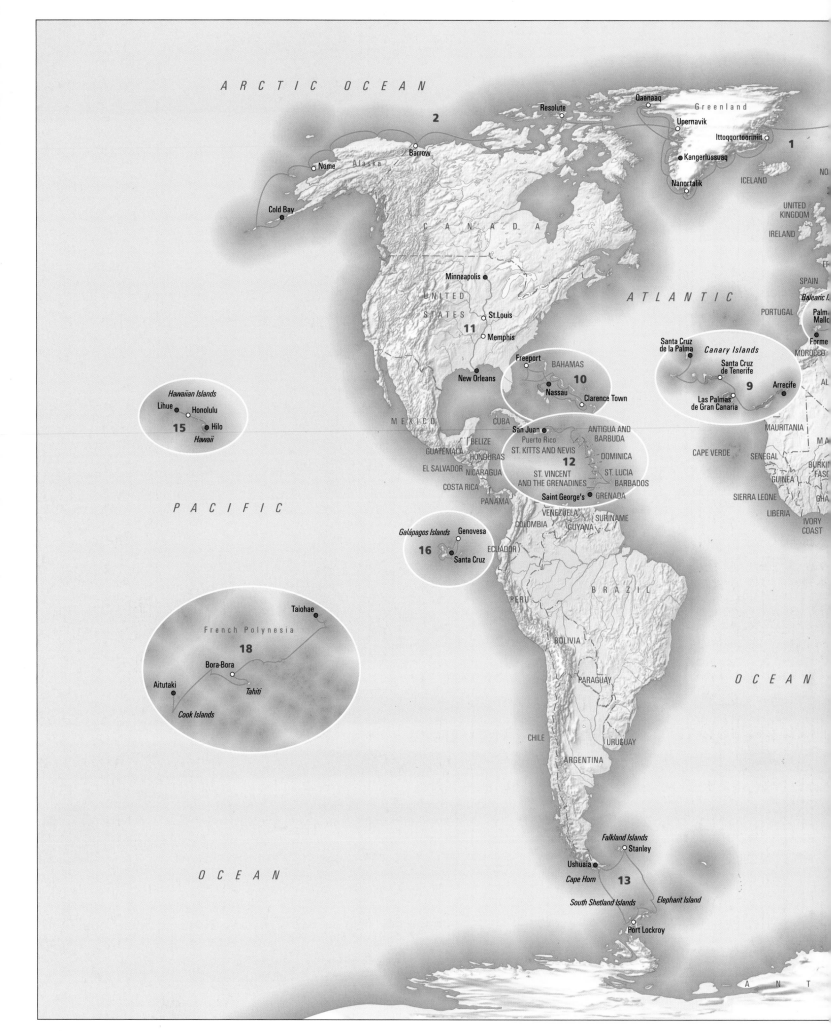

Across the Arctic Ocean

From Svalbard to Greenland

Ice is the dominant feature of the Arctic. It covers most of the sea that surrounds the North Pole, and cloaks the outlying islands. Those small strips of land that manage to break free from the ice for the short duration of the Arctic summer, allowing a sparse life to exist, are few and far between.

As early as AD 985, the Vikings headed north from Iceland to the Greenland coast and established their first settlements there. Accused of murder and exiled from Iceland, Erik the Red was one of the first of the invaders to land on the east coast of Greenland. By the late 12th century, the Vikings had ventured east again and discovered the Svalbard archipelago, lying in the Artic Ocean midway between Norway and the North Pole, but the islands' barrenness discouraged them from settling there. The Viking settlements in Greenland, including the Christian bishops residence at Gardar, survived for a few centuries. It is not clear whether it was famine, disputes with the indigenous Inuit tribes, or disease that finally brought about the demise of the colonists, but by 1550 the settlements had ceased to exist.

From the 16th century, the main motivation for Arctic exploration was to search for a northern route linking Europe and East Asia. The possibilities were the Northwest Passage through North America's Arctic archipelago and the Northeast Passage along Russia's Siberian coast. Both routes were finally established in the 19th century, however they are now relatively unimportant today.

An Inuit wearing a prototype of sunglasses, carved from the ribs of a reindeer.

An iceberg at the mouth of the Scoresby Sund Fjord, on Greenland's east coast.

Young harp seals in their fluffy white juvenile coats. Harp seals live along Greenland's east coast. *Pagophilus groenlandicus* means "ice-loving seal of Greenland" and is the scientific name for the breed.

From the 17th century, the seas around Svalbard and Greenland attracted the interest of whalers. There was a great deal of demand in Europe for whale products at the time: train oil (obtained from blubber, mainly of the right whale species) was used to light lamps, and later in the production of soap, shoe polish, and margarine. Whalebone from the baleen whale was used to make the ribs of umbrellas and corsets. Whalers established many bases along Greenland's west coast, although their relationship with the indigenous population was not always good. Their experiences later proved useful to explorers and missionaries who visited Greenland from 1721. One such was William Scoresby (1789–1857), an English explorer and scientist, and the son of a whaler. Having accompanied his father on several journeys along the coast of Greenland, he sailed there again in 1822 and surveyed and charted some 650 km (400 miles) of jagged coastline with surprising accuracy. He also made detailed and precise notes of the animal and plant life he encountered, and the ruins of some human habitation in north-eastern Greenland.

Explorers were attracted to Svalbard as an easy-to-reach base from which to set off for the North Pole. In the 20th century, the islands played a significant role in research into weather and climate. Since the prevailing conditions resemble those in central Europe during the ice age, studies carried out there are also relevant to the history of the European continent. Svalbard has become a center for scientific research and exploration; over twenty countries, including China and Japan, maintain research stations there.

The cruise ship MS *Hanseatic*, anchored in front of an iceberg near Spitsbergen.

Ny-Ålesund: the northernmost town in the world

Ny-Ålesund is a settlement comprising a number of research stations in the north-west of the island of Spitsbergen. Situated at almost 79° northern latitude, Ny-Ålesund is just 1,200 km (746 miles) from the North Pole. The number of inhabitants here varies greatly. In summer, around 100–150 scientists and technical assistants are based here, but only very few stay in Ny-Ålesund during the winter.

Ny-Ålesund lies on the southern banks of the wide Kongsfjord, which stretches 26 km (16 miles) eastward up to the Kongsvegen glacier. The origins of the settlement date back to 1916, when a mining company opened a coal mine here (this was abandoned, however, in 1929). In the 1920s, Ny-Ålesund became known as the springboard to the North Pole. It was here that polar explorers like Richard E. Byrd, Roald Amundsen, and Umberto Nobile made their last stop before atempting to reach the most northerly point on earth by air.

Top: Spitsbergen is the largest island in the Svalbard ("cold desert") archipelago.
Bottom: Norwegian postal station.

When mining recommenced after World War II, the population became the highest to date with more than two hundred inhabitants. After a serious pit disaster, however, coal mining ceased in 1963.

Scientific research has been undertaken in Ny-Ålesund since 1968. In addition to Norway, the United Kingdom, Germany, France, China, and Japan are all represented with their own research stations. A launch pad for scientific rockets enables exploration of the upper atmosphere to be carried out here, and an ocean laboratory was opened in 2005.

The route takes you through the polar latitudes of the northern hemisphere from Spitsbergen to Kangerlussuaq on Greenland, the largest island on earth. This unique natural space, which seems devoid of human life although it has been settled for thousands of years, is characterized mainly by endless expanses of snow and ice.

❶ Longyearbyen For most visitors to Spitsbergen, Longyearbyen, situated on the southern side of the wide Icefjord, is the entry point to the island world of the Arctic. Planes from Tromsø and Oslo land here, supply ships unload, and cruise ships drop anchor. The settlement, which today totals some 1,800 inhabitants, is the administrative center for Svalbard and is the largest island in the archipelago.

❷ Barentsburg This settlement was named after Dutch explorer Willem Barents, who reached the tip of Spitsbergen's coast in 1596. It is the most important mining center of the whole archipelago. A Russian company mines coal here, which is shipped via the adjacent loading station. The settlement, which snakes up the hilly sides of the fjord in terraces, is almost exclusively inhabited by Russians and Ukrainians but recently it has also become accessible for tourists. It was the Svalbard Treaty of 1920, giving all the nations who signed the treaty the right not just to pursue scientific research on the archipelago, but also to mine its mineral wealth, that has enabled the Russians to establish their presence here.

❸ Ny-Ålesund The journey continues northward along Prins Karls Forland, which rises up to a height of 1,084 m (3,556 ft) and enjoys special protection as the Forlandet National Park, then on to the Kongsfjord and to Ny-Ålesund (see panel, left).

Travel information

Route profile
Length: approx. 9,000 km (5,593 miles)
Duration: min. 6 weeks
Start: Longyearbyen (Spitsbergen)
End: Kangerlussuaq (Greenland)
Itinerary (main locations): Spitsbergen, eastern Greenland, western Greenland

Travel tips
Longyearbyen can be reached by scheduled flight (SAS) from Tromsø (Norway). Circumnavigation of Spitsbergen and the onward voyage to eastern Greenland can only be undertaken on an organized cruise. Although all larger towns in Greenland can be accessed by air, it is advisable to join a cruise to visit the eastern coast; private travel is easier on the west coast where a shipping line visits all the important places between Narsarsuaq and Uummannaq. Year round,

Kangerlussuaq is served by 3–6 and Narsarsuaq by 1–4 flights per week from Copenhagen, and there are direct flights from Baltimore. In summer, flights are available to the east coast (Kulusuk) from Iceland.

When to go
June–August

Accommodation
Larger towns on Greenland have at least one hotel, a youth hostel, or private accommodation. In the south-west, holiday houses can be rented. Camping is possible almost anywhere in Greenland; on Spitsbergen, however, it is only allowed on the campsite at Longyearbyen.

Tourist information
Greenland Tourism
Copenhagen, Strandgade 91, 2 DK-1410 København K.
www.greenland-guide.dk
www.greenland.com

Mining on Spitsbergen

There are several areas containing deposits of coal on the islands. The most productive seams are located in the west of Spitsbergen, embedded in layers of older tertiary rock.

These days the cost of extracting the coal and transporting it are high, making it a less financially viable operation.

The first pits appeared on the Kongsfjord in 1916. In the 1930s, richer deposits were found on the icefjord.

Barentsburg in the south of the icefjord.

Russia has taken advantage of its right to mine coal by operating a mine near Barentsburg. For a time, Barentsburg was the largest settlement on Spitsbergen, accommodating almost 2,000 Russian and Ukrainian inhabitants.

Another important base for coal mining along the icefjord is at Pyramiden, but this was abandoned by the Russian mining company in 2000. Norway also set up a colliery on Spitsbergen, and in the 1980s around 400,000 tons of hard coal a year were mined here.

small island of Lågøya, a popular play area for walruses, which are easy to spot here.

⑤ Vibebukta/Nordaustlandet Via the Straits of Hinlopen, which separate the island of Spitsbergen from Nordaustlandet, the journey continues southward. The narrow straits are frequently blocked by ice, however. The current pushes the drift ice together and piles it up, creating barriers that are impassable. The passage will not normally be free again until July. Look out for polar bears. It is not unusual to see them crossing the drift ice or swimming in the water.

(continued p.26)

1 Walruses on an ice floe; the colossal animals, weighing up to 1,500 kg (3,308 lbs), often use their tusks to drag themselves over the edge of the ice sheet.

2 A sailing boat in the Forlandsundet has dropped anchor in the calm and sluggish salty ice water.

④ Lågøya From the Kongsfjord the voyage continues past the small Moffen Island, known for its large population of walruses. The ocean is often covered with drift ice here, and occasionally the pack ice also stretches as far south as the north of Spitsbergen. When this happens, only icebreakers can force a passage through.

Before long, you reach the island of Nordaustlandet, the second largest island in the Svalbard group. This uninhabited island is protected as a nature reserve. During World War II, the German navy operated a weather station on Nordaustlandet, on the Rijpfjord. Just offshore to the north is the

A curious polar bear peeks into the porthole of a cruise ship. Polar bears are one of the greatest attractions on a Spitsbergen cruise. Nowhere else on earth is it possible to observe and photograph bears in the wild as easily as on a voyage through the drift ice of the fjords and sunds. Seals are the most important

food for polar bears, which have a well-developed sense of smell and can track down seals over a distance of more than 1 km (1,000 yds) or beneath a 1-m (3-ft) thick ice sheet. They often wait at the seals' breathing holes and attack at lightning speed once the seal surfaces.

Arctic wildlife

The inhospitable climate and the sparse supply of foodstuffs are the main reasons for the lack of diversity of wildlife species in the Arctic. In the lakes and ponds of the tundra, the larvae of mosquitoes and small flies flourish; they are the main food for many types of bird, such as the meadow pipit and the pied wagtail. Lemmings and voles live in the tundra in large numbers. Among the larger mammals are the wolf, Arctic fox, and snow hare. Reindeer live on Spitsbergen and Greenland but mainly due to human intervention. Even the presence of musk oxen here is partially due to human introduction.

Top: The polar bear, king of the Arctic.
Middle: Bearded seals live in drift ice areas around the Arctic.
Bottom: An inquisitive Arctic fox.

At the top of the food chain in the Arctic stands the polar bear. It inhabits the shore area, the pack ice belt, and the drift ice, where it preys on its main food source, seals. A skilled diver, it even hunts these animals in the water beneath the ice sheet.
Aside from numerous species of fish and whales, seals are the most common animals in the Arctic Ocean. With its moustache and huge canine teeth, the most impressive type of seal is the walrus. It is, however, present in only a few places along the western and eastern shores of Greenland.

The journey along the southern coast is equally impressive, passing a mighty ice cap which conceals large parts of the island. Unlike most other glacial regions, where valley glaciers predominate, the ice on Nordaustlandet moves over the land beneath it in exactly the same way as the mighty Greenland ice sheet. Although a distinction is made between the southern (Sørfonna) and eastern (Austfonna) ice sheets, the two seem to merge into each other without any visible boundaries.
Videbukt in the south of Nordaustlandet, is a popular anchoring place for cruise ships. If you go ashore here, you can admire the fantastic ice formations close up. Only a small stretch of the coast is free from ice.

6 Hornsund The voyage continues through the narrow straits of the Ginevrabotn to Hornsund fjord. After cruising round the southern tip of Spitsbergen, the entrance to the fjord, which spreads out like the fingers on a hand, soon becomes visible. Several glaciers end in this inlet framed by high peaks, such as the Hornsundtind that rises to 1,431 m (4,695 ft). Polar bears are no strangers to this part of the island, but never try to approach them as they are extremely unpredictable and dangerous.

7 Myggbukta The cruise now proceeds from the Hornsund through the icy North Atlantic to the east coast of Greenland, the largest island on earth. The 900-km (560-mile) voyage across the Greenland Sea, which reaches depths of 4,000 m (13,124 ft), takes a whole day. Even when you reach it, you cannot actually see the coastline as it is cloaked in dense belt of pack ice and getting in close is out of the question. Danmarkshavn, the most northerly of the manned weather stations on the Germanialand peninsula, juts out far toward the east; only for a few weeks in the year can a supply ship put into port here.
A small company of Danish special forces and a dog sled unit are based at Daneborg and patrol the Northeast Greenland National Park from here. The park was originally created in 1974 and was designated an international biosphere reserve

in 1977. It covers virtually a quarter of Greenland and its coastline. Only in Foster Bay, to the south, does the pack ice show sufficiently large gaps in summer to ensure a safe passage. This is usually the most northerly point for cruise ships to drop anchor, giving tourists the opportunity to step onto Greenland soil for the first time. Depending on the weather, it is possible to go on a short hike to the refuge hut of Myggbukta (which has been suitably equipped as a precaution). The area around Foster Bay is part of the national park, which encompasses the entire northeast of Greenland. At an area of some 970,000 sq km (374,420 sq miles), it is the largest national park in the world. Anyone wishing to explore this virgin territory, however, will not get very far without specialist equipment for polar expeditions. In addition, a special administrative permit is required.

8 Kaiser Franz Joseph Fjord One of the special experiences on a Greenland cruise is sailing into the Kaiser Franz Joseph Fjord with its steeply rising rock walls. Many of the surrounding peaks, such as the Angelin Bjerg on Ymer Island, reach heights of between 1,500 and 2,000 m (4,922 and 6,562 ft). The many-branched fjord is linked with King Oscar Fjord to the south. Musk oxen live on these islands. A large number of these giant animals, which are actually related to sheep and not cattle, are found on the island of Traill.

9 Ittoqqortoormiit (Scoresby Sund) The most northerly continuously populated region in eastern Greenland lies on the Scoresby Sund. The bay is some 40–50 km (25–31 miles) wide, more than 700 m (2,300 ft) deep, and offers a safe anchorage even for larger ships. The mouth of the vast fjord is navi-

gable in winter as well, while the side fjords are often covered in ice. The old name refers to the scientist and explorer William Scoresby, who in 1822 became the first European to reach this coast. In the language of the Inuit, the fjord is known as Kangertittivag.

Beyond the Arctic Circle, the area on the northern shores of the Scoresby Sund has the largest Inuit settlement in eastern Greenland. The village of Ittoqqortoormiit (Scoresby Sund) lies right at the mouth of the fjord; a further settlement, Cape Hope or Ittaajimmiit, lies only 20 km (12 miles) to the west at the mouth of a side fjord.

The present population is descended from a group who arrived on a resettlement program during the 1920s; because hunting and fishing in the south of the eastern coastline no longer yielded sufficient food to ensure a traditionally based exis-

tence for the Inuit, they were resettled by the Danish government on the Scoresby Sund.

The climate is relatively mild for eastern Greenland (8°C/46.4°F average July temperature), allowing a rich vegetation to flourish, including mosses and lichens and even flowers and small shrubs. The Scoresby Sund is sometimes even known as the "Artic Riviera" though this is stretching the truth just a little. There are regular flight connections with the settlements in the south and along the west coast of Greenland. A special attraction for tourists are the journeys by dog sleds, which are possible throughout winter and right up to the early summer.

⑩ **Kangalussuaq** From the Nansen Fjord an impressive vista of the Watkin Bjerg unfolds. At a height of 3,700 m (12,140 ft) the highest peak in Greenland towers above the

Gunnbjørn Fjeld. The glaciers emanating from here flow directly into the fjord, which is named after the Norwegian Arctic explorer Fridtjof Nansen. In 1888, Nansen was the first to traverse Greenland's inland ice sheet by sled from east to west. The entrance to the Kangalussuaq Fjord, which is approximately 70 km (43 miles) long and borders the Gunnbjørn Fjeld in the south-west, offers superb views of the precipitous rocky landscape. Polar bears are the largest creatures that inhabit these regions. In summer, Inuit come here to hunt and there are a few huts which serve as accommodation for them.

⑪ **Tasiilaq** Tasiilaq is not only the name of a rugged island, rising to a height of 1,326 m (4,351 ft), but also of eastern Greenland's southernmost community, whose boundaries encircle an area of some 250,000 sq km

(96,500 sq miles), six times the size of Switzerland. The main village in the larger community was once called Angmagsalik or Ammassalik, but is today known by the name of Tasiilaq (about 1,850 inhabitants). Kummiut, Kulusuk, Tineteqilaaq, Sermiligaaq, and Isertoq, with a combined total of 1,166 inhabitants, also belong to the larger community of Tasiilaq.

If normal ice conditions prevail, even larger ships can put into the Tasiilaqfjord during the summer months, from June to October.

The airport at Kulusuk, where between 1959 and 1991 the USA operated a radar station, has regular flights from Iceland during the summer. Internal flights link the community with Kangerlussuaq, Greenland's central airport, which has connecting flights to Copenhagen. The main town of Tasiilaq can easily be reached in only a few

minutes by helicopter from Kulusuk.

The oldest traces of human life in this region date back about 4,500 years. It appears, however, that these early inhabitants were only able to withstand the harshness of the living conditions and the severity of the climate for a few generations. The ancestors of the present population arrived very much later in the coastal region. Ammassalik, or Tasiilaq, was founded in 1894 as a trading and mission station.

Tasiilaq is framed by high mountains; its scattered houses, mostly painted in bright hues, climb up the hillsides and are reflected in the bay, which is generously sprinkled with ice floes, making this one of the most attractive villages on the east coast. A walk full of surprises takes you into the nearby Blomsterdal valley, a popular leisure resort with lakes that in summer are even used for swimming by some of the Inuit.

(continued p.30)

1 Spitsbergen, Magdalen Bay.

2 Narwhals in an ice stream; only the males have tusks.

3 Raudfjord on Spitsbergen in the light of the midnight sun.

4 Icebergs and pack ice in the North Polar Sea.

The Greenland whale is a giant among marine creatures. It can grow to a length of 18 m (59 ft) or more and its tail fin alone can be up to 8 m (26 ft) wide. Its vast mouth gives it an awesome appearance, but in fact it has no teeth and uses its bone plate (baleen) to sift its food, minute marine creatures, from

the water. The Greenland whale is perfectly happy underwater, but from time to time it has to surface in order to fill its lungs with air. Making it easy for whalers to track down their prey, this has been the undoing of many a whale. Since 1946, the Greenland whale has been protected by law.

Hunting, Inuit style

There are still some Inuit on Greenland who have remained faithful to their traditional lifestyle and live predominantly from fishing and hunting. They hunt marine animals, especially seals, but also walruses and whales. The hunt on land is less important in terms of food supply, but it serves to provide fur from polar bears, Arctic foxes, and snow hares. In order to hunt large game, several hunters will band together in a larger group and go out for several days. They use mostly dog sleds to transport them across the snow of the mainland and on the ice sheet, while they use kayaks or *umiak* on the water.

Top: Narwhals are easy to hunt in readily maneuverable kayaks.
Middle: An Inuit team leader at the back of the sled.
Bottom: Hunting birds with a fishing net.

Kayaks are lightweight hunting boats consisting of a solid framework (made from wood or bones) covered with seal skin. If a seal skin apron is secured firmly around the waist of the kayaker, water cannot get into the boat. The *umiak* is built in a similar fashion but is considerably larger and open at the top. It can hold several seal hunters. In the past, every part of the hunted animal was used and transformed into a multitude of useful objects.

12 Nanortalik At Cape Farvel we reach the most southerly point on Greenland. Several settlements were established on the initiative of missionaries on land surrounding the adjacent fjords and on the rocky offshore islands, mostly in the 19th century. Up until this time, the local Inuit population had never lived in large settlements or towns. The main village in the region, and the most important anchorage, is Nanortalik, which was founded in around 1830. As elsewhere on Greenland, seal-hunting and fishing play an important role in the local people's survival.

Surprisingly, this is a good place for a northerly "country" walk. The mild climate here enables willow shrubs to grow to some 300–500 m (984–1640 ft) and there is even the odd tree surviving in particularly sheltered spots, such as the Kangikitsoq Fjord.

Narsarsuaq, situated at the northern end of a long fjord, has an airport and is the ideal starting point for an excursion to the former Viking settlement of Gardar. After a boat trip across the fjord, a short walk takes you to the 12th century ruins of Gardar, near Igaliku, the residence of the first Christian bishop in Greenland. The foundations of the cathedral

church, erected around 1200, are still visible today. The Vikings, who came to Greenland in the tenth century, made the "green land" their new home. Aside from nearby Brattahild, the area around Igaliku was their most important settlement. The Viking farmstead of Herjolfsnes, as well as the remains of numerous other buildings, have also been excavated. They provide evidence of the flourishing wealth of the settlement.

13 Nuuk (Danish Godthåb) Greenland's capital city was founded in 1721 and moved to its present location on a rocky peninsula seven years later. Now numbering nearly 15,000 inhabitants, the city has changed its appearance considerably over the last fifty years or so, with the building of huge apartment blocks, high-rise office blocks, and supermarkets. All Greenland's important institutions have their offices here: parliament and local

government, the radio station, and the university, as well as the country's largest hospital. The enormous apartment blocks, which were built in the 1960s, were supplemented by more appealing examples of modern architecture, such as the cultural center Katuaq. Away from the business center, older and smaller buildings can still be found, painted in red or yellow. The Church of the Redeemer (1849) stands here, commemorating the city's founding

father, the Norwegian mission-ary Hans Egede.

14 Sisimiut With around 5,200 inhabitants, Sisimiut, also known by its Danish name of Holsteinsborg, is the largest town in Greenland north of the Arctic Circle. It is the center for the import, processing, and export of the much sought-after Greenland shrimp. The town was founded in 1724 by Hans Egede and as such is one of the earliest settlements in the country, although there were whalers' bases in the area even before this.

15 Uummannaq This village is situated in a fjord of the same name on an island surrounded by many others whose peaks rise to a height of well over 1,000 m (3,281 ft). The region enjoys a sunny, dry climate and offers many opportunities for walking and kayaking. The edges of the inland ice sheet are not far away.

1 The cruise ship MS *Clipper Adventurer* passes an iceberg on Greenland's west coast.

2 Icebergs near Tasiilaq Island.

3 Eye-catching log cabins in Nuuk.

Dog sleds

In winter, dog sleds are still an indispensable means of transportation in the north of Greenland. No other transport method has proven itself so well suited to the rough terrain. The sleds were originally made from walrus teeth or animal bone; iron runners only came into use after the first contact with Europeans.

Inuit with a dog sled.

The famous sled dogs, which work in teams of several animals are extremely hardy. They can reach speeds of around 30 km/h (20 mph), while average travel speeds are around 12–15 km/h (7–9 mph). It is not unusual for them to cover distances of up to 70 km (43 miles) a day. The sleds often carry loads of 300–400 kg (660–882 lbs). When there is an incline, however, passengers have to get off and walk next to the sled or help push.

16 Uummannaq (Dundas) The northern section of Greenland's west coast is navigable for ships only for a short period in summer because of the long duration of the ice drift. Cape York, the trading station for hunting equipment, was founded in 1910 and was then known as Thule.

The USA initially set up a weather station here during World War II, and in 1946 they added a landing strip for their air force. Further expansion of the base severely affected the traditional lifestyle of the Inuit. They were no longer able to hunt and finally had to abandon their ancestral lands. During the Cold War, several thousand US soldiers served at this military base.

17 Qaanaaq Lying some 80 km (50 miles) north of Uummannaq, this small village totals around 600 inhabitants and was founded in the 1950s, when the Inuit had to abandon their territories around the military air base of Thule.

The village is situated on the northern shore of a wide fjord that cuts deeply inland. Whether it can be reached by ship depends on the depth of the ice cover on the sea. Qaanaaq is not only the most populous village in the north of Greenland, it is also the largest community in terms of the area it covers. The com- mune of Qaanaaq comprises an area about eight times the size of Belgium. The inhabitants of Qaanaaq are Inughuit, an inde- pendent tribe of Inuit with a sep- arate language. Fishing and hunting on land and at sea are the cornerstones of their exis- tence.

Another village within the com- munity, Siorapaluk, situated about 50 km (31 miles) north- west, has around 70 inhabitants. Cruises usually end their north- ward journeys here because of the increasingly thick ice cover on the ocean.

18 Ilulissat Ilulissat (Danish Jakobshavn) is one of the most visited tourist destinations in Greenland. The name of the set- tlement means "icebergs" and, indeed, the icebergs that drift in large numbers across the fjord in the Disko Bay area make for an impressive backdrop. Depending on the angle at which they are seen, it might appear that the entire fjord is covered in ice, but on closer inspection the blue waters of the fjord can be seen shimmering between the white giants.

These vast masses of ice originate in Sermeq Kujalleq, an outlet gla- cier fed by the inland ice sheet. The pressure on the ice here is so strong that the glacier is forced to flow into the fjord at a rate of up to 22 m (72 ft) a day. Every few weeks, the glacier calves and vast chunks of ice break away. The huge icebergs, often hundreds of feet high, drift off slowly towards Disko Bay. As the fjord is less deep there, the icebergs start to pile up and can only pass the barrier once they have broken up into smaller pieces. Watching the ice- bergs calve and following their journey through the fjord is cer- tainly one of the highlights of a Greenland cruise.

19 Kangerlussuaq For many vis- itors who arrive by plane, the entry point into Greenland is this village, which lies in a sheltered spot in a wide valley that is the continuation of the 170-km (106- mile) long Kangerlussuaq Fjord. The village was founded in 1941 as a transatlantic stopping point for the military. Since the late 1960s the town has become Greenland's most important transport hub. From here, a chal- lenging long-distance path leads to the edge of the inland ice sheet.

1 A herd of musk oxen at Kangerlussuaq.

2 The high art of navigation: ice- bergs are treacherous because they are usually very much larger under- neath the water surface.

3 Dried cod in Ilulissat.

Ny-Ålesund This collection of Arctic research stations at the Kongsfjord in the north-west of Spitsbergen is the most northerly settlement in the world.

Lågøya This small island in north Spitsbergen is the ideal spot for walrus watching … but only from a safe distance. They may look as though they can't move fast, but they are unexpectedly nimble and dangerous!

Forlandsundet The bay is free from ice only during summer. The mountains either side of the straits between Barentsburg and Ny-Ålesund rise to a height of 900 m (2,953 ft).

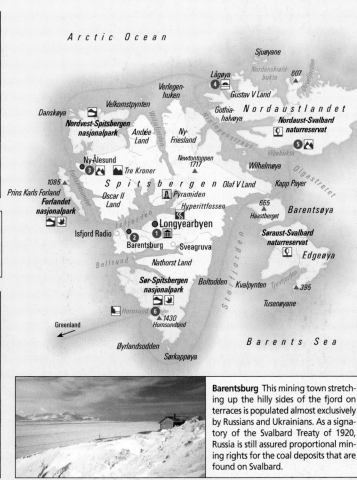

Longyearbyen Spitsbergen's capital is situated on the wide icefjord and is the entry point for many tourists and polar expeditions. Shown here is the island of Nordenskjoeld near Longyearbyen.

Hornsund Mighty peaks, some of which reach heights of more than 1,400 m (4,593 ft), line the fjord, which fans out like the fingers of a hand. Several glaciers feed into it. Cruise ships are frequently seen here during the short Nordic summer.

Barentsburg This mining town stretching up the hilly sides of the fjord on terraces is populated almost exclusively by Russians and Ukrainians. As a signatory of the Svalbard Treaty of 1920, Russia is still assured proportional mining rights for the coal deposits that are found on Svalbard.

Uummannaq The island town in the fjord of the same name, where drifting icebergs can often be seen, is surrounded by peaks rising to 1,000 m (3,281 ft). The climate is dry and sunny, making it ideally suited for outdoor activities.

Ilulissat The Ilulissat (Jakobshavn in Danish) icefjord attracts large numbers of visitors who come to see the icebergs and the Kujalleq glacier that feeds into the sea here.

Nuuk The capital of the largest island in the world, known as Godthåb in Danish (1721), has around 15,000 inhabitants. Practically all Greenland's important institutions have their headquarters in mostly modern, purpose-built office blocks, erected in the 1950s. Traditional old buildings have become a rare sight.

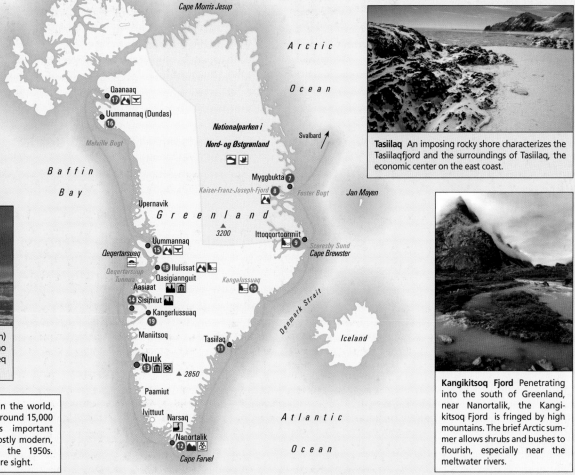

Tasiilaq An imposing rocky shore characterizes the Tasiilaqfjord and the surroundings of Tasiilaq, the economic center on the east coast.

Kangikitsoq Fjord Penetrating into the south of Greenland, near Nanortalik, the Kangikitsoq Fjord is fringed by high mountains. The brief Arctic summer allows shrubs and bushes to flourish, especially near the meltwater rivers.

The Northwest Passage

Through the North American Arctic

The navigation of the Northwest Passage cost the lives of many sailors and Arctic explorers and is still a fascinating adventure today. This legendary sea route along North America's coastline leads through fields of sea ice, pack ice, and icebergs on its way from the Atlantic to the Pacific.

Soon after the discovery of America by Christopher Columbus in the late 15th century, seafarers were already boldly making their first attempts to sail northward around the New World in search of a sea route to East Asia. At the beginning of the 16th century, in appalling conditions, explorers like Gaspar Corte-Real and Sebastian Cabot reached the islands of the Canadian archipelago. However, all attempts to find a route through the maze of narrow sounds and fjords failed, the way often blocked by impregnable pack ice; yet even the ill-fated 19th-century expedition led by English explorer John

Franklin, which cost the lives of the whole crew, did not discourage others from making further attempts. The subsequent decade-long search for Franklin's missing expedition contributed considerably to what was known about the Far North.

The first person to prove the existence of the Northwest Passage was Norwegian explorer Roald Amundsen. With just a tiny ship and a small crew he successfully navigated the northern coast of the American continent between 1903 and 1906. However, the conquering of the passage, during which Amundsen and his crew spent two winters stuck in the ice,

A young Inuit from Victoria Island.

did little to lessen its dangers. It was not until 1942 that a second expedition, led by Henry Larsen, an officer of the Royal Canadian Mounted Police (RCMP), aboard the *St Roch*, succeeded in navigating the route, this time in the opposite direction, sailing from west to east. Nowadays, modern technology and navigational aids allow a safe passage, though only for a few weeks each year, and even then there is no guarantee that it will be possible to follow the planned route. The first voyage with a cruise ship took place in 1984.

The Northwest Passage has never become important commercially because its navigation is still difficult and plagued by uncertainty today, although use of the passage has become a necessity for the mining industry, which exploits many of the natural resources that are found in

The 1,800-km (1,200-mile) Iditarod dogsled race takes place in Alaska every year.

Huge icebergs float south from Disko Bay. Around nine-tenths of the ice mass is hidden underwater.

the Canadian Arctic. Even so, the number of mining companies using the passage is limited to isolated examples, such as the Polaris Mine on Bathurst Island, where lead and zinc ore are extracted. In contrast, the oil from the Prudhoe Bay oilfield is transported by pipeline.

For people in the far-flung settlements of the North, the arrival of a ship is a special event; but although there are no roads to connect the region to southern Canada, the settlements are no longer as cut off from the rest of the world as you might expect. Almost all research stations and Inuit settlements are within reach of South Canada by air. It is true that modern technology has helped make life and travel in the Arctic easier, but the magic of the landscape, the solitude, and the peace remain undisturbed. It is not just the sparkling surface of the sea ice in the estuaries and fjords, the strangely shaped icebergs, and the towering pack ice that make this place so fascinating and beautiful, the tundra also blazes with bright hues during its short flowering season. The play of shades from violet to pale pink across the night sky is also an incredible sight. As the nights grow longer and darker, the haunting glow of the Northern Lights appears: flickering shards of light filling the sky.

Even today, despite all the recent technological advances, life in the far north remains indisputably hard. The biggest challenge of all is the inhospitable climate. In winter, temperatures can be expected to drop to around -40°C (-40°F) or lower, and even in May, when the sun reaches a higher point in the sky, the thermometer only just manages to struggle above freezing.

A snowy owl in its ground nest watches over its numerous offspring.

Roald Amundsen

In 1903, the Norwegian polar explorer Roald Amundsen (1872–1928) set sail with a six-man crew with the aim of navigating the Northwest Passage. His

Conqueror of the Northwest Passage.

ship, the *Gjøa*, was a modified fishing vessel of just 47 tonnes (52 tons). When he reached Herschel Island in 1905, the passage had finally been conquered. Amundsen was also first to reach the South Pole, in 1911. He died in 1928 when his plane crashed while on a rescue mission to find fellow Arctic explorer Umberto Nobile.

The cruise begins in Greenland and crosses the Canadian Arctic to the point where the Norwegian explorer Roald Amundsen began his successful navigation of the Northwest Passage. It then continues to Alaska and ends in the Aleutian Islands on the border with Russia.

❶ Kangerlussuaq This town has the largest airport in Greenland and is the arrival point for most visitors. The cruise through the islands of the Arctic departs from the Kangerlussuaq Fjord, which is approximately 170 km (106 miles) long. The route then passes numerous glaciers that drop abruptly and steeply into the estuary. Extending from the Greenland Ice Cap, they cut deep into the rock, carving out a path into the fjord.

❷ Sisimiut When open sea is reached at the mouth of the fjord, the route follows the rocky coast northward. After crossing the Arctic Circle, the small town of Sisimiut soon comes into view. The fish factory and cold-storage buildings around the port leave you with little doubt as to how the local population earns its living. A particular export are the

highly sought-after Greenland crabs, which are sold to countries all over the world. Back in the 18th century, Dutch whalers established a base here, as did the Danish missionary Hans Egede, in 1724. The current settlement, originally named Holsteinsborg, was founded four decades later under the patronage of Count Ludwig Holstein. Living in an urban environment necessitated a big lifestyle change for the local Inuit population, but nowadays most enjoy the comforts that modern life brings.

❸ Ilulissat Previously known by its Danish name of Jakobshavn (Jacob's Harbor), this settlement, the third largest in Greenland, is one of its most popular tourist destinations. Ilulissat (meaning "the icebergs" in Inuit) is a very appropriate name as the surrounding landscape is dominated

Fishing off Greenland

The sea off the west coast of Greenland has the highest proportion of fish in the entire North Atlantic. Fishing is carried out from all the towns along the coast, with the main center in the region around Disko Island and the adjacent Disko Bay in the south. Whaling was previously carried out here, notably by the Dutch, but is no longer of economic significance, un-

Above: Fishing boat in Disko Bay.
Below: Crabbing in Sisimiut.

like crabbing which has become increasingly important. The rich stocks of Greenland deep-sea shrimp in Disko Bay today are also a mainstay of the local economy. Traditional fishing methods are still used alongside the more modern. The Inuit venture far out to sea in their boats, which include sea kayaks. The kayaks may be small but they are extremely versatile, robustly made with frames originally of whalebone but now also of wood, and covered in seal skin. The *umiak* (meaning "women's boat" and kayak means "men's boat") has a similar construction, but is larger and more open.

local wildlife: the tundra landscape of the Svartenhuken Peninsula is home to herds of reindeer and musk ox. The landscape to the north of Upernavik is even wilder, with a glacier flowing directly into the sea.

For the people of Upernavik, the sea is the basis of their existence, and even today most families still earn their living from fishing and seal-hunting. The most northerly open-air museum in the world has been set up in the buildings of the former Upernavik trading post to inform visitors about the development of the town and the traditional life of the Inuit people.

5 Pond Inlet The route now leads through the narrow Pond Inlet to the settlement of the same name in the north of Baffin Island. Here, in Eclipse Sound, the route enters Canadian territory for the first time. Founded just a few decades ago and named
(continued p.40)

1 Icebergs off western Greenland.

2 Glaciers in the Ilulissat Fjord.

by these white giants, floating slowly from the fjord into Disko Bay. The Greenland Ice Cap, up to 3 km (2 miles) deep in places, ensures a steady supply of ice. Propelled by the force of its own weight, the ice cap glides into the fjord via one of its many outlet glaciers. When the ice reaches the

open water of the bay it breaks up, forming icebergs.

4 Upernavik The municipality of Upernavik (Springtime Place) is made up of several small groups of buildings hugging the jagged cliffs of Greenland's north-west coast, and has a total of around

three thousand inhabitants. The main settlement, with around a thousand inhabitants, is located on one of the many small rocky islands off this part of the coast. The area around Upernavik, especially the nesting cliffs of Apparsuit, offer an excellent opportunity for watching the

Walruses are the largest species of seal in the northern hemisphere. They inhabit the waters of the Eastern Canadian Arctic and Northern Greenland. These giant semi-aquatic mammals do not eat fish but dive for mollusks which they dig out from the sea bed with their canine teeth, and then suck

out the meat, pressing on the shell with their powerful upper lip. They also forage for starfish, sea urchins, and worms on the sea floor. Their tusks can grow

after an English astronomer, Mittimatalik means "the place where Mitima is buried" and is Pont Inlet's Inuit name; Inuit form the majority of the 1,300 inhabitants. A whaling station was established here at the beginning of the 20th century but abandoned after just a few years.

Despite the inhospitable climate, people have been living in the region around Pond Inlet for at least four thousand years. Archeologists have found evidence in the area of both the Dorset culture and the later Thule people, who were the ancestors of the modern Canadian Inuit. In 1929, two missions, Anglican and Catholic, were established in the settlement to foster and support Christianity in the region.

As with most of the settlements in the Arctic, the scattered buildings of Pond Inlet are plain and functional, with little architectural charm. However, this simplicity only serves to make the location of the settlement, with its spectacular mountain backdrop, all the more impressive. To the south, the peaks climb to over 1,500 m (4,922 ft), while to the north, on the towering Bylot Island, the peaks are just as steep and even higher at over 2,000 m (6,562 ft). Pond Inlet is the source of several vast glaciers, which surge inexorably toward the sea. Both Eclipse Sound and the nearby Pond Inlet, which sepa-

rates Bylot from Baffin Island, are littered with icebergs and sea ice even during the summer months. It is not only the views of this Arctic landscape that will fascinate you, the wildlife of the estuaries is also captivating. Beluga, narwhals, and occasionally even Greenland whales can be seen in the waters nearby, and sperm whales and orcas are also sighted occasionally. Other marine mammals worth looking out for include walrus and various types of seal, including the ringed seal.

Most of Bylot Island is within Sirmilik National Park, one of Canada's newest national parks, established in 1999. The island is well-known as a bird sanctuary: hundreds of thousands of thick-billed murres and black-legged kittiwakes nest on its cliffs, and there is also a large population of greater snow geese. Bird- and whale-watching excursions leave from Pond Inlet and boat tours for anglers are also on offer, as well as trips by snowmobile and dogsled during the spring. You can learn more about the bird sanctuary on Bylot and the Sirmilik National Park at the Nattinak Visitor's Centre in Pond Inlet.

6 Dundas Harbour The route continues along the rocky west coast of Bylot Island through the narrow Navy Board Inlet to the north of Lancaster Sound,

the 80-km (50-mile) wide main entry point to the Northwest Passage. The channels of the passage rarely exceed 300 m (984 ft) in depth, so at a depth of over 1,000 m (3,281 ft) this represents the deepest section of the route. A little further on you reach Dundas Harbour, located at a northerly latitude of nearly 75° on the south-east coast of Devon Island, the largest uninhabited island in the world. The RCMP opened up an outpost here in 1924 as part of a government move to curb foreign activity, including whaling, but abandoned it in 1932. Inuit families were relocated to the island in

1934, but although they chose to leave in 1936, finding the conditions too harsh, sovereign rights to Dundas Harbour are still disputed to this day. The area to the north of Dundas Harbour reaches altitudes of 1,900 m (6,234 ft) and is completely covered by glaciers. Prehistoric finds dating back to the Dorset and Thule cultures have been discovered in the coastal region, proving that it has been inhabited for thousands of years.

Dundas Harbour is the ideal place to learn about Arctic wildlife. Walruses and seals on the coast and musk ox on the land make for impressive photo

opportunities. It might be a good idea, however, not to get too closely acquainted with the polar bears that also live here, though these dangerous predators are rarely seen on land as most of their prey lives on the ice.

7 Beechey Island This island, in Wellington Channel, was discovered in 1819 by the English seafarer William Edward Parry and named after Frederick William Beechey, an officer from Parry's crew. Beechey Island played an important role in the history of exploration in the Canadian Arctic. In 1845, the polar explorer John Franklin thought the

island's protected port would be a good place to anchor his ship for the first winter of his expedition, but it ended in tragedy. When rescuers arrived in 1851 they discovered the graves of three crew members marked with stones but no clue as to the fate of the remaining crew.

In the 1980s, the remains of the three men, which were well-preserved in the permafrost, were exhumed and scientifically examined. It emerged that the men had probably died of lead poisoning: the cans of food that they lived off for months on end had been poorly soldered with lead. Evidence of lung disease was found too, which also could have proved fatal.

In 1979, Beechey Island was declared a site of territorial historical significance by the government of the Northwest Territories. Today, like most of Northeast Canada, it belongs to the territory of Nunavut, formed in 1999. The graves of the three sailors are still a special point of interest for visitors to the Arctic.

⑧ **Resolute** Located on Cornwallis Island at the northern end of Resolute Bay, the so-called "hamlet" of Resolute is one of the most northerly settlements on earth and has around 250 inhabitants, the majority Inuit. Despite the small size of the settlement, its airport is big enough to cater for large planes and acts as an important hub for air traffic in the Canadian Arctic.

Resolute is a reminder to visitors of how difficult life was in the region before the Northwest Passage was finally opened. The town is named after HMS *Resolute*, one of the many ships that took part in the search for the missing Franklin expedition. The *Resolute* was locked in the ice for two winters; in order to avoid a third winter of darkness and cold, Captain Belcher took the decision to abandon ship and the crew returned to England aboard a rescue ship. The *Resolute* was found in good condition by American whalers in 1855 and freed from the pack ice.

The hamlet of Resolute is important as a location for weather and research stations. The Canadian government assumed control of the original Inuit settlement only in the 1950s and 1960s. Today, Inuits live alongside scientists and engineers in the hamlet, and can still hunt according to their traditions.

During the 1960s and 1970s, the Magnetic North Pole was located on the nearby Bathurst Island, only 150 km (93 miles) to 200 km (124 miles) west of Resolute. This made the town an excellent base for research teams investigating the earth's magnetic field. Since then, the magnetic pole has moved north beyond the latitude of 80°.

1 Nomadic polar bears searching for prey.

2 A dogsled team in the Arctic ice desert.

3 A big event for the whole village: cutting up a Beluga whale.

4 An Inuit fishing in the ice.

Captain Scott

The English naval officer Robert Falcon Scott (1868–1912) was Amundsen's greatest rival in the race to the South Pole and led a successful British expedition into Antarctic waters between

Discovery Hut, built by Scott's 1901–1904 expedition, at Hut Point.

1901 and 1904. His second expedition, however, which began in 1910, ended tragically. In order to reach the South Pole, the main goal of the expedition, he used ponies and dogs to haul the sleds, unlike Amundsen, who used only dogs. The ponies died in the cold, slowing Scott down, and he finally reached the Pole in January 1912 only to find that Amundsen had already arrived a month earlier. Scott and his men died in the terrible conditions on the return journey to the coast. They were found six months later just 20 km (12 miles) from their supply depot.

Despite this, weather stations and geophysical research facilities continue to be located in Resolute, which is now also the starting point for both the biennial Polar Race and the annual Polar Challenge, in which teams race to the Magnetic North Pole. Resolute also gained importance as the transport and provisions base for the Polaris Mine on Bathurst Island, for a time the most northerly ore mine in the world. Non-ferrous metals such as lead and zinc were extracted here until the mine became nonprofitable and closed in 2003.

9 Franklin Strait This strait is named after the explorer John Franklin (see page 34), who led an expedition into the islands of the Canadian Arctic in 1845 while attempting to prove the existence of a sea passage between the Atlantic and the Pacific. His ships, HMS *Erebus* and HMS *Terror*, commanded by Captain James Fitzjames and Captain Francis Crozier respectively, were sighted north of Baffin Island by whalers, but were soon lost in pack ice. Several expeditions set out to search for the missing crews, but their sad fate was not known until 1859 when a diary was found. It emerged that Franklin and his crew spent the

first winter near Beechey Island and then sailed to Peel Sound and Franklin Strait. In September 1846, the ships again became trapped in the ice, this time in Victoria Strait. While attempting to head south on foot, all members of the expedition perished. The route continues past King William Island. The Northwest Passage Territorial Historic Park at the settlement of Goja Haven reminds visitors of the history of exploration in the passage and surrounding area with information boards and artifacts. The

town is named after *Gjøa*, the vessel in which Roald Amundsen navigated the passage for the first time between 1903 and 1906. Amundsen found it an ideal place to drop anchor and conduct research into the earth's magnetic field. The historic park provides visitors with an insight into the life and work of the famous polar explorer, who spent three winters here.

10 Cambridge Bay Cambridge Bay, named for the English Duke of Cambridge and also known as

Ikaluktutiak ("place of many big fish") is on the south coast of Victoria Island and, thanks to its sheltered position at the end of the bay, offers good anchorage. The small settlement, with around 1,500 inhabitants, mostly Inuit, has developed into a center for arts and crafts. The Nunavut College of Fine Arts offers courses in the techniques and styles of Inuit art to inhabitants and tourists alike. Jewelry production is also popular, using mostly local stones such as the easily worked serpentine and the

Inuit whaling

Whaling has long played an important part in the livelihood of the people living along the Arctic shoreline. Unlike the European whalers who ransacked the seas fairly indiscriminately, during the 19th century in particular, the Inuit limited themselves to waters close to the coast.

Top: Bringing a whale to shore.
Middle: Cutting up a whale.
Bottom: Whale meat is a staple food for the Inuit.

Smaller whales were shot in narrow bays and then slaughtered on the beach. The catch was cut up and shared out among the community according to set rules and tradition. Whales provided meat, fat, and blubber; whale oil was used to power lamps, while decorative objects and tools were made out of the bone. Although manufactured food products now reach even the most isolated of townships, whaling is still important for the local inhabitants. If whales are shot in the bay or become stranded on the beach, everyone gets involved.

bones of marine mammals. Copper, found in some parts of the island, has also been used traditionally by the Inuit and other metals and modern materials further enrich Inuit art.

In the area around Cambridge Bay, visitors can see the remains of old Inuit dwellings, built out of rock and earth and known as *quarmaq*. One of the sights of the bay itself is the wreck of the *Maud* (named after the Queen of Norway and later renamed the *Baymaud*), the ship built for Amundsen's second Arctic expe-

dition, which was sold to the Hudson's Bay Company in 1925 and sank in 1930. A lighthouse has provided safe passage into the bay since 1947.

Originally a trading post for the Hudson's Bay Company and a small police station, Cambridge Bay was developed in the 1920s as a Canadian government post for this part of the Arctic. The Inuits, previously widely spread over the area, did not settle here until the 1950s.

Cambridge Bay is an ideal place to learn more about Arctic flora

and fauna. Venturing onto the slopes in an off-road vehicle, you might be lucky enough to see whole herds of musk ox.

⑪ Ross Point The route westward along the southern coast of Victoria Island heads through Dease Strait and Coronation Gulf. If you have a chance to go ashore at Ross Point, take the opportunity to fit in a short walk around the area, far from any kind of settlement, to see some of the plant and animal life of the tundra. The most impressive animal you could see here is the musk ox, which frequently roams in small groups or even entire herds.

⑫ Holman Island After some 250 km (155 miles), the route, often narrow in places, opens out into the Amundsen Gulf, marking an end to the most difficult section of the Northwest Passage. This area is also the border between the Canadian Inuit territory of Nunavut and the Northwest Territories. The community of Ulukhaktok is home to the most northerly golf course on the planet, and welcomes international competitors every summer when it plays host to its own tournament. Despite its remote location, the island has

become a magnet for artists, who are especially attracted by the traditional Holman Art Prints. Lithographs, etchings, linocuts, and other graphic techniques are used to create motifs symbolic of the Arctic world. Dancing and drumming are also important elements of community life in Ulukhaktok. Before the current settlement was established, the area was a trading post and some buildings still remaining from this time can be visited on Read Island.

⑬ Herschel Island The route continues through the vast Amundsen Gulf to the Beaufort Sea, passing the delta formed by the Mackenzie River before reaching Herschel Island. Lining the coast are great piles of driftwood bleached pale gray by the salt water of the sea. The driftwood, which is pushed northward from Canada's forest region across the Mackenzie and out into the sea, is a precious source of timber for building and burning in this area, which is barren of trees.

1 Musk oxen can often be seen in the Canadian Arctic.

2 Icebreakers in the Beaufort Sea.

Spring in the Arctic

Spring is often considered the most beautiful season in the Arctic. The darkness of winter is over, and from the end of March the days become longer than the nights until the sun stays above the horizon day and night. The thermometer still clearly shows temperatures below 0°C (32°F), the land is covered in snow as far as the eye can see, and sheets of ice float on the sea, but the sunlight brings with it a comforting feeling of warmth.

The welcome warmth of the sun in such harsh conditions affects the variety of plant life. The tundra plant species vary depending on how much

Arctic and tundra bird life (from top to bottom): Arctic tern, American golden plover, sandpiper.

sunlight or shade the land receives. They are also affected by the amount of water and the gradient of the land. As the sun warms the top layer of soil, penetrating just a few inches below the surface, small trickles and pools are formed by the snowmelt. The tundra then unfurls into a vibrant display of blossom for a few short weeks.

The local name for Herschel, *Qikiqtaruk*, means simply "island" in Inuit. During the short summer, the tundra here is a blaze of color. Though just a few square miles in size, the island with its sheltered port was regularly frequented by whalers and scientific researchers, and, with an Inuit settlement already in existence there, became a supply center for the entire region.

⑭ Barrow The line of longitude 141° west is crossed at Barrow 80 km (50 miles) west of Herschel Island, marking the border between Canada and Alaska. People began arriving at Prudhoe Bay to look for crude oil as early as the 1940s, but it was not until 1968 that exploitable sources were discovered. The crude oil is pumped across almost 1,300 km (808 miles) to Valdez on Alaska's southern coast through the Alaska pipeline, which was completed in 1977.

As the largest settlement on the northern coast and the USA's most northerly city, Barrow is an important supply town for oil fields in the area. In summer, the pack ice briefly retreats from the coast, allowing boats access to the port to offload goods and supplies for the settlement.

Some 15 km (9 miles) north of Barrow is the headland known as Point Barrow, or Nuvuk in the local language, the USA's most northerly point and the departure point for many historic Arctic expeditions.

⑮ Point Hope Point Hope is perched on a headland that juts west into the Chukchi Sea. The small town has a population of less than a hundred people, mainly Inuit. Among the attractions here are beautiful cult objects carved out of whalebone.

From here the route continues south to the Bering Strait, which, along with the Bering Sea, Island, Glacier, and Land Bridge, was named for the Danish-born sailor Vitus Jonassen Bering (1681–1741), who explored the area. Cape Prince of Wales, the most westerly point of the entire American mainland, is a mere 100 km (62 miles) from Cape Deshnev, the easternmost point of Asia.

⑯ Diomede Islands The two countries of Russia and the USA almost meet here. At the closest land approach, Little Diomede (American) and Big Diomede (Russian) are just 3 km (2 miles) apart. It is the only place where the two nations share a border. The International Dateline also bisects the channel between the two islands.

⑰ Nome This town played an important role in Alaska's history during the gold rush. Word got around quickly when gold was discovered in nearby Anvil Creek in 1898, and prospectors came from all over the world, hoping to strike it lucky. Today, Nome is most famous as the destination for the Iditarod Trail Sled Dog Race, held in honor of the dogsled team that brought the serum to bring to an end the 1925 diptheria epidemic among the Inuit.

⑱ Gambell Lying on the northwestern tip of St Lawrence Island, Gambell is almost wholly inhabited by Siberian Yupik, the indigenous people of the northeast Russian Federation.

⑲ St Paul Island St Paul is one of the four Pribilof Islands *(continued p.46)*

1 Ice floes drift in the Bering Sea.

2 Two teams from the Iditarod dogsled race make a stop in Unalakleet.

The tufted puffin (*Lunda cirrhata*), which is common along the American Pacific coast from Alaska to California, is very closely related to the Atlantic puffin. Its most striking feature is its breeding plumage: pale yellow tufts of hair protruding above its eyes.

situated in the Bering Sea between Alaska and Siberia. Like most islands in the region, they are volcanic and provide breeding grounds for seabirds and seals. The Pribilof Islands are inhabited by Aleuts, whose homeland also includes the Shumagin and Aleutian islands and the western part of the Alaska Peninsula.

20 Dutch Harbor The small town of Dutch Harbor lies on the Aleutian Island of Amaknak and is connected by a bridge to the adjacent Unalaska Island.
The Russian Orthodox Church in Unalasaka is worth visiting. It is protected as a cultural monument dating back to the time when Alaska was part of Russia. The Aleutians came under Russia's influence in the 18th century when Russian fur trappers established settlements on the island, brutally oppressing and sometimes murdering the inhabitants. Missionaries from the Russian Orthodox Church arrived later and built their first church here in 1825.
Despite being somewhat removed from world affairs, the Aleutians did not escape the effects of World War II. While the USA tried to protect the islands by building military bases, they

could not prevent attacks by Japanese fighter planes, and on the morning of June 3, 1942 Japanese aircraft attacked Dutch Harbor.

21 Cold Bay The passage continues from Unalaska, past the Krenitzin Islands to Unimak Island, the largest of the Aleutian Islands. Pavlof, a huge volcano and one of many on the Alaska Peninsula, towers a vast 2,862 m (9,390 ft) above the bay, though it is often obscured by mist.
Like the islands in the area and vast regions of the Peninsula, Unimak is protected as a

National Wildlife Refuge. Many North American animal species can be found here, ranging from the enormous brown bear to the silver fox.
Cold Bay lies at the outermost end of the Alaska Peninsula, with its airport an important transport hub for the south-western part of the state. The town's development was closely linked to the local airport. It was built during World War II for better defense of this isolated part of the USA against Japanese attack. At that time, it was also used as a stopover point for the transportation of cargo between the

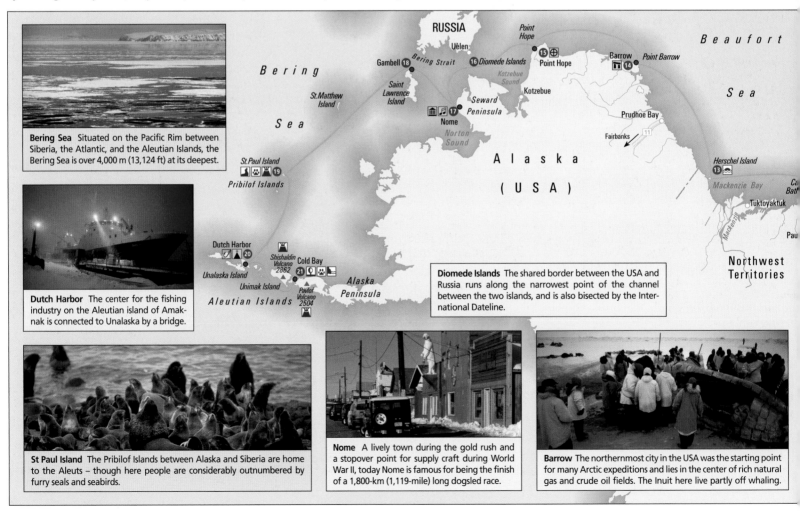

Bering Sea Situated on the Pacific Rim between Siberia, the Atlantic, and the Aleutian Islands, the Bering Sea is over 4,000 m (13,124 ft) at its deepest.

Dutch Harbor The center for the fishing industry on the Aleutian island of Amaknak is connected to Unalaska by a bridge.

Diomede Islands The shared border between the USA and Russia runs along the narrowest point of the channel between the two islands, and is also bisected by the International Dateline.

St Paul Island The Pribilof Islands between Alaska and Siberia are home to the Aleuts – though here people are considerably outnumbered by furry seals and seabirds.

Nome A lively town during the gold rush and a stopover point for supply craft during World War II, today Nome is famous for being the finish of a 1,800-km (1,119-mile) long dogsled race.

Barrow The northernmost city in the USA was the starting point for many Arctic expeditions and lies in the center of rich natural gas and crude oil fields. The Inuit here live partly off whaling.

USA and Soviet Union. Today, the town of Cold Bay is mainly inhabited by employees of the airport, military aerial surveillance, and meteorological service.

With its offshore islands, mighty volcanoes, and rocky coasts rich in coves and bays, the area surrounding Cold Bay is home to some of Alaska's most impressive scenery. Pavlof has erupted some forty times in the last 200 years and is one of the most active volcanoes in Alaska. The Izembek National Wildlife Refuge is a special animal haven, containing several lagoons that form the habitat of wild geese and migratory birds.

The cruise through the North American Arctic comes to an end in Cold Bay. Many passengers make the return journey from here by plane.

1 The American Pribilof Islands in the Bering Sea.

2 A Russian Orthodox church on St Paul Island.

3 An iconostasis in the Russian Orthodox church on St Paul Island.

4 A colony of furry seals on the Alaskan coast.

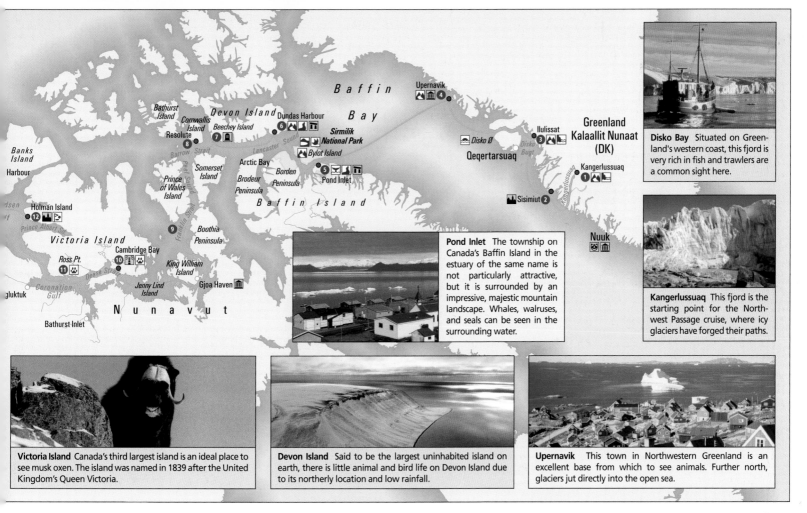

Pond Inlet The township on Canada's Baffin Island in the estuary of the same name is not particularly attractive, but it is surrounded by an impressive, majestic mountain landscape. Whales, walruses, and seals can be seen in the surrounding water.

Disko Bay Situated on Greenland's western coast, this fjord is very rich in fish and trawlers are a common sight here.

Kangerlussuaq This fjord is the starting point for the Northwest Passage cruise, where icy glaciers have forged their paths.

Victoria Island Canada's third largest island is an ideal place to see musk oxen. The island was named in 1839 after the United Kingdom's Queen Victoria.

Devon Island Said to be the largest uninhabited island on earth, there is little animal and bird life on Devon Island due to its northerly location and low rainfall.

Upernavik This town in Northwestern Greenland is an excellent base from which to see animals. Further north, glaciers jut directly into the open sea.

Hurtigruten
By mail ship from Bergen to the North Cape

Originally established as a *hurtig* (express) route for mail deliveries and general supplies for remote settlements in the far north of Norway, the *Hurtigruten* became semi-redundant when the road network was extended and is now a popular cruise route from Bergen on the southern end of Norway's west coast to the North Cape and into the midnight sun.

In holiday brochures, the *Hurtigruten* is sold as "the most beautiful sea voyage in the world" by the Norwegians. The name just means "fast connection" translated literally, and is applied to the post ship route between Bergen in Norway's southwest and Kirkenes on the Russian border. The line was founded by a private shipping company in the summer of 1893, when Captain Richard With set off on board the D/S *Vesteraalen* from Trondheim to Hammerfest. He had been making this journey for years and had kept a detailed log; the entries provided invalu-

able for those who later voyaged in these waters, which were not entirely free from danger. With's observations made it possible for him to travel along the Norwegian coast at night, resulting in a considerable saving in time which, in turn, was rewarded with state subsidies.

For the inhabitants of the remote areas of Norway, the new mail line was a real benefit. At last it was possible to do without arduous journeys on rough, unmade roads. As early as 1898, the southern end of the route was extended to Bergen and in 1911 the northern end reached the iron-

A sailing boat moored in Bergen.

ore town of Kirkenes. The "Imperial Road No. 1" service is still operating today. The mail line not only guaranteed deliveries to remote villages during the severe winters, but also improved competition outside the larger cities and increased social cohesion, so the Hurtigruten is still subsidized by the government.

With the development of the road network, however, as well as the use of planes, the mail line became increasingly less important. The shipping lines looked for a new source of income and discovered tourism, which had already been gaining considerably in importance. Instead of the basic postal ships, modern cruise ships now ply the route, at least during the summer months, in order to satisfy the high expectations of today's demanding tourists. Altogether twelve ships operate the route, which is approxi-

The vessels of the Hurtigruten, shown here at Trondheim, are well-equipped modern cruise ships.

Svolvær, the largest town and most important fishing village on the Lofoten islands, lies between the sea and the mountains on the southern side of Austvågøy Island, in the Vestfjorden.

mately 4,630 km (2,877 miles) long. During the course of the eleven-day voyage they drop anchor in thirty-four ports.

The special attraction of a journey via the Hurtigruten is the natural beauty of the countryside. You can admire the rugged coastline with its remote fjords, the steep hillsides and snow-covered mountains, the red fishing huts along the shores, and the wide expanses of the ocean. The air smells of salt and algae.

North of the Arctic Circle, the Arctic twilight holds a special fascination during winter, while in summer the midnight sun is the biggest draw. The motion of the ship lulls passengers on their voyage through a dreamy landscape made even more romantic by the magical light. Between February and April, the brilliance of the snow and the sunshine often create intense light conditions.

The journey starts in Bergen, which is still an important trading center today. White wooden houses and narrow alleyways characterize the old parts of town. After a fire, Ålesund was rebuilt in the early 20th century in art nouveau style. The vibrant houses of Kristiansund are scattered across three islands. Trondheim, Norway's third-largest city, has an impressive old town, which is dominated by the medieval Nidaros Cathedral. The journey continues along the coast, past beautiful scenery such as the Seven Sisters waterfall. Tromso is known as "the gateway to the polar sea" and is a busy trading town, just as it was when explorers stocked up on provisions before setting off into the unknown. Beyond the Arctic Circle, the North Cape awaits its visitors with magnificent views of the midnight sun and the final destination at Kirkenes on the Russian border.

The post ship carries its passengers through the impressive world of the Norwegian fjords.

Edvard Grieg

In Bergen, Edvard Grieg's villa, Trold-haugen, gives visitors a fascinating glimpse into the life of the composer. He studied in Leipzig, where he published his Opus No. 1 before returning

Edvard Grieg's living room in his villa, Troldhaugen.

to Bergen in 1862. In 1866 he moved to Oslo, where he helped to set up the Norwegian musical academy. The following year he moved to Denmark, where he composed his most famous work, the Piano Concerto in A Minor Op. 16.

The journey on the Hurtigruten line from Bergen to the North Cape and beyond follows the course of the coastline, taking in the spectacular fjords. A number of interesting port towns are included in the program of visits, but the main attractions of this sea voyage are the wonders of nature: lonely, wild coastal landscapes, mighty glaciers, steep mountainsides, and roaring waterfalls.

❶ Bergen Norway's second largest city is the starting point for a journey on the Hurtigruten. The "town between the seven mountains" is proud of its history. Following a famine in the 13th century, the merchants joined the German Hanseatic League and the Tyske Brygge (German Bridge) took over trading control. The Hanse office on the waterfront, a row of wooden buildings and warehouses, developed into a separate residential area. In 1702, a large fire destroyed the buildings, which were rebuilt in their original form. The Bryggen Hanseatic wharf was designated a UNESCO World Heritage Site in 1979.

The 12th-century St Mary's church, with its baroque pulpit dating from 1676, is also worth seeing. The wooden stave church at Fantoft was erected in 1150 in Fortun in Sogn, then dismantled and rebuilt at Fjøsanger near Bergen in 1883. The Rosenkrantz Tower affords superb views of the city. From Bergen the trip continues northward along the coast.

❷ Ålesund Ålesund is one of Norway's most important fishing ports. The town is spread across several islands; in the south the Sunnmøre mountain range rises steeply above the fjord. More than 418 steps lead up from the port to the Aksla Mountain; from here you can enjoy magnificent views of the coastline. Ålesund is the starting point for the journey into the Geirangerfjord.

Travel information

Route profile
Length: approx. 4,630 km (2,877 miles)
Duration: 12 days
Start and end: Bergen

Itinerary
Day 1: Bergen; Day 2: Florø, Måløy, Torvik, Ålesund, Geiranger (in summer), Molde; Day 3: Kristiansund, Trondheim, Rørvik, Stokksund; Day 4: Brønnøysund, Sandnessjøen, Nesna, Ørnes, Bodø, Stamsund, Svolvær; Day 5: Stokmarknes, Sortland, Risøyhamn, Harstad, Finnsnes, Tromsø, Skjervøy; Day 6: Øksfjord, Hammerfest, Havøysund, Honningsvåg, Kjøllefjord, Mehamn, Berlevåg; Day 7: Båtsfjord, Vardø, Vadsø, Kirkenes (return journey from here), Vadsø, Vardø, Båtsfjord, Berlevåg; Day 8: Mehamn, Kjøllefjord, Honningsvåg, Havøysund, Hammerfest, Øksfjord, Skjervøy; Day 9: Tromsø, Finnsnes, Harstadt, Risøyhamn, Sortland, Stokmarknes, Svolvær, Stamsund; Day 10: Bodø, Ørnes, Nesna, Sandnessjøen, Brønnøysund, Rørvik; Day 11: Trondheim, Kristiansund, Molde; Day 12: Ålesund, Torvik, Måløy, Florø, Bergen

When to go
The best time to travel is during the summer months, June to August.

Tourist information
Hurtigruten ASA
Havnegata 2, box 43
N-8514 Narvik
Norway
Tel. 76 96 76 00
Fax. 76 96 76 01
Booking: 810 30 000/
booking@hurtigruten.com
www.hurtigruten.com

2

3

A major attraction for gourmets is Bergen's fish market, located right next to the port, equally popular with locals and visitors. In the open air, canny market traders loudly extol the virtues of their fresh fish and other seafood, selling smoked salmon and shrimp rolls. Sea bream, cod, and herring are displayed for sale on the stalls. Giant langoustines reach out with their red pincers and the scales of plump salmon shimmer in the light. Truly a feast for the senses!

Fresh fish and crustaceans are delivered daily by the fishermen and are of the highest quality, though this is also reflected in their high prices.

Top: Delicious salmon.
Middle: Fresh rosefish from the surrounding waters.
Bottom: Lobster for gourmet palates.

At the beginning of the 13th century, when famine forced the people of Bergen to enter into a treaty with the Hanseatic League, the whole of the catch was sent for export. In exchange for grain, flour, salt, and malt, they had to salt and dry their entire catch of fish and send it abroad.

Trondheim was the most important spiritual center in northern Europe. The mainly Gothic Nidaros Cathedral, erected over the tomb of St Olav, is the most important medieval structure in the country and is the coronation church of the kings of Norway.

5 Bodø North of the Arctic Circle, the ship calls at Bodø. Among the interesting sights here are an aviation museum and the Salten Museum. From Bodø the journey continues to the Lofoten Islands.

6 Svolvær The ship drops anchor in the port of Svolvær, (continued p.54)

1 On the northward journey, the ship passes through the long and narrow fjords along the coast, here the Geirangerfjord.

2 The Seven Sisters waterfalls in the Geirangerfjord.

3 The past comes to life on Bergen's picturesque waterfront and the narrow alleyways of Tyske Brygge.

3 Geirangerfjord As you sail through the fjord, you will have superb views of the Seven Sisters, Suitor and Bride's Veil waterfalls. A bus tour from the village of Geiranger to the summit of the Dalsnibba Mountain is one of the best land excursions available on the cruise. The bus jogs along in first gear to the top of the 1,500-m (4,922-ft) high mountain, but the views from the summit make the arduous journey well worthwhile. From the Geiranger-fjord the ship returns to Ålesund and the coast. The next stop is at Trondheim.

4 Trondheim Norway's former capital has an impressive historic old town. Until the Reformation,

In summer, the ships of the Hurtigruten line travel across the Geirangerfjord. Probably the best known of Norway's fjords, it extends some 15 km (9 miles). At its sides, steep cliff faces rise up to about 800 m (2,625 ft). From the 1,500-m (4,922-ft) high Dalsnibba Mountain, accessed via a pass, superb panoramic views

extend across the fjord and the magnificent mountain scenery. At the end of the fjord is Geiranger village, with 250 inhabitants. With its hairpin bends (center of the picture) and viewpoints, the Ørneveien ("Eagle Way") pass to the Norddalsfjord in the north is one of Scandinavia's most breathtaking mountain roads.

Northern Lights

In the Middle Ages, the Northern or Arctic Lights had a formidable reputation across Europe: the flickering light in the sky was seen as a harbinger of death. Today, this natural spectacle excites mainly holidaymakers who have come to the far north to admire this extraordinary natural phenomenon. On a cruise with the Hurtigruten line in autumn or winter, you are guaranteed to see the Northern Lights, especially at Tromsø. The light flickers in restless patterns of white, green, yellow, and red, and lights up the entire sky.

Scientists explain the Northern Lights as the interplay between sun and earth. The electrically charged particles in a sun storm, such as electrons and protons, are deflected toward the poles by the earth's magnetic field. At a height of about 100 km (62 miles), they collide with gas particles consisting of nitrogen and oxygen. These countless collisions cause the magnifi-

The Northern Lights above Hammerfest.

cent vibrant spectacle in the Arctic sky. Rays of light shoot up in wide arcs, while large parts of the sky seem to be on fire. After a major sun eruption, this natural spectacle can be observed as far south as northern Germany.

The true majesty of the Northern Lights, however, can only be appreciated north of the Arctic Circle. Today, any activity can be predicted fairly accurately, but the Lights can only be seen when the sky is clear or only partly cloudy, since they play way above the clouds.

the most important fishing village on the Lofoten Islands. The small town, which has around 4,000 inhabitants, is renowned for its picturesque waterfront and its artists' workshops. Documents from World War II are on display at the Lofoten War Museum. The Lofoten Islands are still at the center of cod fishing in Norway today. Steep cliffs rise up out of the sea that teems with life. More than five thousand fishermen and their ships arrive every year in January and remain in the coastal waters until April in search of cod. From Svolvær the cruise ship returns to the mainland coast.

7 Harstad This town, located on the island of Hinnøya, the southernmost of the Vesterålen Islands, developed as a result of trade and the extraction of oil. The church of Trondenes, the best-known sight here, is the most northerly stone church in the world, completed around 1434. Known for its rich decoration, it contains a tryptych by the Lübeck artist Bernt Notke. Also worth a visit is the church of Harstad, which was built in the mid 20th century and features modern stained glass.

8 Tromsø North of the Arctic Circle, Tromsø is one of the most important ports on the Hurtigruten. Its 60,000 inhabitants live in an area of 2,558 sq km (987 sq miles), covering both the mainland and the offshore islands, making Tromsø one of the largest towns in Europe by surface area. When Tromsø received its city charter in 1794, its location on a small island off the mainland, to which it is connected by a bridge, and its ice-free port soon led to an economic boom. The city is still an important trading center today, dealing in fish and fur products, and has shipyards and fish-processing factories. On the same degree of latitude as the

north of Alaska, Tromsø owes its ice-free port to the warm waters of the Gulf Stream. From 25 November to 21 January, the sun never rises here, but on the other hand, from 31 May to 23 July, it never sets completely either. These extremes determine the city's rhythms. In summer, Tromsø is a lively and bustling place around the clock. Its vast student population of more than seven thousand (from its university, four colleges, seven grammar schools, and forty-three other schools) party until late into the light night, ensuring the city is in no danger of losing its reputation

as the Paris of the North. In winter, everyone withdraws into the pubs and bars and celebrates the Arctic night.

The Ishavskatedralen, or Arctic Cathedral, is one of the must-sees on every tour of the city. With its extraordinary gable shape, it is reminiscent of the structures used by Nordic fishermen to dry their fish, but its futurist architecture also symbolizes the Arctic night, the Northern Lights, and the midnight sun. A vast stained glass window portraying Jesus with arms outstretched, designed by Viktor Sparre, covers the entire east wall.

Whale-watching

Whale-watching, observing whales in nature, is one of the most popular activities in the cold waters of the north. With a little luck, you might see one of these mighty mammals from the deck of a Hurtigruten ship, but sighting a whale is more or less guaranteed if you take a trip with one of the specialist organizations in Narvik, Norway's whale-watching center. On these trips, you approach the whales in small boats, getting as close as 100 m (328 ft), but it is left to the animals themselves to decide whether they wish to come any closer. In order not to disturb the whales, the organizers avoid revving up their boat engines and will not drive through the middle of a group of whales.

Off the coast at Narvik, the main species you can spot are sperm whales. These huge animals reach a length of up to 20 m (66 ft) and a weight of 35 tonnes (40 tons). After a dive that can last for up to two hours, the sperm

An orca in the waters of the Tysfjord, south of Narvik.

whale surfaces for about ten minutes in order to breathe, the first jet from its blowhole shooting up to 5 m (16 ft) into the air. Only the males can be seen as far north as this. They meet up with the females for mating farther south. Orca (killer whales) can be seen in the waters off Tysfjord, around 60 km (37 miles) south of Narvik. Between mid-October and January the whale population is said to be between 600 and 1,000.

ern coast of Norway makes a living from fishing. Nearby is the Øksfjordøkulen Glacier, Norway's fifth largest and the only one to calve directly into the sea.

⑪ Hammerfest Until the 1990s, when it was surpassed by Honningsvåg, Hammerfest was the most northerly town in the world. The sun does not set here between the middle of May and the end of July, while in winter darkness reigns for months. This is also why, in 1891, it became the first town in Europe to be fitted with electric street lights. The grave chapel next door to the church of St Michael is the only building to have survived World War II; the mosaic image in the church consists of 10,000 individual pieces. The Royal and Ancient Polar Bear Society with its 200,000 members enjoys a legendary reputation. It is a

1 Rocky coastal scenery near Svolvær on the Lofoten Islands.

2 From the Hurtigruten ships, you can take an excursion (by smaller boat) into the Holandsfjord and to the Svartisen Glacier.

3 Wildly romantic: the world of the Vesterålen Islands.

"Gateway to the Arctic" is how Tromsø styles itself, an appropriate epithet since thanks to its northerly location, the town became the starting point for numerous Arctic expeditions in the late 19th and early 20th centuries. The Polar Museum commemorates Norwegian explorer Roald Amundsen, who passed through the town aboard the *Gjøa* and the *Maud*, and, on 18 June 1928, rushed off to help search for the crew of Italian researcher Umberto Nobile, whose airship the *Italia* had crashed on its return from the North Pole. Amundsen never

returned from his rescue mission. A central space in the Polar Museum is devoted to the story of the Arctic explorer Fridtjof Nansen, who also set off from Tromsø on his legendary expedition in 1893. He planned to be frozen into the pack ice on his ship, the *Fram*, in order to drift across the North Pole into the North Atlantic. After one year, however, Nansen had to accept that he would not reach the North Pole this way. His attempt to reach the Pole by dog sled also failed and it was not until 1895 that Nansen and his companion Hjalmar Johansen reached Franz

Josef Land, where they had to spend one more winter before they were able to return.

⑨ Skjervøy This Sami settlement is scattered across several islands, although most of the houses are found on Skjervøy Island. Fridtjof Nansen dropped anchor here with the *Fram*. The village prospered thanks to its trade with the city of Bergen. The wooden church dates back to 1721.

⑩ Øksfjord With just over 500 inhabitants, this small town in a sheltered position on the north-

curiosity because there are, in fact, no polar bears at all on the Norwegian mainland.

⑫ Honningsvåg/North Cape At the Hurtigruten's northernmost point, the ship drops anchor in the fishing port of Honningsvåg. The small town comes to life only in winter, when cod come to the Norwegian coast to spawn and hundreds of fishing boats return from the high seas with their valuable catch.

There is little of interest to be seen on the journey across the island of Magerøya, where the sparse and treeless landscape is a reminder of the proximity of the Arctic Circle. Some Sami have established their homes along the tourist route and sell their souvenirs to visitors here. The Sami have to rely on such additional income because they cannot survive from breeding reindeer alone. They only spend the summer on Magerøya with their herds; in September they drive their animals through the sound back to the mainland. Some 25,000 Sami live in the county of Finnmark today.

When more and more Norwegian farmers thrust northward, an attempt was made to assimilate the Sami, but the tribe vehe-

mently fought the repression of their culture and refused to give up their traditions. It was not until the 1960s that the Sami's call for cultural independence was finally heard and they were granted the right to retain their own language and culture.

At the tip of the island of Magerøya, lies the North Cape, the second most northerly point in continental Europe (after Knivskjellodden, a nearby spit of land). It was named by Richard Chancellor, a 16th-century English explorer who passed it while looking for a sea passage. Few others ventured here, apart from some daring explorers who scaled the cliff face. A steel globe has been erected to mark this northerly spot, which has become a magnet for tourists, with more than 200,000 coming here every year. Other than the globe and a fantastic view out to sea from the viewing platform, there is just a car park, a visitor's center and an underground souvenir shop. The journey now continues to Vardø.

⑬ Vardø The town is not far from Hornøy Island, in the extreme north of Norway. Like most island settlements, Vardø once survived by fishing. Today,

the small village is being developed into an important NATO base. Its most impressive structure is the 2,800-m (9,187-ft) long car tunnel that runs under the Arctic Sea, connecting the island with the mainland. The octagonal fortress, Vardøhus Festning, dates back to 1734–1738. Vardø is the starting point for the final section of the journey on the Hurtigruten line.

⑭ Kirkenes This remote town, the finishing point of the Hurtigruten, is situated in the far east of the Norwegian county of Finnmark, only 10 km (6 miles) from the Russian border. The town owes its rapid rise at the beginning of the 20th century to iron ore mining. Since 1908, Kirkenes has been the point where ships on the Hurtigruten turn around and return to Bergen.

1 At the North Cape on the island of Magerøya, a steel globe marks the much-visited northern tip of Europe. The view from the platform is incomparable.

2 The weather in the far north does not always show its most clement side, but all the ships are equipped with stabilizers and so stay relatively smooth even when the sea is rough.

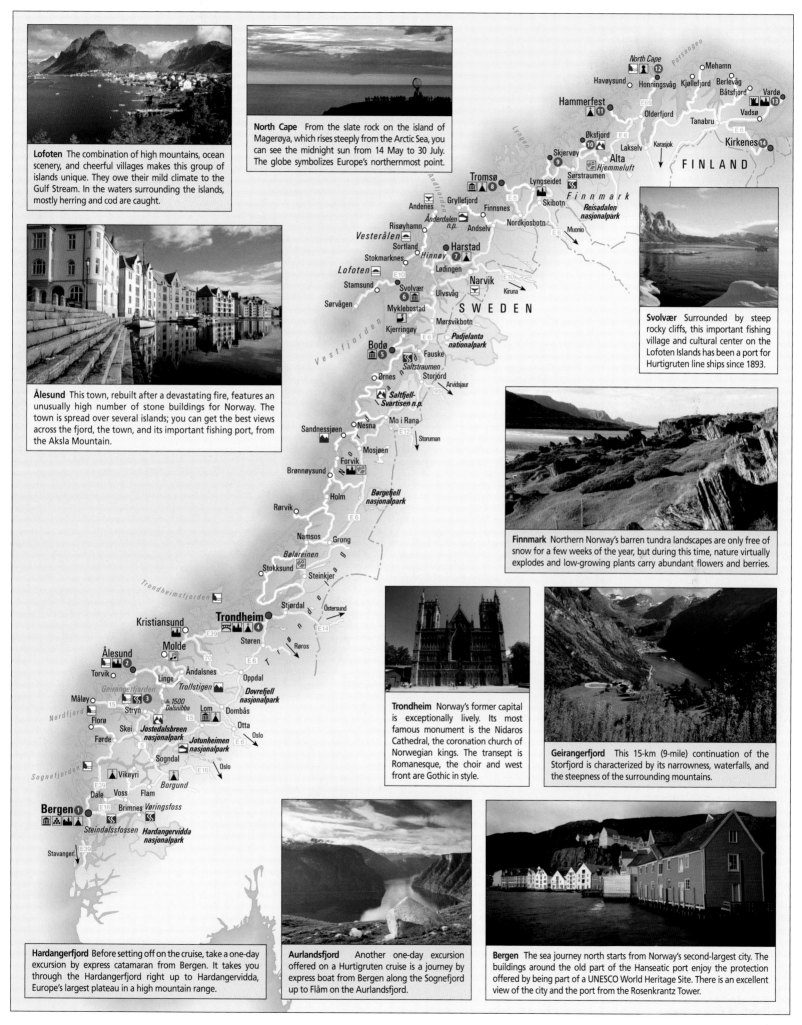

Lofoten The combination of high mountains, ocean scenery, and cheerful villages makes this group of islands unique. They owe their mild climate to the Gulf Stream. In the waters surrounding the islands, mostly herring and cod are caught.

North Cape From the slate rock on the island of Magerøya, which rises steeply from the Arctic Sea, you can see the midnight sun from 14 May to 30 July. The globe symbolizes Europe's northernmost point.

Ålesund This town, rebuilt after a devastating fire, features an unusually high number of stone buildings for Norway. The town is spread over several islands; you can get the best views across the fjord, the town, and its important fishing port, from the Aksla Mountain.

Svolvær Surrounded by steep rocky cliffs, this important fishing village and cultural center on the Lofoten Islands has been a port for Hurtigruten line ships since 1893.

Finnmark Northern Norway's barren tundra landscapes are only free of snow for a few weeks of the year, but during this time, nature virtually explodes and low-growing plants carry abundant flowers and berries.

Trondheim Norway's former capital is exceptionally lively. Its most famous monument is the Nidaros Cathedral, the coronation church of Norwegian kings. The transept is Romanesque, the choir and west front are Gothic in style.

Geirangerfjord This 15-km (9-mile) continuation of the Storfjord is characterized by its narrowness, waterfalls, and the steepness of the surrounding mountains.

Hardangerfjord Before setting off on the cruise, take a one-day excursion by express catamaran from Bergen. It takes you through the Hardangerfjord right up to Hardangervidda, Europe's largest plateau in a high mountain range.

Aurlandsfjord Another one-day excursion offered on a Hurtigruten cruise is a journey by express boat from Bergen along the Sognefjord up to Flåm on the Aurlandsfjord.

Bergen The sea journey north starts from Norway's second-largest city. The buildings around the old part of the Hanseatic port enjoy the protection offered by being part of a UNESCO World Heritage Site. There is an excellent view of the city and the port from the Rosenkrantz Tower.

It may be hard work, but exploring the Danube Delta by rowing boat is rewarding for nature lovers.

Eastern Europe

Down the Danube from Vienna to the Black Sea

The Danube cruise takes you from Vienna to the Balkans. The river is lined with the capital cities of almost all the countries it passes through, and bisects the vast Pannonian Plain. Just before the Romanian border, the Danube squeezes through the Iron Gate, then flows on through the Walachia region to the Black Sea.

You could hardly wish for a more perfect central theme for a journey: a river, the second largest on the continent, rich in history and fringed with diverse and largely untouched landscapes, and in between, lined up like pearls on a necklace, are the cities: some are bustling metropolises, others dreamy small jewels, flanked by mighty fortresses and ruins. Several places date back to antiquity and were of major importance, such as Carnuntum, where there was a large Roman camp, Tác-Gorsium (not far from Lake Valence), or Histria, on the

Black Sea. Reminders of the great days of the Habsburg Empire are everywhere, as are those of more recent history, which brought so much suffering and destruction to the Balkans.

To sing the praises of Vienna or Budapest, the two cities on the first stretch of the journey, would be to state the obvious; each one makes a travel destination in its own right. The attractions of the Slovakian capital, Bratislava, increase each year and even Belgrade has a few surprises in store, revealing plenty of charm despite all the recent

A Woolly Pig on the Pannonian Plain.

upheavals. Many of the smaller towns that line the great river also have a special magic: fortified Hainburg, with the remains of the ancient Roman settlement of Carnuntum nearby; the old bishops' town of Esztergom; Szentendre with its bohemian flair; or the thousand-year-old baroque town of Baja. The many fortresses and defensive structures along the route bear witness to wars past: Devín, which guards the spot where the Morava flows into the Danube, about 45 km (28 miles) east of Vienna; Visegrád, the "upper castle" of the kings of Hungary, in a prominent location on the right bank of the Danube, at the point where it bends; the fortifications at Komárno, in Slovakia, or those at Ilok or Petrovaradin in Novi Sad. There are also fortresses in many capital cities, such as the Royal Palace in

Pelicans in the Danube Delta. This unique riverscape, home to more than three hundred indigenous species of bird, is one of the largest bird paradises on earth.

For many places in the Danube Delta, ships are still the only public means of transport today.

Budapest, the castle in Bratislava, and the fortress in Kalemegdan, in the heart of Belgrade, flanked by two rivers.

Meanwhile, a rather more poetic mood is conjured up by the endless, fertile expanses of the Pannonian Plain in the south of Hungary, and the Voyvodina Region, located between Budapest and Belgrade, where the Danube is fed in rapid succession first by the Tisza, then the Sava and Greater Morava, and the river swells majestically to its full size. Just a short way downriver, a breathtaking backdrop is formed by the 100-m (328-ft) high rocky walls of the Derdab Gorge, better known as the Iron Gate. At the end of its long journey, the river Danube and its many branches pour into the Black Sea, sustaining a magnificent natural habitat in its estuary, which to this day remains little disturbed by human activity.

The importance of the Danube in terms of both cultural and natural history has not escaped the attentions of UNESCO. A number of cities and areas have been included in its register of World Heritage Sites: the historic center of Vienna as well as the palace and gardens of Schönbrunn; the old town of Budapest; the bridge at Mostar and its environs; and the Danube Delta, are especially worthy of protection. Another reason that Eastern Europe is such a fascinating place to visit is that many places seem to be undergoing massive change. Everywhere, historic monuments and streets are being restored, new museums opened, the infrastructure improved, and new markets created. All this is helping to lay the groundwork for the lands around the Danube to have a highly promising future as a tourist destination.

View from the Romanesque Fishermen's Bastion across Budapest and the Danube.

Most Danube cruises start at either Passau or Vienna. When conflict broke out in the collapsing Yugoslav federation in the early 1990s, Budapest became the destination for Danube river cruises; but with the re-opening of the Liberty Bridge in Novi Sad in 2005, the Danube is once again navigable as far as Tulcea, on the edge of its delta.

1 Wien The former heart of the Habsburg Empire still retains much of the sparkling charm of the former "imperial and royal" monarchy. Already a large city with a population of one million by the 19th century (now nearly two million across the entire metropolitan area), Vienna has a wealth of historic buildings, monuments, and art treasures dating from every period. Especially worth seeing are St Stephen's Cathedral, the Hofburg Palace, baroque Josefsplatz, the Spanish Riding School, the Karlskirche, Belvedere Palace, and Schönbrunn Palace. You can best experience the essence of Vienna in a Heurigen wine bar, in a coffee house, or on the Naschmarkt.

2 Carnuntum-Petronell On the southern banks of the Danube are the ancient remains of the Roman town of Carnuntum. During its heyday, the military camp and the civilian town numbered some fifty thousand inhabitants. The Archaeological Park of Carnuntum comprises the richest finds from antiquity on Austrian soil.

3 Hainburg Austria's most easterly city was destined to be a border fortress thanks to its location on the Porta Hungarica, a gorge and natural gateway through which the Danube flows as it leaves the country. Of its defensive structures, only the 2.5-km (1.5-mile) long city walls and the gates are preserved.
The nearby Donauauen National Park (Danube flood plains) is definitely worth a visit (see panel, opposite). Only a few miles away, on the opposite bank of the Danube, lies the capital of Slovakia.

4 Bratislava See page 62.

5 Čunovo Just under 15 km (9 miles) south of Bratislava, on a peninsula in the Danube (already broad at this point), stands the Danubiana Art Museum. Its architecture alone lends a futuristic feel to the museum, which also has a sculpture park. A special attraction for sports enthusiasts is the water sports center with its artificial white-water runs for rafting and canoeing.
From Čunovo, the journey continues through the Danube plains, a flat, dry landscape that in some parts is reminiscent of the Hungarian *puszta* (Pannonian Plain).

6 Komárno This village, situated at the point where the Váh River flows into the Danube, has always been of considerable importance strategically. The Romans had a military camp here, known as Brigetio. Hungary's King Stephen I had a fortified earth settlement built in the same

Travel information

Route profile
Length: approx. 1,800 km (1,119 miles) (incl. excursions)
Duration: at least 12–14 days
Start: Vienna
End: Danube Delta or Constanţa
Itinerary (main locations):
Vienna, Bratislava, Esztergom, Visegrád, Budapest, Mohács, Vukovar, Novi Sad, Belgrade, Drobeta-Turnu Severin, Tulcea and Danube Delta, Constanţa

When to go
The winters are generally cold and, near the river, also damp; in summer in the Danube Delta the climate is hot continental, and oppressively humid. Spring and autumn are therefore the best times of year to travel.

Information on Danube cruises
www.ddsg-blue-danube.at
www.bluedanubeholidays. com

www.rivercruisetours.com
www.danuberivercruise.com
www.europeanrivercruises. com

Tourist information
Tourist offices:
Austria:
www.austria.info
Lower Austria:
www.niederoesterreich.at
Vienna: *www.wien.info*
Slovakia:
www.slovakiatourism.sk
Bratislava:
www.bratislava.sk
Hungary:
www.hungarystartshere.com
Budapest:
www.budapestinfo.hu
Croatia:
www.kroatien.hr
Croatia/Osijek-Baranja:
www.tzosbarzup.hr
Serbia:
www.serbia-tourism.org
Belgrade:
www.Beograd.org.yu
Romania:
www.romaniatourism.com

spot, and during the 19th century the Habsburgs transformed the town, strengthening its fortifications and making it a major center of defense for the Empire. Several fortresses were erected on both sides of the river to accommodate some 20,000 soldiers. At the end of World War I, when the Treaty of Trianon was signed in 1920, the Danube was declared the border between the states of Hungary and Czechoslovakia, and since then the town has been divided into two. The former old

town on the northern shore is today part of the Slovak town of Komárno. When you cross the Elizabeth Bridge, you reach the Hungarian town of Komárom, where three mighty forts form a unique attraction for military historians. The largest of them, Monostor, has an area of 40,000 sq m (430,400 sq ft) and comprises 14 wings with 640 rooms, linked by 4-km (2.5-mile) long corridors. You can visit this labyrinth of bastions and casemates, ditches and tunnels, extremely modern in its

day, on a guided tour. After Štúrovo, the river winds its way into Hungarian territory.

7 Esztergom This ancient town forms the western gateway to the Danube Bend. The Romans had a military camp here named Solva, built on the rocky terraces above the river. According to the Nibelung legend, Attila, the much-dreaded king of the Huns, is supposed to have resided here, while it is documented historically that Grand Duke Géza lived

here also. His son was crowned in the year 1000 to become Hungary's first king, Stephen I. In the period that followed, Esztergom ranked as the most important palatinate within the empire. It also became the seat of the archbishop and has, for the most part, been the center of the Roman Catholic Church in Hungary ever since. Built in the 19th century, the neoclassical cathedral is a physical sign of clerical power and a symbol of the city. Highlights to see inside are the treasury and the Renaissance Bakócz Chapel, built from red marble, from the remains of the church that originally stood on the site of the present basilica.
(continued p.63)

1 High above the Danube rises Bratislava Castle, originally built in the 15th century but modified several times since. On the right is the tower of St Martin's Cathedral.

2 Vienna as it is rarely seen: the skyline on the northern banks of the Danube has a markedly futuristic appearance.

Donauauen National Park

Just a few miles beyond the Vienna city limits, an area of flood plains several miles long follows the northern banks of the Danube. This ecologically valuable habitat became famous in

The Danube flood plains: an almost untouched natural idyll covering over 9,000 ha (22,239 acres).

Europe in the early 1980s for the successful campaign waged against a nuclear power station, and was designated a national park in 1996. Exploring this central European primeval forest, which covers an area of more than 9,000 ha (22,239 acres), on foot, in a horse-drawn carriage, or even in a canoe, is a unique adventure.

Bratislava

This historic city became the seat of Slovakian government again in 1993, when Slovakia became an independent republic, making Bratislava one of Europe's youngest capital cities.

With approximately 500,000 inhabitants, Bratislava has developed into an important political, economic, and cultural center. The Old Town has been revitalized and spruced up. The pedestrianized streets buzz with life, first-class restaurants and Viennese-style coffee houses have sprung up around the renovated historic buildings, while shopping streets feature brand names and designers of international renown. The city's historical sites include Michalská Brána (St Michael's Tower), the old Town Hall, and the Primatial Palace, and especially St Martin's Cathedral, its most important sacred building, where numerous Habsburg rulers were vested with the Hungarian crown; for a time the city, then known as Pozsony, was the capital of Hungary. Worth a separate tour in its own right is the castle, which was built in 1430 on the orders of King Sigismund, remodeled into a baroque residence by Empress Maria Theresa, and finally, in 1958, after nearly 150 years of decay, carefully restored to its former glory.

Bratislava is already the most densely populated central European city and

Top: Michalská Street and Michalská Gate.
Bottom: Primatial Palace and Old Town Hall (right).

new districts are springing up in its outskirts at breakneck speed. On top of all this development, due to the large amount of heavy-goods traffic that moves through the city, in an east-west direction, a great deal of money and effort have been expended recently in the building of new motorways.

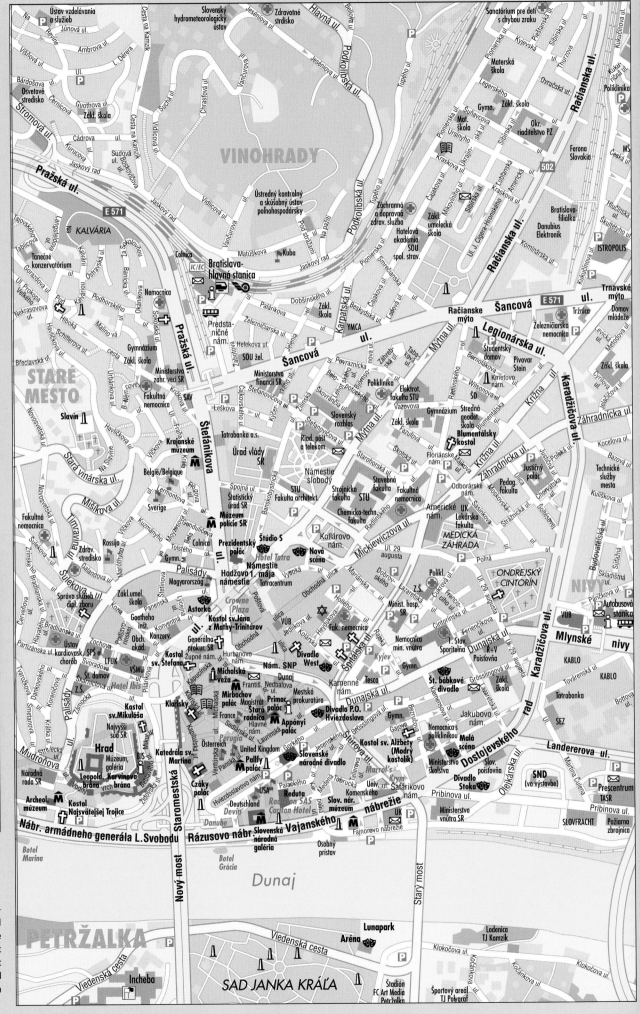

Also worth seeing, immediately adjacent to the cathedral, are the ruins of the archbishop's palace, originally the ancestral seat of the Árpád dynasty, part of which has now been opened as a museum. You can enjoy superb views of the cathedral and across the city from the Danube bridge. The voyage continues for a just few miles more before we reach the next town, Visegrád.

8 Visegrád On the southern shores of the narrow Danube Bend, nestling in a picturesque loop in the river, lies yet another town of great historical importance for Hungarians. The Romans appreciated the strategic benefits of its location, as did the later Slavs, who named the place Upper Castle (Visegrád), and the

Magyars. In response to the Mongols' invasion in 1241–1242, Béla IV had the citadel built on top of the hill and, at its foot, a fortress, together with the Salomon Tower, which still survives today. In the early 14th century, Charles I of Anjou moved his residence to Visegrád, which also housed the Hungarian coronation insignia for more than two hundred years. The palace was extended by King Matthias Corvinus, and has been restored to its original glory over the last few decades.

9 Szentendre With Budapest just 20 km (12 miles) away, this picturesque riverside town in Pest county attracts more than its fair share of visitors, especially in the summer. Wandering through the winding cobbled

streets, across the small squares, and up flights of steps in the car-free center of the town, you will soon understand the reason for this. Dainty houses with vibrant, lovingly maintained baroque and rococo façades, a dozen churches, nearly twice as many museums, and of course its location right next to the river make this small town a true gem, and even the countless souvenir shops and the hordes of visitors cannot detract from that. The main square (Fö tér) is a good place from which to set off on a walk around town. You will soon come across some of its many galleries and museums. Thirteen galleries showcase the works of contemporary local artists alone. In terms of its many museums, Szentendre has some unusual

ones. Those with a sweet tooth will enjoy the marzipan museum. There is also a wine museum, the House of Folk Art, a museum of stonework, and Hungary's largest open-air ethnographic museum.

10 Budapest "Queen of the Danube" and "Paris of the East" are just two of the many enthusiastic epithets for Hungary's imposing capital city. Few cities are able to arouse fond nostalgia to quite such a degree as Budapest. As early as the 15th century it was at the heart of central Europe's Renaissance culture, but it acquired its most glamorous flourishes in the *fin de siècle*. After the 1867 Austro-Hungarian Compromise between the Hapsburgs and the

Hungarians, its architectural history was lovingly recreated to further the glory of the new nation-state. There are neogothic residential buildings, neoclassical palaces, sugary sweet, neobaroque palaces, and, as is the case with the parliament building, even a generous dash of ancient Byzantium. The cupolas above the thermal baths were adopted from the Orient, and Andrássy út soon became the local equivalent of the Champs Élysées. With such a vivid pot-pourri of delights, comprising a Castle Hill dating at least in part from medieval times, around one thousand monuments, ancient ruins, and more than two hundred museums and galleries, spiced up with a lively cultural and gastronomic scene, and peppered with plenty of green
(continued p.65)

1 The Danube Bend, seen from the Castle Hill in Visegrád.

2 Esztergom is where the first Hungarian king was crowned. It has been the spiritual heart of Catholic Hungary for a thousand years.

3 Reopened in 2001: the old iron road bridge between Hungarian Esztergom and Slovak Štúrovo.

One of the classic postcard views of Budapest: the Chain Bridge (Széchenyi Lánchíd), completed in 1849, was the first fixed link across the Danube River between the separate districts of Buda and Pest. In the background, the famous Parliament building, opened in 1902, can be seen on the Pest shore of the Danube.

spaces and fashionable shopping streets, Budapest has no problem at all keeping even its most demanding visitors happy. With this many attractions, it is hard to get bored even when you are staying for some time.

What you must do, no matter how little time you have, is to journey by funicular railway (Sikló) up to the castle, visit the Royal Palace, which has been extended several times, together with the National Gallery, the Matthias Church, and the white Fishermen's Bastion, and perhaps go for a stroll in the fortified Vár district. Also not to be missed in Pest, on the east bank of the Danube, are the National and Applied Arts museums, St Stephen's Basilica dating from the second half of the 19th century, the Great Synagogue, built in the Ottoman-Byzantine style, the market halls, the Parliament, and the Opera. And don't forget the traditional coffee houses: the Central, Astoria, and Gerbeaud cafés are especially worth a visit. Finally, you should not miss a trip out to Heroes' Square and a stroll through the City Park.

⓫ **Paks** Just 100 km (62 miles) south of Budapest, this village is also worthy of mention, especially because of its exceptionally attractive Church of the Holy Spirit, built in wood in 1990 to a design by Imre Makovecz, the master of popular Magyar architecture. If you are interested in contemporary art, you should also pay a visit to the adjacent Paks Gallery.

⓬ **Kalocsa** This 1,000-year-old episcopal see, famous for its paprika as well as its embroideries and folk costumes, features an imposing basilica church built in the Italian baroque style, which has a well-stocked treasury and library. Also worth seeing are the ethnographical Viski Museum, a museum dedicated to the history of paprika, and a museum publicizing the work of Miklós Schöffer, a pioneer of cybernetic *son et lumière* computer art.

Farther south, the ship passes the village of Bogyiszló, the port of Szekszárd, which lies above and away from the Danube. In Szekszárd, the capital of the county of Tolna, the remains of an 11th-century Benedictine abbey were excavated in the 1970s. Attractive baroque and neoclassical buildings adorn the center of the village. The main square is dominated by a rococo church, said to be the largest single-nave Catholic church in central Europe. First-class vines flourish on Szekszárd's seven hills, and you can try the wines at a wine tasting.

⓭ **Baja** Only a few miles south of Szekszárd lies the port of Baja, where people have been living off the river for hundreds of years. Here, Hungarians, Serbs, Danube Swabians, and the Croat Bunjevci people have peacefully cohabited for centuries. During the Baja festival, on the second Saturday in July, the famous Baja fish soup (*halászlé*) simmers in some two thousand cauldrons over open fires in the main square. A detour from here takes you to the Duna Dráva National Park (see panel, right).

⓮ **Mohács** For Hungarians, this little town is still inextricably linked with traumatic events: on August 29, 1526, around twenty thousand Hungarian soldiers fell victim to the superior strength of the Turkish forces, on the right bank of the Danube. A votive church on the main square, built in the Byzantine style, commemorates their defeat, which marked the beginning of a 150-year period of foreign rule. The history of the town and battle is documented in the Dorottya Kanizsai Museum. To remember the dead, a park with carved wooden memorials was established in the nearby village of Sátorhely.

⓯ **Kopački Rit** Having crossed into Croatia, the journey continues through the historic region of Baranya. Privately owned by the Habsburg dynasty until 1914, it is renowned as an excellent hunting ground, which is probably one of the main reasons that many of the nobility built their castles here in the past. Near the Drau estuary, the Kopački Rit region of marshes, pastures, and forests ranks as a jewel among European landscapes, invaluable as a refuge

1 An excursion into the puszta plains is not complete without a visit to one of the traditional horse-riding displays, such as this one in Kalocsa.

Duna Dráva National Park

The Gemenc Forest, which stretches over 50,000 ha (123,550 acres) from Szekszárd almost as far as Baja, is part of the national park that continues at Mohács. The park covers what is left of the flood plains and wetland meadows that once bordered the entire course of the Danube, before the

A paradise for nature lovers: the Gemenc Forest, covering 50,000 ha (123,550 acres).

flood defenses were built. Ponds, swamps, ox-bow lakes, and alluvial banks characterize this protected area of great ecological importance, which is home to numerous rare animal species. Access is by ship; from Bárány-fok and Pörböly the park is also accessible by narrow-gauge railway.

for many threatened animal and plant species. Flooded for several months every year, the area is home to wild boar, fallow and red deer, and wild cats. Numerous species of fish spawn here and around 270 different bird species make their nests, including rare black storks and sea eagles. Approximately 229 sq km (88 sq miles) of the region have been a nature reserve since 1967.

Farther south-west lies Osijek, the capital of the Slavonia region, which has around 115,000 inhabitants. A dynamic center of industry, it is a mix of central European bourgeois *joie de vivre* and Pannonian melancholy. Its location on the Drau's right bank, 22 km (14 miles) from the point where it flows into the Danube, made the town an important trade and traffic hub, which was already of strategic importance in Roman times. In the 16th century, after their victory over Hungary, the Turks chose Osijek as their main base. During their rule, a mighty fortress was erected and the town became a thriving city with an oriental influence. Today the town center is the Upper Town. Despite the destruction wrought by bombing in the early 1990s, it still exudes an air of the Austro-Hungarian Empire, with its many attractive houses built in various historicist and art nouveau styles.

16 Vukovar A visit to this little town, located just under 30 km (18 miles) south-east of Osijek, at the confluence of the Vuka and Danube rivers, serves as a reminder of the horrors of war. As early as 1231 Vukovar received its charter as a free royal city, and from 1745 it became the administrative center of the Srijem area. In 1991–1992, within 100 days, 90 percent of the buildings were destroyed by bombing, and most of the inhabitants were either killed or expelled. Entire streets of the once charming baroque town center are still awaiting repair and renovation today. Yet, about two-thirds of the residential houses have now been restored, and the fields, vineyards, and forests in the environs have been cleared of landmines. Important historic buildings, such as the former Grand Hotel, the Srijem County Palace, and the Franciscan monastery, have also been restored to their former glory. The municipal museum has returned to the baroque castle of the Counts of Eltz, and once again documents the rich archaeological and sociological heritage of the city and its hinterland.

17 Ilok Croatia's most easterly town lies 40 km (25 miles) beyond Vukovar in another wide loop of the Danube on the Fruška Gora Hills, a densely wooded mountain

range designated a national park on its Serbian side. It is dotted with numerous well-known Orthodox monasteries. In the 15th century, the strategically important village was fortified against the advancing Ottomans and these fortifications still characterize the townscape today. In the old town, the baths (hamam) and a dervish tomb are reminders of Turkish rule, which lasted for 130 years, while its Catholic heritage is represented by the Franciscan monastery, which houses

the tomb of St Capistran, a 15th-century itinerant preacher, in its chapel. Also worth seeing is the municipal museum in the Odescalchi Palace, a baroque building with wine cellars branching out in all directions.

18 Novi Sad The capital of the autonomous province of Voyvodina lies just under 30 km (18 miles) east of Ilok in the Pannonian lowlands bordering the Danube. The second largest Serb city, with around 300,000 inhabitants, it

was founded in around 1700 by traders and craftsmen. During the Turkish occupation it was considered the center of intellectual resistance. Bearing witness to the town's spiritual and intellectual pre-eminence are several Orthodox churches, thirteen colleges, and the literary association Matica srpska, which was founded in 1828. The art gallery of the same name houses an extensive collection of Serb paintings and illustrations. Other places worth seeing are the Voyvodina Museum as

Excursion

Bucharest

Thanks to its chic boulevards and architecture, as well as its lively intellectual scene, Romania's capital enjoyed a reputation as the "Paris of the East" in the 1920s. But World War II, the decades of the Ceauşescu dictatorship, and the earthquake of 1977 made such glory fade into oblivion. Named after a shepherd called Bucur ("the cheerful") who built the first little church here according to legend, near the small Dâmboviţa River, this city of some two million inhabitants

Ceauşescu's "House of the People" is today used as the seat of Parliament (Palatul Parlamentului).

has only begun to remerge since the end of the Communist regimes. Vast squares, such as Piata Universitatii or Revolutiei, bear witness to the modernization frenzy that raged here, yet a pleasant contrast is created by expansive green parks dotted with lakes, such as Parcul Cişmigiu.

In the 15th century, Bucharest became the winter residence of the Walachian princes; from the mid 17th century they made the town their permanent seat, and in 1861 it became the capital of unified Romania. Even during a brief tour, you will be struck by the huge variety of building styles. These range from the ruins of the 15th-century Curtea Veche, the old royal court of the town's founder, Vlad Ţepeş to Orthodox churches and monasteries, villas in the style of the Second Empire, the late-19th-century apartment blocks in the Calea Victoriei, swanky Stalinist palaces, and the Communist-era concrete-panel buildings. In stark contrast stands the Village and Ethnographic Museum (Muzeul Taranului Roman), which comprises 300 original structures from all over the country. On the subject of museums, well worth a visit are the National History Collection and the National Art Museum.

well as the collection of historic buildings around the main square, especially the Town Hall, the Bishop's Palace, and the Cathedral Church (saborna crkva). Novi Sad's emblem is the Petrovaradin Fortress on the right bank. Covering an area of 100 ha (247 acres) and comprising a 16-km (10-mile) long system of tunnels and casemates, this complex became the historic location where the Habsburg troops led by Prince Eugene fought and won against the Turks. Today, it is

home to artists' workshops and the municipal museum.

⑲ Belgrade The capital of Serbia, situated on the Sava estuary and of strategic importance for thousands of years, stands on the site of a Roman settlement. An important traffic hub and industrial town, today it has a population of more than 1.1 million inhabitants. The Danube divides the city into two parts, the Old Town and New Belgrade, adjacent to the historic district of

Zemun, which is under autonomous administration. The main attraction is the powerful Kalemegdan Fortress. Much fought over, especially by the Habsburgs and the Turks, the fortress has Celtic and Roman origins, but in its present form dates back mainly to the 18th century. Especially worth seeing in the fortress, which has today been transformed into a municipal park, are the massive towers and entrance gates, the moat, the bridges, the clock tower, and the Roman springs, as well as the vast military museum (Vojni Muzej). The artists' quarter, Skardarlija, is a pleasant place to stroll and admire its 19th-century buildings.

⑳ The Iron Gate/Derdap East of Belgrade, fed by the rivers Tisza, Sava, and Great Morava, the Danube reaches its full breadth, flowing initially through fertile lowland plains. At Golubac, guarded by a well-preserved medieval fortress, the Derdap National Park begins, one of the most visited areas in Serbia. Its main attraction is the magnificent gorge more than 100 km (62 miles) long known as the Iron Gate, at the entrance to the Carpathian Mountains. Its rocky sides reach a height of over 500 m (1,640 ft), while the river is almost 90 m (295 ft) deep here. Carved into the rockface on the right-

hand side is the Tabula Traiana, only visible from the water, evidence that a Roman road once ran along here. The hydroelectric Iron Gate dam, just before Kladovo, was opened in 1971, turning the river into a 150-km (93-mile) long reservoir. The journey continues across the reservoir right up to the sluices near Orşova, where nearly all the Danube cruises drop anchor. From here, a detour to Bucharest is worthwhile (see panel, opposite).

㉑ Drobeta Turnu Severin In this sleepy little town, the Romans once built a 1,100-m (3,609-ft) bridge across the Danube, to its south bank, something of a wonder of the world at the time. The Iron Gate Museum has a scale model of the legendary bridge, which is well worth seeing.
(continued p.70)

1 Whether in Hungary, Serbia, or Romania, the river is still the principal source of food for the countries that border it.

2 The Derdap Gorge, also known as the Iron Gate, is the most spectacular valley of the Danube, breaching the foothills of the southern Carpathian Mountains.

3 A fisherman proudly presents his catch: two fresh sturgeon.

The giant pelican flocks in the Danube Delta are just one of Romania's many spectacular natural sights. Of the country's surface area, 8.3 percent or almost 200,000 ha (494,200 acres) in total have now been declared nature reserves. The best known internationally of these eleven regional parks (and even

parks) is the biosphere reserve and UNESCO Natural World Heritage Site of the Danube Delta. The eastern white pelican seen here is the more common of the two European species of pelican. Only very few pairs of Dalmatian pelicans, an endangered species, live in this region.

The voyage continues along the southern edge of the Walachia Region, the Danube here forming first the border between Romania and Serbia, and then Bulgaria, past the towns of Calafat, Corabia, Zimnicea, Giurgiu, and Oltenița. These are only of relatively minor interest for tourists. There is more to see in the Dobrudja, when the Danube turns northward in a wide arc.

22 Tulcea Already serving as an anchorage and trading center in Phoenician and Roman times, this port is of only marginal interest to visitors today. However, it is the starting point for excursions into the Danube Delta. Nearby the river divides into three main branches, which together form a landscape that is unique in Europe: a labyrinth of lakes, swamps, canals, and reed islands, covering 4,500 sq km (1,737 sq miles), where hundreds of bird species nest. While the two outer branches, the Chilia and the Sfântu Gheorghe, snake their way to the Black Sea in endless meanders, the central branch (Sulina) flows to the coast in a straight line. On this branch you also reach Romania's easternmost village, Sulina, from where there are connections by ship to Constanța.

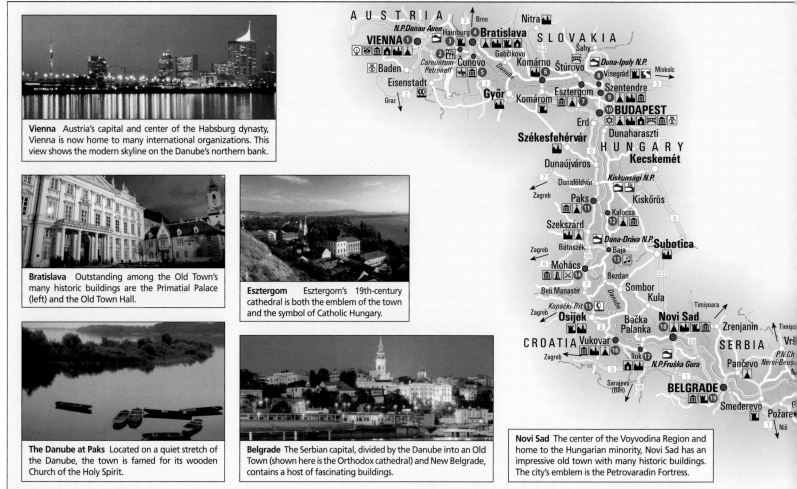

Vienna Austria's capital and center of the Habsburg dynasty, Vienna is now home to many international organizations. This view shows the modern skyline on the Danube's northern bank.

Bratislava Outstanding among the Old Town's many historic buildings are the Primatial Palace (left) and the Old Town Hall.

Esztergom Esztergom's 19th-century cathedral is both the emblem of the town and the symbol of Catholic Hungary.

The Danube at Paks Located on a quiet stretch of the Danube, the town is famed for its wooden Church of the Holy Spirit.

Belgrade The Serbian capital, divided by the Danube into an Old Town (shown here is the Orthodox cathedral) and New Belgrade, contains a host of fascinating buildings.

Novi Sad The center of the Voyvodina Region and home to the Hungarian minority, Novi Sad has an impressive old town with many historic buildings. The city's emblem is the Petrovaradin Fortress.

23 Constanța Romania's largest sea port was founded by Greek settlers in the sixth century BC. It has much to offer the visitor today: a picturesque old town complete with lighthouse and beach promenade, ancient remains, minarets, church towers, and cupolas. In addition, Constanța is the focal point of the Black Sea beach resorts.

About 50 km (31 miles) north from here is Histria, a fascinating place of ruins, whose columns and walls bear witness to the history of the region, from Greek via Roman to Byzantine times.

From Constanța, you can return to Bucharest (see page 67) via road or rail, and from there take a flight home.

1 Rangers ensure that no one endangers or desecrates the natural habitat in the Danube Delta. Seen here is one of their observation huts.

2 It is easy to lose your sense of direction on the seemingly endless watercourses of the Danube Delta.

3 A romantic experience on every occasion: sunset on the reed-lined banks.

Budapest Hungary's capital shines with a wealth of diverse architectural styles. Shown here is a view of Parliament from the Fishermen's Bastion.

Duna Dráva National Park Rare animal species, such as the otter and the wild cat, live in the protected water-meadows.

Tulcea In ancient times, this port was already an important trading town for the Phoenicians and later the Romans. An industrial city on the Sfântu Gheorghe branch of the Danube, today it has also taken on a significant tourist role as the starting point for excursions into the Danube Delta.

The Danube Delta The Danube's estuary has a landscape that is unique in Europe. You can explore this unusual world on a tour by boat.

Bucharest The former "Paris of the East" lost much of its original charm with the erection of monumental buildings, such as the Parliament building, during the Ceaușescu years.

Histria Admire remains from the Greek, Roman, and Byzantine periods in these ancient ruins.

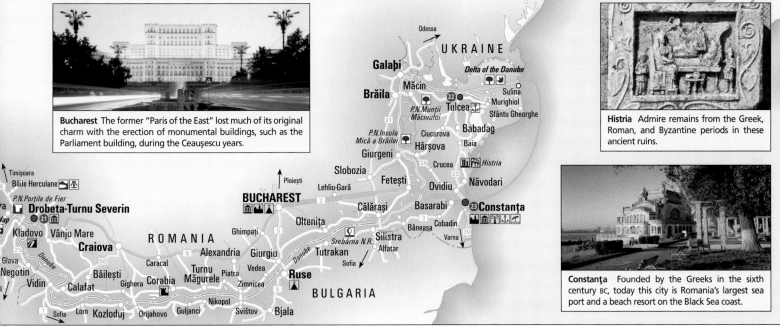

Constanța Founded by the Greeks in the sixth century BC, today this city is Romania's largest sea port and a beach resort on the Black Sea coast.

Playa de Ses Illetes: Formentera's best-known beach captivates with its fine, white sand and crystal-clear waters.

Route 5

Spain

Jewels of the Mediterranean: the Balearic Islands

The Balearic Islands enjoy around 300 days of sunshine per year. With so much sun, and a choice of some 180 beaches ranging from long, flat sandy stretches (*platjas*) to small, sandy bays (*calas*), and shingle beaches over-looked by rocky cliffs, it's hardly surprising that up to seven million holiday-makers flock every year to Mallorca's popular resorts. Parts of Ibiza are just as lively, but life is a little more sedate on Menorca and Formentera. Amid all the pleasure seeking, some visitors overlook the natural beauty of the islands.

Many artists, from Chopin to Miró, have been drawn to Mallorca (or Majorca as it is also known), the largest of the Balearic Islands, by the atmospheric quality of its light. Sunseekers and water lovers flock to the beaches, while nature lovers explore the island's beautiful countryside on foot or by bicycle, and night owls enjoy the dance and night clubs. Even so, Mallorca is far from being a European Florida, nor is it simply devoted to nightlife culture. True it is a

holiday paradise, but one that has pre-served its identity, language, culture, archi-tecture, festivals, customs, and traditions. Despite having much in common, there are considerable differences between Mallorca and its three sister islands of Menorca to the north and Ibiza and Formentera to the south. The latter two are also known as the Pityuse Islands (pine-tree covered islands). Ibiza is infamous for its nightlife, which continues round the clock, but life is more

Inside the Miró Museum in Palma de Mallorca.

relaxed on Formentera, which draws peo-ple who want to chill out or escape the rat race. With its numerous prehistoric sites, Menorca is like an open-air museum, and nearly half of the island is a nature reserve. Long before the Balearic Islands became such a popular holiday destination for sun-hungry tourists, they were a desirable prize for Phoenician and Greek sailors. In 123 BC, the Carthaginians were replaced by the Romans under Consul Belarius, who gave his name to the islands. After the Romans, the islands were successively occupied by the Vandals, Visigoths, and Franks, before the Moors settled here in 903. The Moors were extremely influential, their rule last-ing for almost 300 years, until the 13th cen-tury, when they were forced to retreat before the Spanish during the Reconquest. Since then, apart from interludes under British control, the Balearic Islands have

The cliffs rise steeply at Cap de Formentor in north-east Mallorca. At the tip of the Formentor peninsula, wind and water have created spectacular rock formations.

The lighthouse at Cap de Cavalleria on Menorca stands high above the sea.

been an autonomous province of Spain. About 700,000 people live on the islands, which have an overall area of 5,014 sq km (1,935 sq miles). They speak Mallorquin, a version of Catalan and an old literary language, closely related to Castilian Spanish. Towns and villages often have both Spanish and Mallorquin names. Most of the islands are hilly or even mountainous, with Mallorca's Puig Major (Major Peak) the highest at 1,443 m (4,734 ft). The climate is moderate Mediterranean, with dry, warm summers and mild winters, which is why the almond trees start flowering as early as the end of January. Tourism, the service industries, and construction have made the islands one of the most prosperous Spanish provinces. However, the contribution of agriculture to the islands' economy has been much reduced as a result, and the fishing industry increasingly suffers from overfishing in the Mediterranean. The main foodstuffs grown and produced on the islands are tomatoes, citrus fruits, apricots, almonds, olives, carob, and wine. Pigs are bred in the holm oak woods and in the *macchia* (scrubland).

Numerous festivals are celebrated on the islands. In Palma, for example, Epiphany, the Day of the Three Kings, is a noisy affair, with ships' sirens blasting out and firework displays. Artá is known for its festivals, such as its Easter procession and the spectacular fiesta of San Salvador in early August. Sineu holds a lively spring festival on the first Sunday in May and at Pollença, as elsewhere, a mock historic battle between the *cristians i moros* (Christians and Moors) takes place each year. Petra, meanwhile, is famous for its almond blossom festival, Vilafranca de Bonany for its melon festival, and Binissalem for its wine festival.

Mallorca: The Plaça Espanya in the center of Felanitx, with the Church of Sant Miquel.

Prehistoric cultures

It is likely that settlers from the Iberian peninsula arrived on the Balearic Islands as early as the late Bronze Age, in the third millennium BC. Evidence of their presence can be seen in the remains of places of worship and the *navetas*, megalithic chamber tombs resembling the upturned hulls of ships. During the late Bronze Age, the Talaiot (from Arabic *atala-ya* = guard tower) culture developed on the Islands. It is characterized by round, tower-like stone buildings built from blocks of limestone, similar to the *nuraghen* on Sardinia. There are

Large monuments provide evidence of the megalithic culture on Menorca:
Top: Son Bon Torre d'en Groumes.
Middle: *taula* near Binissafúller.
Bottom: the Naveta des Tudons near Ciutadella.

several hundred such structures on both Menorca and Mallorca, but it is only on Menorca that you find large numbers of *taulas*, large slabs of stone several feet high topped by another flatter slab, resembling large T-shaped stone tables. It is still not known whether these prehistoric structures originally served a religious or an astrological purpose.

The cruise around the Balearic Islands begins in Ciutadella on Menorca, from where you head inland, across the island to Maó on the east coast, and from there take the ferry to Palma de Mallorca. After a tour of Mallorca, another ferry takes you to Ibiza and to its capital, Eivissa, from where you make the short trip to the island of Formentera.

① Ciutadella With its characteristic Spanish-Moorish architecture, the old town of this Menorcan port has retained much of its former charm. Above the waterfront, around the Plaça des Born, are the town hall, mansions with English-style sash windows, the Teatro Municipal des Born, and the 17th-century Church of Sant Francesc. The entrance to the port is dominated by the Castell de Sant Nicolau (17th C.). However, Ciutadella's emblem is the Gothic Cathedral (13th/14th C.), Menorca's most important religious building.

Not far from Ciutadella are the fine sandy beaches of Cala Macarelleta, Cala Morell, Cala Blanca, Cala n´Bosch, Cala des Talaier, Cala Turqueta, and Cala d'Algayarens, with their many water sports and leisure facilities. Five km (3 miles) to the east, on the road to Maó, stands Menorca's most significant prehistoric structure, the Naveta des Tudons, and 3 km (2 miles) farther along is the Torre Trencada, a 3-m (10-ft) high *taula* with a stone circle and caves.

② Ferreries From Ciutadella, take the C721 road across the island to Ferreries, where the Church of Sant Bartomeu (17th/18th C.) is worth seeing. South of the village are the ruins of the 4,000-year-old settlement of Son Mercer de Baix. South-west from here, you can hike through the charming Barranc d'Algendar Gorge. Several miles long, it is flanked by steep rocky cliffs some 80 m (262 ft) high. The gorge leads to the Cala Galdana on the south coast, a resort tightly packed with hotels.

③ Es Mercadal Renowned for its excellent restaurants, this village of whitewashed houses is dominated by its windmill, which has also been converted into a restaurant. The remains of an enormous Moorish water cistern, *l'aljub*, is still in use today and forms part of the modern water system. Climb

Travel information

Route profile
Length: approx. 400 km (249 miles)(without flights)
Duration: 10 days
Start: Ciutadella (Menorca)
End: Eivissa (Ibiza)
Itinerary (main locations): Ciutadella , Alaior, Palma de Mallorca, Valldemossa, Pollença, Manacor, Eivissa, Formentera

Transport tips
Driving is on the right and seat belts are obligatory. The alcohol limit is 0.5%. Yellow road markings mean no stopping, and the police are very strict about speeding. It is illegal to use a mobile phone while driving.

When to go
The islands are suitable for a holiday almost all year round. You can generally swim in the sea from May to October.

Accommodation
On Mallorca especially, there are hotels at all price levels, from 50 € to more than 200 €. Information on *fincas*: Associacio Agroturisme Balear, *www.agrotourismobalear.com*. There are few campsites on Mallorca; Ibiza has three, Menorca two, but Formentera none.

Tourist information
www.spain.info
www.illesbalears.es
www.balearicsislands.com

❺ Maó From Alaior the road continues in a virtually straight line directly to Maó, also known as Mahón, the capital of Menorca. Among the city's main attractions are the Church of Santa Maria with its magnificent organ and the Claustre del Carme, once the cloisters of a monastery but today a market hall. The port basin, 1.2 km (¾ mile) wide and 6 km (4 miles) long, is lined with restaurants, bars, and boutiques. There are several prehistoric sites in the Maó area also, such as Taula de Trepacó and the remains of the prehistoric settlement of Talati de D'Alt. From Maó a ferry takes you to Palma de Mallorca.

(continued p.80)

to the top of the nearby Monte Toro for some excellent panoramic views of the island. It is Menorca's highest mountain at 357 m (1,171 ft) and is crowned by a statue of Christ.

From Mercadal, you can take a detour to Cap de Cavalleria. The most northerly point on Menorca, it rises up 90 m (295 ft) and is topped with a lighthouse. Another worthwhile excursion is to the pretty fishing village of Fornells, on the beautiful Bay of Fornells. Its attractions include a superb sandy beach, and the local specialty, *caldereta de langosta*, a delicious stew of langoustines.

❹ Alaior From Mercadal, the road leads to Menorca's third largest town, famed for its Mahón cheese and its shoe manufacture. The old churches of Santa Eulária and San Diego are worth a visit, and afterwards you can take a stroll among the cypress trees in the tranquil *cementiri* (cemetery). Nearby are the prehistoric sites of Torralba d'en Salort and Torre d'en Gaumés, the largest complex of its kind on Menorca.

1 View of Ciutadella's waterfront promenade in the west of Menorca.

2 The large port of Maó is used by both the navy and the fishing trade.

3 The Cala Macarelleta is one of Menorca's most beautiful bays. It can be reached on foot by a track, but many visitors arrive by boat.

The construction of La Seu Cathedral in Palma de Mallorca, the capital of the Balearic Islands, was begun in the 13th century. It is one of the most beautiful sacred buildings in the world. La Seu derives from sedes, meaning "seat" in Latin. The seat in question is generally taken to be the seat of the bishops

It is built on the foundations of a mosque that belonged to the Almudaina Palace, once the residence of Mallorca's Moorish rulers. Over the centuries,

Palma de Mallorca

Situated at the end of the wide bay of Palma, on Mallorca's south-west coast, is the undisputed center of international holiday traffic in the islands, Palma de Mallorca. The Mallorquins refer to the capital of the Balearics simply as La Ciutat ("the town").

With its medieval town center, the *centro historic*, Palma is one of Spain's most attractive cities. It is dominated by the Gothic La Seu Cathedral, one of the most magnificent churches in the world. In a stunning location in front of the lake in the Parc de la Mar, it stands on the foundations of an earlier Moorish mosque and looks out over the bay. The wide nave is very impressive due to its height (44 m/144 ft). The two main bell towers (67.5/221 ft and 47.8 m/157 ft) are unfinished. The superb rose window on the apse is 11.5 m (38 ft) wide and contains over a thousand pieces of stained glass.

Aside from the cathedral, there are another thirty churches in the city, including Sant Francesc, which has Europe's longest cloister and houses the tomb of Ramón Llulls, known as the "Spanish Luther" (1235–1315). Among the secular buildings of note are the Palau Reial de l'Almudaina (13th C.), which was built by Mallorca's first king, Jaume I (1276–1311), on top of the Moorish Alcazar, and the late-Gothic merchants' exchange Sa Llotja (15th C.), as well as the remains of the Banys Arabs (Moorish baths), to which should be added a total of seventy-two former city palaces, all with beautiful inner courtyards.

Visitors stroll, shop, and enjoy the nightlife along the plane-tree-lined ters Pelaires and Sa Nostra, and of course, the Fundació Pilar i Joan Miró. Aside from strolling along the Passeig des Born, allow time for shopping in the Avinguda Jaume III and in the narrow streets and alleyways leading off the Plaça Major. Culinary delights are on offer in the Mercat Olivar, and in the maze of streets between Sa Llotja and the Passeig Marítim, Palma's club scene reigns supreme.

The Castell de Bellver, commissioned in 1309 by Jaume II stands on a hill overlooking the town. Dominating the bay of Palma, the castle was built in a strategically important position. For a time, the fortress held political prisoners. From the castle's roof, you can enjoy magnificent views across Palma de Mallorca and the Serra de Tramuntana mountain range.

Below the Castell de Bellver and the Fundació Pilar i Joan Miró (opened in 1993 and displaying three thousand of the artist's works) is the Palicio Marivent. It is the Spanish Royal Family's official residence in Majorca, which they visit quite frequently.

Palma lies at the northern tip of the Badia de Palma, the second largest bay on Mallorca, lined with sandy beaches. It is here that mass tourism began, with its attendant blight of "costa-style" apartment and hotel developments. It led to the airport of Son Sant Joan,

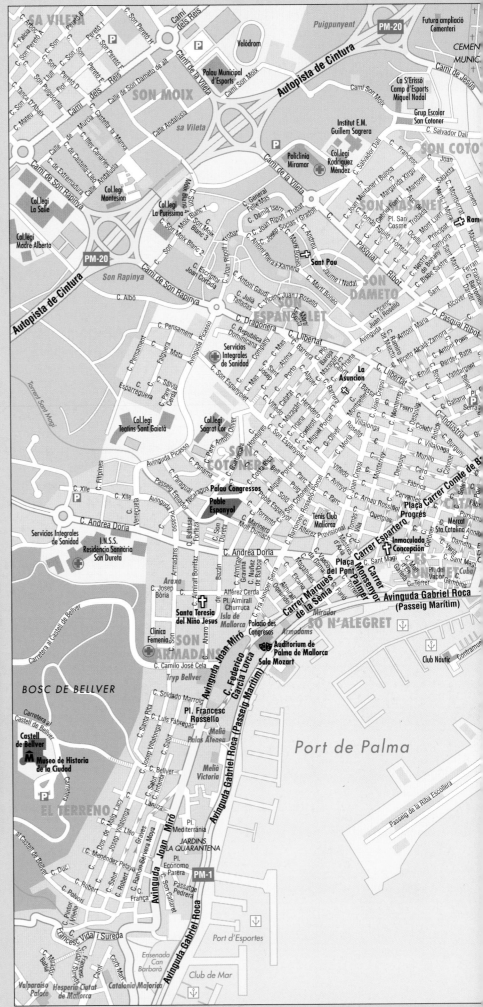

The La Seu Cathedral towers above the port of Palma de Mallorca.

Passeig des Born and around the picturesque squares Plaça Major, Plaça Cort, and Plaça Weyler. The squares are lined with buildings with superb art nouveau façades, such as the Teatro Principal, the Gran Hotel, and the Museu d'Art Espanyol Contemporani. Museums worth visiting include the Museu de Mallorca (ethnography and the period under Moorish rule), Casal Solleric (modern art), the cultural cen- south-east of Palma, completed in 1997, becoming Europe's largest charter airport. From here it is only a stone's throw to the three best-known holiday resorts on the east coast of the bay: Can Pastilla, Ses Maravelles, S'Arenal. This stretch of coastline offers just about everything you could want in terms of beaches and water sports, including a fairly raucous nightlife, especially at Ses Maravelles.

Badía de Palma

Fincas

The Spanish word *finca* originally referred to any rural property, from a farm to a country estate, often incorporating plantations where citrus fruit, olives, or grapes were cultivated; in more recent years, plants such as aloe vera have also been grown to suit demand.

Mass tourism on the Balearic Islands has meanwhile introduced the term into estate agents' speak, where it mostly refers to a (rural) holiday apartment or bed-and-breakfast place. For the proprietors, the only way to maintain or renovate the often neglected, centuries-old buildings, constructed in the style typical of each island, is to let the property short-term to holidaymakers. Most of the *fincas* are located in Spain's classic holiday regions, such as the Balearic and Canary Islands.

Top: a *finca* near Muro.
Bottom: a *finca* and windmill near the small town of Algáida.

Some still operate in traditional ways, giving guests the opportunity to experience and help with the cultivating, harvesting, and processing of whatever is grown on the estate. And children are bound to enjoy seeing any of the various domestic animals that are typically reared on the estates, such as chickens or oxen. A stay in a finca is a good alternative to a package holiday on the heavily built-up coast. That's if you can afford it: it is not cheap.

6 Palma de Mallorca See pages 78–79.

7 Portals Nous The road along the west coast of the Badia de Palma leads first to Portals Nous, which provides anchorage for some impressive yachts and boasts a waterfront promenade lined with elegant restaurants and bars. Children may like to visit Marineland on the road to Palma Nova.

8 Palma Nova/Magaluf These two villages have now virtually merged into one and are very popular with British visitors. Among the attractions are the Platja de Palma Nova, the Aquapark leisure center, a diving center, and the submarine *Nemo*, which dives to a depth of 20 m (66 ft). Continuing south down the spit of land to the west of the Badia de Palma, *platjas* and *calas* follow one after the other down to Cap de Cala Figuera. All the resorts along the west coast of the bay are under the administration of the small town of Calvía, which received an ecology award from the EU in 1997.

9 Andratx From Palma Nova, the C719 continues to Andratx, past the resorts of Santa Ponça

Sa Calobra

The spectacular "snake road" winds its way in breathtaking bends through the precipitous mountain world, at one point even turning back underneath itself at an angle of 270 degrees. Winding its way down through the hills it ends at the Cala de sa Calobra, where the Torrent des Pareis River emerges from a huge gorge formed by erosion, and flows out into the sea.

and Peguera. In nearby Cala Fornells, the holiday complex created by the architect Pedro Otzoup is worth a visit. Andratx itself is generally a much quieter place, though it livens up on Wednesdays with the weekly market selling local products. The Castell de Son Mas with its

talaias (defensive towers) now houses the town hall and hosts cultural events. A short distance farther south is Port d'Andratx situated in a beautiful deep bay where countless luxury yachts drop anchor opposite the residential area of Cap de sa Mola. Before continuing on to Vall-

demossa, a trip to Sant Elm is a real must. From here, the ferry takes you to the Parc Natural on the island of Sa Dragonera (15 minutes). More than 320 species of plants are to be found here, and many rare bird species breed on the island, including the black Eleonora's falcon.

Back in Andratx, the road winds its way parallel to the coast up to Banyalbufar, one of the most idyllic villages on Mallorca, with steep flights of steps and alleyways on either side of the road, terraced gardens that betray their Moorish origins, and superb views out to sea. Nearby are the ruins of former *talaias*, such as the Mirador de Ses Animes and the Mirador de Ricardo Roca.

From Banyalbufar, you can take a short trip inland to the town of Puigpunyent in the heart of the Serra de Tramuntana. Rising to a height of 1,026 m (3,366 ft), the nearby mountain Puig de Galatzó lies in the nature park Reserva Puig de Galatzó, which contains some spectacular waterfalls and a nature trail.

10 Valldemossa Back on the C710, the road leads to this much-visited mountain village on the 1,062-m (3,484-ft) high Puig de Teix with its famous Carthusian

monastery, where the monks' cells had already been converted into two- and three-room apartments by the 19th century. Frédéric Chopin and George Sand lived here between 1838 and 1839, putting Valldemossa firmly on the map for visiting music and literature lovers across the world ever since. A Chopin festival is staged here every year in August. Nearby, in the Port de Valldemossa, the Son Marroig, once the summer residence of the Austrian Archduke Ludwig Salvator, stands in splendid isolation. It is famous for its views and the concert performances held at sunset.

11 Deià Thanks to its location and the beautiful quality of the light, this idyllic mountain village has long been a haven for artists, musicians and writers. Famous residents have included Robert Graves, Ernst Fuchs, Arik Brauer, Eric Clapton, and Mike Oldfield. North of Deià, in the tranquil village of Lluc Alcari, the houses cling to the rocks like swallows' nests.

12 Sóller/Port de Sóller This small town lies in a basin enclosed by steep mountain slopes and surrounded by orange, lemon, and

fig plantations. The Church of Sant Bartomeu is of interest as are the façades of the surrounding houses. Every year, the historic reenactment of "Cristians i Moros" and "Ses valentes dones" commemorating the victory of the women of Sóller over Turkish pirates causes plenty of excitement on the beach. On the coast, just a few miles away from the town of Sóller lies Port de Sóller, which you can reach by car or on an historic tram. The lively port is known for its almost circular bay as well as its street cafés and excellent restaurants. Back on the C710 once more, after passing the 1,445-m (4,741-ft) high Puig Major, a winding road branches off to the left, towards the Cala

1 Typical karst (limestone) outcrops in the rocky landscape of the Cala Sa Calobra.

2 Fishing nets in the Port de Sóller.

3 Son Marroig, the former country estate of Archduke Ludwig Salvator, lies high above the Costa Brava Mallorquina.

4 The mountain village of Valldemossa, popular among visitors, situated at 437 m (1,434 ft).

1

Stunning caves

The Balearic Islands attract visitors for their sun, sea, coastline, and beautiful countryside, but are equally fascinating below ground. Mallorca especially has hundreds of caves, including the

In the Cova de Can Marça on Ibiza.

famous Coves del Drac near Portocristo. The highlight is a visit to the underground lake, 177 m (581 ft) long and 40 m (131 ft) wide, where you can glide across in an illuminated boat while listening to classical music. A similar spectacle is on offer at Ibiza's Cova de Can Marça near Port de Sant Miquel. Smugglers once used it as a hideaway, but today an artificial waterfall splashes gently amid stalactites and stalagmites, accompanied by a *son et lumière* show.

de sa Calobra and the Torrent de Pareis gorge.

⑬ **Pollença** In Roman times, this little town was the island's main center, and it is still considered its secret capital today. The Plaça Major is one of most attractive squares on Mallorca. Not far from here is the Font de Gall, the cockerel fountain. The "penitents' stairway" takes you up 364 steps to Mount Calvary, from where, at a height of 170 m (558 ft), you can enjoy superb views across the town and the sea. At the northern edge of the town, a two-arch Roman bridge has survived the ravages of the centuries. This is where spectacular performances of the historic Cristians i Moros festival take place every year. An excursion to the headland of Cap de Formentor, the most northerly point on the island, offers spectacular views.

⑭ **Alcúdia** From Pollença, the road continues along the coast of the Badia de Pollença to Alcúdia, once the Moorish capital of the island and the gateway to the La Victoria peninsula and the Cap d'es Pinar. In the village you can still see the two town gates and walls dating from the 13th century. Below the walls stands the

2

Church of Sant Jaume. The bay between Pollença and Alcúdia/ Cap d'es Pinar is nearly 30 km (19 miles) long and fringed by seemingly endless beaches.
From Alcúdia the route turns south to Inca, Mallorca's third largest town, famed for its traditional cellar restaurants and its leather products. From here the road veers away from the coast to Sineu in the heart of the island. Among its attractions are the old village church and the Palacio Real, now used as a convent. If you can plan your journey accord-

ingly, try to be in Petra for the almond blossom festival (February 12) on the way to Manacor, and then continue to Vilafranca de Bonany for the melon festival on the second Sunday in September, the village is renowned for its sugar-sweet melons.

⑮ **Manacor** Despite being the second largest town on Mallorca and a hub for transport on the island, Manacor has remained almost untouched by mass tourism. It is known for its imitation pearls made from natural

products. A worthwhile detour from here is to the coast at Portocristo, and especially to the Coves del Drac, spectacular caves with thousands of floodlit stalactites and the largest underground lake in Europe (see panel, left).

⑯ **Felanitx** South of Manacor lies the sedate little town of Felanitx. The 13th-century Church of Sant Miquel has a magnificent façade and a grand flight of steps leading up to its portal. The surrounding maze of narrow streets and alleyways is enchanting.

17 Santanyi Farther south still is the village of Santanyi, where artisans, gallery owners, and restaurateurs have made their home, largely to serve the German residents living in the surrounding area. Not far from here is the Cala Figuera, one of Mallorca's most beautiful resorts. A short detour will take you past the old windmills near Ses Salines to the coastal village of Còlonia de Sant Jordi. The route then continues towards Campos and from there to the market town of Lluc- major and the nearby 549-m

(1,801-ft) high Puig de Randa, which is crowned by not just one but three monasteries.
The return journey from here is via the large and bustling resort of S'Arenal and on to Palma de Mallorca, where a scheduled ferry takes you across to Ibiza.

18 Eivissa Founded by the Carthaginians, Ibiza's capital, also known as Ibiza Town, is one of the oldest in the Mediterranean. The old town is characterized by its white cube-shaped houses, enclosed by defensive

walls and dominated by the cathedral. Eivissa consists of two parts: the upper town, Dalt Vila, and the lower town with its former fishing quarter Sa Penya and the old port district of La Marina. For many visitors, the tour of the town starts here, past the monument to the corsairs in the Passeig des Moll, diagonally opposite the Church of Sant Elm. The narrow Carrer de la Verge runs through the Sa Penya quarter with its many boutiques, which have made the charming slightly neglected look of Ibiza so

famous. Dalt Vila (meaning High Town) is surrounded by well preserved 16th-century defensive walls. You can enter via one of three impressive gateways, including the Portal de ses Taules. The Cathedral of Sant Maria de las Nieves towers into the sky forming the focal point of the Dalt Vila, framed by the bishops' palace and an archaeological museum. On the way back down to the lower town, you pass the Chapel of Sant Ciriac, dedicated to the town's patron saint, and the baroque Church of Santo Domingo.

1 The mighty ramparts of the upper town of Eivissa look down onto the port below.

2 Cruise ships such as the *Aida* frequently drop anchor in the port of Eivissa, on Ibiza.

3 High above the steep cliffs of the Cap Jueu on Ibiza's south-west tip, the Torre del Pirata offers views of the uninhabited islands of Vedranell and Es Vedrá.

4 Small bays nestling between protective rocky cliffs, such as the beach of Sa Caleta shown here, are typical of Ibiza's south-west coast.

Nightlife

Beachlife and nightlife merge almost seamlessly into one on the Ballearics, especially on Mallorca and Ibiza. They party till late on the beaches and in the bars, cafés, and clubs. Mallorca is far

A live performance at the El Divino disco on Ibiza.

surpassed, however, by the Ibiza club scene, where the fun is virtually around the clock. Fast music, frenetic dancing and light shows, all kinds of beauty contests… just about anything goes here. At El Divino you can dine in its terrace restaurant with fine views of the port, and then work off all those extra calories in the club below.

19 Cap Jueu The journey now continues in a south-westerly direction, via Sant Josep de sa Talaia and Cala d'Hort, to the south-western tip of the island at Cap Jueu. A short walk takes you to the 18th-century Torre del Pirata, high above the steep cliffs. The route then continues parallel to the coast, past the modern holiday complex of Cala Vedella and on to Sant Antoni de Portmany.

20 Sant Antoni de Portmany One of Ibiza's largest tourist destinations, the old part of San Antonio, as it is also known, is certainly worth seeing though the town has now been crowded out with over 90 hotel complexes. They attract a mainly youthful clientele, which makes for an exceptionally lively, and often rowdy atmosphere, and not just at night, but also in the daytime on the surrounding beaches along the bays of the Badia de Sant Antoni, such as Cala Tarida, Cala Comte, Cala Bassa, Cala Grassico, Cala Salada, and Punta Sa Galera.

21 Santa Eulària des Riu If you'd like to escape the hurly-burly of Eivissa to explore the island for at least some of the time, you should head east to Santa Eulària, a much quieter village, despite the Passeig de S'Alamera, a tree-lined avenue full of hippie stalls which attract the tourists. Towering over the little village are the white walls of the Church of Santa Eulària (16th C.), on top of a 52-m (171-ft) high hill. Another hippy market held every Wednesday in Es Canyar, 6 km (4 miles) away, is also a tourist magnet. South of the village, the usually overcrowded Cala Llonga stretches along the coast, while Cala Parda lies to the north, and not far from here is the holiday village of Punta Arabi.

From Santa Eulària the road leads on to Sant Carles de Peralta, where an arts and crafts market is held on Saturdays. Farther north is Es' Port on the Cala de Sant Vicent, an enchanting natural landscape that has also fallen victim to the demands of tourism.

From the small inland town of Sant Vicent de sa Cala, continue through the Serra de la Mala Costa to the village of Sant Joan de Labritja, a haven for those in search of a place to chill out. From there, the road leads west to Sant Miquel de Balansat and via Santa Gertrudis de Fruitera back to Eivissa.

22 Formentera From Eivissa, a ferry crosses to Port de la Savina

on Ibiza's small sister island of Formentera, covering just 100 sq km (39 sq miles). The atmosphere is distinctly laid-back and nude sunbathing is accepted on many of its beaches, reputed to be among the best in the entire Mediterranean. In the north of the island lie the beaches of Illetes and Llevant and the Parc Natural de Ses Salines nature reserve. The longest beach, the Platja de Migjorn, stretches for several miles. It is made up of several small sandy bays separated by rocks. Pinewoods alternate with cornfields and vineyards, and dotted here and there are isolated *fincas*. The scent of rosemary, lavender, and thyme seems to fill the air everywhere along the road from La Savina to Sant Francesc, and from there to Sant Ferran de ses Roques and El Pilar de la Mola in the most easterly part of the island, which is ideal for cycling and rambling.

1 The Punta de Sa Ruda
La Mola rears up out of the sea at Formentera.

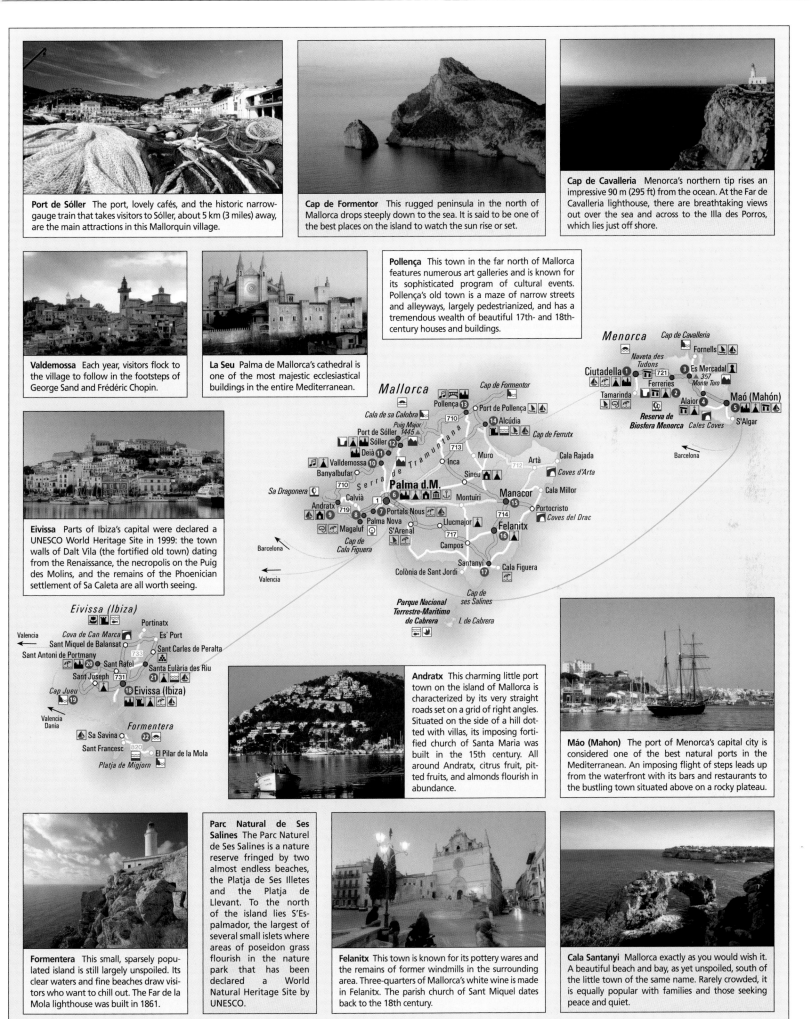

Port de Sóller The port, lovely cafés, and the historic narrow-gauge train that takes visitors to Sóller, about 5 km (3 miles) away, are the main attractions in this Mallorquin village.

Cap de Formentor This rugged peninsula in the north of Mallorca drops steeply down to the sea. It is said to be one of the best places on the island to watch the sun rise or set.

Cap de Cavalleria Menorca's northern tip rises an impressive 90 m (295 ft) from the ocean. At the Far de Cavalleria lighthouse, there are breathtaking views out over the sea and across to the Illa des Porros, which lies just off shore.

Valdemossa Each year, visitors flock to the village to follow in the footsteps of George Sand and Frédéric Chopin.

La Seu Palma de Mallorca's cathedral is one of the most majestic ecclesiastical buildings in the entire Mediterranean.

Pollença This town in the far north of Mallorca features numerous art galleries and is known for its sophisticated program of cultural events. Pollença's old town is a maze of narrow streets and alleyways, largely pedestrianized, and has a tremendous wealth of beautiful 17th- and 18th-century houses and buildings.

Eivissa Parts of Ibiza's capital were declared a UNESCO World Heritage Site in 1999: the town walls of Dalt Vila (the fortified old town) dating from the Renaissance, the necropolis on the Puig des Molins, and the remains of the Phoenician settlement of Sa Caleta are all worth seeing.

Andratx This charming little port town on the island of Mallorca is characterized by its very straight roads set on a grid of right angles. Situated on the side of a hill dotted with villas, its imposing fortified church of Santa Maria was built in the 15th century. All around Andratx, citrus fruit, pitted fruits, and almonds flourish in abundance.

Máo (Mahon) The port of Menorca's capital city is considered one of the best natural ports in the Mediterranean. An imposing flight of steps leads up from the waterfront with its bars and restaurants to the bustling town situated above on a rocky plateau.

Formentera This small, sparsely populated island is still largely unspoiled. Its clear waters and fine beaches draw visitors who want to chill out. The Far de la Mola lighthouse was built in 1861.

Parc Natural de Ses Salines The Parc Naturel de Ses Salines is a nature reserve fringed by two almost endless beaches, the Platja de Ses Illetes and the Platja de Llevant. To the north of the island lies S'Espalmador, the largest of several small islets where areas of poseidon grass flourish in the nature park that has been declared a World Natural Heritage Site by UNESCO.

Felanitx This town is known for its pottery wares and the remains of former windmills in the surrounding area. Three-quarters of Mallorca's white wine is made in Felanitx. The parish church of Sant Miquel dates back to the 18th century.

Cala Santanyi Mallorca exactly as you would wish it. A beautiful beach and bay, as yet unspoiled, south of the little town of the same name. Rarely crowded, it is equally popular with families and those seeking peace and quiet.

A well-deserved lunch break for a mule in the picturesque village of Ía on Santorini.

Greece

Island-hopping from Ándros to Kythnos

The Cyclades Islands rise out of the shimmering deep blue sea in a spectacular range of shapes and sizes. Mountainous and rugged, edged by sandy beaches and coves, picturesque whitewashed villages cling to their slopes, or cluster around their natural anchorages, and ferries cross back and forth between them during the summer months.

The Cyclades Islands form a ring in the Aegean Sea; their name is derived from the old Greek word *kyklos* ("ring" or "circle"). Apart from the two volcanic islands of Santorini (also known as Thíra) and Milos, the Cyclades are formed from the peaks of a mountainous landscape that is now submerged. They enjoy a mild, dry climate, but the land is not particularly fertile. People settled on the islands as early as the Neolithic Age, but they gained in importance when the ancient Greek city-states began to trade with Crete and Asia Minor. The total number

of islands in the Cycladic archipelago depends on how you define an island, as opposed to merely a rock in the sea. Only 31 out of a total of 150 have a surface area covering more than 5 sq km (2 sq miles), but according to some sources there are over 200 islands. The largest and most important of these in ancient times was Náxos. North of Náxos, the small island of Delos achieved a special status from around 1000 BC, when it became a sanctuary for Apollo, the god of medicine and healing, and the Sun. The Delos cult of Apollo attracted devotees from all over

Fruits of the Mediterranean: a still life with pomegranates on Santorini.

The Church of Agios Minas in Santorini's capital, Thíra. The houses are built on the rim of a crater.

Greek coffee houses (*kafenia*) are still male territory, just as they always have been: this *kafenia* is on the island of Amórgos.

Greece, and in much the same way its wealth of ancient remains attracts tourists today.

Yet ancient temples and statues are only one of the reasons to visit these islands. Romantic bays and beaches entice the visitor, as does the superb range of water sports. Add to this the villages with their traditional whitewashed houses, nestling against the hillsides, each with countless alleyways, doorways, and flights of steps leading up to them. The cuisine is local and seasonal yet always varied; it includes fish dishes, fresh vegetables, sheep's cheese, and olives. The islands' wines are full-bodied and aromatic. The wine-growers grow their vines close to the ground to protect the leaves and grapes from drying out in the heat and wind. Many visitors take the opportunity to visit more than one island during their stay,

taking advantage of the large ferries and increasingly popular hydrofoils that operate during the summer months. Island-hopping is an ideal way to get to know the islands, spending several days on one of the more popular islands, such as volcanic Santorini or elegant Mykonos, and then crossing to one of the less touristy islands such as Amorgós, Folégandros, or Sérifos.

Tourism has changed life on the Cyclades Islands, but the growing number of visitors has also put a stop to the mass migration to the cities that was taking place. Just a few decades ago, when fishing and agriculture were no longer able to provide sufficient income, the younger generation began to abandon the islands in droves, leaving them in danger of becoming deserted and the beauty of the white villages threatened with decay.

On Amorgós, donkeys and mules are indispensable: a monk from the Hozoviótissa Monastery.

The landscape and culture on the Cycladic Islands are very varied. The major resort islands, such as Mykonos or Santorini, enjoy a bustling and lively scene, while life on many of the lesser known islands, where the local population still outnumbers the tourists, is a much quieter affair. Today, most of the smaller islands are deserted, such as Delos, with its magnificent ruins and statues.

❶ Ándros The most northerly of the Cyclades Islands, Ándros also has the largest surface area in the archipelago, at 380 sq km (147 sq miles) and there is plenty to see here. Visitors who have already been to some of the more southerly islands in the Aegean get their first surprise in the port of Batsi. They never expect to see so many green fields and hillsides, as well as bubbling springs and rushing streams. The island's green woods, parks, and gardens attracted wealthy shipowners from Athens as well as retired sea

captains who settled on Ándros in the 19th century, after the end of Ottoman rule. The fact that the island is so close to Athens was an added bonus.

The island's greeness is best appreciated if you make your way from the port town of Batsi across the mountain ranges to the east side of the island.

The old town of Chora, the island's capital, situated on a headland between two beaches, is entered via an historic archway revealing a maze of narrow alleyways, whitewashed houses, and churches.

The remains of a fortress commemorate its architect, the Venetian Martino Dandolo. The

Serenissima (the Republic of Venice) ruled here from the 13th century until 1537, when the island was taken by Barbarossa (Red Beard), the name by which the Ottoman corsair Khair ad-Din was more commonly known. Promoted to the rank of admiral by Sultan Suleiman, he conquered many islands in the Aegean for the Ottoman empire.

Particularly worth seeing in the old town are two museums, the Archaeological Museum and the Museum of Modern Art, which were gifted to the town in the 20th century by the Goulandris shipping family, via the Vasilis and Elsa Goulandris Foundation. Also worth seeing on Ándros is the

Travel information

Route profile
Length: approx. 800 km (497 miles)
Duration: about two months
Start: Ándros
End: Kythnos
Itinerary: Ándros, Tínos, Mykonos, Delos, Syros, Páros, Antíparos, Náxos, Amorgós, Íos, Santorini, Anáfi, Mílos, Sifnos, Kythnos
NB The spelling of place names varies, and some have several different names.

When to go
Spring or autumn

Transport tips
Ferry schedules are subject to change. The route is best undertaken by yacht (many charters are on offer).

Accommodation
Most islands offer a range of facilities, but smaller islands may only have pensions and private accommodation.

Tourist information
www.iles-cyclades.com
www.cyclades-islands.com
www.greece.cruise-charter.net/cyclades

beaches around the *chora* and the southern and south-eastern coastline are typically crowded with throngs of tourists, yet there are stretches along the mostly treeless coasts and bays where you can still be entirely on your own.

Four of the museums are well worth a visit: the Nautiko Moussio (featuring the history of shipping since the Minoan period), the Archaeological Museum, the Ethnographic Museum, and Lena's House, part of the Folklore Museum, which is a 19th-century

defensive tower dating from the Hellenic period, and other places to visit include Orthodox monasteries containing iconostases, and mountain villages perched high on windswept rocky outcrops.

② Tínos A narrow stretch of water is all that separates Ándros from Tínos. Covering 194 sq km (75 sq miles) and with green valleys and several beautiful sandy beaches, Tínos is the third largest of the Cyclades. From the Kechrovounou convent, there are magnificent panoramic views of the island, which is famous for its dovecotes. The church of Panagia Evangelistria is a place of pilgrimage for followers of the Greek

Orthodox religion. In 1823, a nun named Pelagia had a series of visions of the Virgin Mary and an icon of the Virgin was subsequently found near the remains of a Byzantine chapel that had burned down nearly a thousand years earlier. The new church was built on the site and completed in 1830. It has a magnificent arched façade with two flights of stairs on either side. Hundreds of thousands of pilgrims climb the road from the port to the church each year, some on their knees, and on the Virgin's festival days, March 25 and August 15, the icon is carried down to the port.

The dovecotes (*peristerionas*) are quite extraordinary: they are

stone buildings that house agricultural produce or livestock in the lower levels, while the upper levels are decorated with a latticework of openings that allow the birds to fly in and out. Dovecotes are found on other islands, but Tínos has the greatest number of these impressive *peristerionas*, around eight hundred. The doves were bred for their meat and their droppings were used as fertilizer.

After crossing the valley at Kambos, you reach the marble quarries near the sculptors' village of Panormos in the north-west of Tínos. Museums showcase the work of local artists, and the village is also home to a school of

sculpture, as well as galleries and shops where you can buy pieces at reasonable prices.

③ Mykonos A hundred years ago, it was lovers of ancient Greek history who stopped at Mykonos on their way to nearby Delos, where they visited the sanctuary of the cult of Apollo. As an added bonus, they could also enjoy the outstanding beauty of Chora, the island's main town. *Chora* is the name that is often given to the most important village or town on a Greek island. Artists and bonviveurs soon followed and in the last fifty years, it is the rich, chic, and fashionable who have flocked to the island. The long

1 Chora, the beautiful old town on a headland on Ándros.

2 Seagulls follow a fishing boat in the bay of Kionia on Tínos.

3 Tínos has more of these unusual stone dovecotes than anywhere else.

4 One of the most attractive villages in the Cyclades is Mykonos Town.

5 Above the water: Little Venice in Mykonos Town.

6 An island emblem: the windmills of Mykonos.

middle-class home. Architecturally, the most unusual building on Mykonos is the Church of Panagia Paraportiani, which literally means "at the gates of the castle" (the castle is no longer standing). Since the Middle Ages, the church has been altered and increased in size thanks to several extensions. It now appears as a unified whole beneath frequently applied coats of limewash.

One of the most important mythical and historical sites in Greece now awaits you to the south-west of Mykonos on the island of Delos.

4 Delos A row of marble lions, symbols of Apollo the sun god to whom the island was dedicated by the Greeks, are there to greet or rather snarl at you. There were probably nine or twelve of them at one time. They guard the Sacred Way, the processional path along which pilgrims made their way from the port to the Sacred Lake. The lake is now dry, it was filled in in 1926, but it played a role in the creation myth of the Delos cult. Zeus had fathered twins, Apollo and Artemis, with the goddess Leto. His wife, Hera, flew into a rage

and stirred up the animosity of all the towns and islands of Greece against Leto, demanding that they grant her no place of rest in which to give birth. Only the rather pitiable, small Delos (a mere 3.8 sq km/1½ sq miles) would take her, and then only on the condition that Leto's son would have his first temple built there. After a long and difficult birth, Leto produced her two divine children at the Sacred Lake, and immediately the island began to flourish, with rocky cliffs, olive trees, and even a river, all cloaked in a golden light.

What is certain is that the island was an important religious center

from the seventh to the first century BC. In 543 BC, the ruler of Athens, Peisistratos, had all the tombs moved from Delos to the adjacent island of Rínia for religious purification. Later Delos gained independence from Athens, and in 166 BC the Romans declared it a free port. However, the town never recovered from the attack by Mithridates VI from the kingdom of Pontus (on the Black Sea), who rose against Rome in 88 BC.

The help of a guide is useful to explain the island's historic background when visiting the remains of the temples and residential areas. Of particular artistic value

are the mosaics in the House of Dionysos (the god is depicted riding on the back of a tiger) and the House of the Dolphins. The museum with its model of the ancient town is a good source of information.

5 Syros At 86 sq km (33 sq miles), Syros is almost exactly the same size as Mykonos, although in political terms it enjoys far greater importance as the island's capital, Ermoúpoli, is also the capital of the Cyclades. It was a closely fought contest as to which town should be named the capital of the new kingdom of Greece, Athens or Ermoúpoli, after the

country's liberation from Turkish rule in around 1830.

Ermoúpoli was founded in the 1820s during the Greek War of Independence, and named after the god Hermes, the patron of traders and voyagers. Viewed from the sea, it lies in a natural amphitheatre surrounded by hills. Closer inspection reveals spacious town squares, neo-classical buildings, elegant mansions, and picturesque flights of steps. On the eastern side of the town, the blue cupola of the Orthodox cathedral glints in the sun, while on the steeper western side, the Catholic Agios Georgios Cathedral rises above the fortress-like monastery

walls. In the town below there is an archeological museum and the Apollo theatre, which is a copy of La Scala in Milan, along with a number of coffee houses (*kafenia*) and markets.

In the area immediately surrounding the town, life has a distinct rural feel. The green and fertile south is the most attractive part of the island. Both the village of Episkopi, situated high up in the hills, and Possidonia, farther to the south are pleasantly surprising with their many parks and villas dating back to the 19th century. If in search of a beach resort that has remained largely untouched by tourism, make your way to the village of Kini; but if you prefer something smarter, try Galissas with its wide beach, a few miles to the west.

6 Páros The south-eastern islands of the Cyclades are perennially popular with tourists: Páros and the larger adjacent island of Náxos, Íos and Amorgós, and Thíra/Santorini, as well as the multitude of small islands in between. The islands here are larger, their beaches longer, and there are more of the typical white buildings in the villages.

In Páros you can visit the quarries from which Páros marble has been exported since the eighth century BC. The island's capital, Parikia is an attractive example of typical Cycladic architecture, especially its old town, the Kastro district, but little remains of the Venetian castle to the east of the town, except for a sturdy tower, built using stone from ancient temples. The Panagia Ekatontapiliani however is magnificent. It integrates two chapels from the earliest days of Christianity, dating from the fourth century AD. The "church of a hundred doors" (the literal translation of its name) is a sixth-century cross-vaulted church and one of the islands' most important Byzantine structures. It has suffered earthquake damage and has been altered extensively over the years, but was restored to its original form in the second half of the 20th century. The main church has three aisles and a marble altarpiece containing 17th-century icons. A font in the shape of a cross is still preserved in the baptistry; it was originally only used to baptize adults. The Panagia Ekatontapiliani was erected on the foundations of an ancient pre-Christian temple. In the early days of Christianity, spiritual leaders would congregate on its marble steps and around the bishop's throne in the apse. It has no bell tower, instead the church bells hang suspended from the strong branches of a cypress tree.

Visitors come to Páros for its beautiful beaches and picturesque villages, and the bars and restaurants around the port are normally very lively at night, but it is also a good place from which to venture inland and explore some of the villages in the island's interior. You can visit the small mountain village of Lefkes on the slopes of Agios Ilias, with its shady cafés and picturesque flights of steep steps. The Moussio Laikou Politismou tou Aigaiou, a private museum devoted to the culture

(continued p.94)

1 Apollo's lions stand guard on the once sacred island of Delos.

2 The port and capital of the Cyclades: Ermoúpoli on Syros.

3 The fishermen mend their nets tirelessly, as here on Syros.

4 One of the most popular destinations on Páros is the waterside village of Náousa.

5 The ancient Panagia Ekatontapiliani in Parikia on Páros.

Parikia, capital of the island of Páros and a ferry port, lies on a beautiful bay fringed by mountains. It is also known for its houses, some of which incorporate ancient columns. The peaceful twilight mood by the old windmill opposite the port is slightly deceptive as at this time of day the old town's alleyways and

squares are lively and bustling, with shops that open late and restaurants, bars, and discotheques around the busy Market Street and the waterfront promenade permanent hives of activity. The main beach of Parikia and many of the hotels are found north of the town.

The Colossus of Náxos

To see this large marble figure, you have to travel across the mountainous north of Náxos to the tiny fishing and holiday village of Apóllonas, almost at the extreme northern tip of the island. The countryside here is magnificent, with silvery olive groves, deep valleys, and remote mountain peaks. The mountain villages along the way all have something to offer, such as Apiranthos with its four museums. The high road through the mountains

Top: The Kouros of Flerio.
Bottom: The Kouros of Apóllonas, measuring nearly 11 m (36 ft).

starts to narrow until the last stretch is a mere track leading through a dense forest past an ancient marble quarry above Apóllonas. This is where the enormous statue (11 m/36 ft, around double the size of the Kouros of Flerio) is to be found. It was never finished by its ancient creators, probably due to faults found in the marble, but even in its rough-hewn and incomplete state this Kouros is impressive. There is speculation as to what the figure would have become – a young man perhaps, or the god Dionysos? The hint of beard would seem to support the latter interpretation.

of the Aegean, is a special attraction here. Its founder, the hotel owner and collector Giorgios Pittas, created the museum and made it part of his hotel, Lefkes Village. It provides an excellent overview of thousands of years of farming, fishing, and rural crafts on the island.

Páros has its fair share of beach resorts, the most attractive are in the Bay of Náousa in the north, with others farther east on the Langeri peninsula, such as the village of Kolymbithres with its amazing rock formations, and on the east coast near Longaras and Chrissi Akti, and finally in the south at Akrotiri and Alyki.

7 Antíparos This island is much quieter than Páros, but since Antíparos also boasts some extensive sandy beaches it has long been a tourist destination in its own right rather than just a target for daytrippers. Covering a total area of around 35 sq km (14 sq miles), it is situated off the west coast of its larger sister island of Páros. The two islands were linked by a spit of land until the Neolithic Age. At the southern end of the island, steps descend some 90 m (295 ft) down to Spilion Agiou Ioannou, the cave of St John, one of the most frequently visited in Greece.

8 Náxos Spend a day in Náxos, capital of the largest of the Cycladic Islands (448 sq km/173 sq miles). Start by visiting the Archeological Museum in the morning to admire the extensive collection of early Cycladic figurines, then

take a stroll through the atmospheric old town in the afternoon, and finally wend your way to the Portara, on the Palateia peninsula north of the port basin, in the evening. The Portara, a huge marble portal, is the emblem of Náxos and the only remaining part of a vast temple complex that was planned in the sixth century BC in praise of the god Apollo. With long views across the town and the sea, the 6-m (20-ft) high stone structure is an atmospheric place for a walk in the early morning. Zeus was worshipped in a cave below the 999-m (3,278-ft) high Mount Zas (Zas is modern Greek for Zeus). According to legend, Zeus was born on Crete, but grew up here.

Dionysos, the god of wine, is also claimed as a "local god" on Náxos. Vases and drinking vessels depict the famous legend of how the young Dionysos managed to escape from pirates on board their ship, causing the deck and masts suddenly to become overgrown with vines, and in panic the pirates jumped into the sea. The collection of marble figurines in the Museum of Náxos is the second largest after the collection in the Museum of Cycladic Art in Athens. They date back to the Cycladic culture of the Bronze Age in the third century BC. The figures mostly depict female and abstract, ranging in size from a few inches to life size. They were mostly found in graves on Náxos, Páros, Tínos, and Amorgós. Before it was destroyed by the Persians in 490 BC, Náxos was the

central power base in the Aegean. The island was later forced to submit to the rule of Athens, but started to take on a significant role again when the Venetians made the island the center of their Duchy of Náxos in 1207, and built the castle that is still preserved there today. The Catholic cathedral was also built around this time, in the highest part of the castle district. North from here, in the Bourgos district, there are more than forty Orthodox churches and chapels, while

farther on towards Portara, recent excavations have uncovered the remains of an ancient settlement, which you can now visit as an open-air museum.

A large statue approximately 6 m (20 ft) long and similar to the Colossus of Náxos (see panel, left), known as the Kouros of Flerio, can be seen in Melanes, near the town of Náxos. It is displayed in the garden of its owners' home. The church of Panagia Drossiani in the middle of the island, near the mountain village of Moni, is

steep donkey path from the coast or a short bus ride.

If island tradition is to be believed, most of the churches and chapels on Íos (said to number 365) were donated by repentant pirates, who once made up a large proportion of the population. More interesting than the often fairly old churches to some visitors are the long beaches, (continued p.98)

1 A stunning sight at dawn as well as dusk: the temple gate on Náxos.

2 A church near Apiranthos on Náxos.

3 View of Náxos and its Venetian fortress.

4 Clinging to the rocks: the Hozoviótissa Monastery on Amorgós.

5 Amorgós: a church near Profitis Elias.

6 Windmills on Íos.

one of Europe's oldest Christian churches and is famous for its Byzantine frescoes.

9 Amorgós With cliffs rising up steeply from the sea below, the long, narrow island of Amorgós is wild and beautiful. Covering 120 sq km (46 sq miles), this easternmost island in the Cyclades can be explored by car in just a few days, or on foot in a week or two, provided you are ready to tackle some uneven terrain and steep inclines. The effort will be well

worth it for some amazing sights: the small white houses in the island's *chora* seem to scramble up the almost vertical walls of the mountain, while on the southern coast, the 11th-century Hozoviótissa Monastery, seems to hang in space from a steep cliff that drops directly to the sea.

10 Íos Continue westward to reach Íos. You may need to change ship once more on Páros or Náxos as not all the islands are linked directly by ferry. The ferries

may also dock at some of the smaller islands that belong to the Lesser Eastern Cyclades, such as Kato Koufonisi and Epano Koufonisi, Schinoussa, and Iráklia. They were once also known as Eromonisia, the "abandoned" or "lonely" islands, but today each has a small population numbering one or two hundred people, swelled in summer by the tourists who like to stop off en route.

Íos, meanwhile, has an area of 108 sq km (42 sq miles). Despite its well-maintained roads and

numerous hotels, away from the *chora* it still has the allure of unspoiled nature. In the 1970s, the hippies discovered Íos and put it firmly on the hippy trail, enjoying the partying at night as well as the peaceful rural life in the countryside.

Accommodation is available in the port town of Gialos, situated on a deep bay fringed by a sandy beach. A little way inland from the port of Íos is the island's picturesque *chora* with restaurants, clubs and bars. It is accessible via a

Ía on Santorini is a picture-postcard Cycladic village. The houses are built into the hills at the northern tip of the island at such a steep angle you would think they must be glued to the rock. Nearby, there are a number of "cave houses" available for rent, carved into the soft tuff stone. On the side that faces the crater,

hotels, restaurants, pensions, terraces, and cafés are built into the steep walls, tightly packed together; each one offering its customers spectacular views of the vast caldera. ... A dream of Atlantis, the mythical sunken continent that may lie beneath the ocean

The Minoan Pompeii

It was one of the greatest archaeological finds of the 20th century: in 1967, on the island of Santorini, the researcher and archaeologist Spyridon Marinatos (1901–1974) found under a layer of stones several feet thick, the remains of a wealthy merchants' town, dating back some three and a half thousand years. Marinatos excavated many of the ruins, finding everyday objects, and works of art, including large murals that were perfectly preserved. He was able to prove that the fall of the Minoan culture on Crete was also caused by the powerful volcanic eruption that created Santorini. One of the ancient cities excavated, Akrotíri is also known as the "Minoan Pompeii" but unlike Pompeii no dead were

Akrotíri was preserved under deep layers of volcanic ash: it can be visited under a protective roof covering.

ever found here. It is presumed that the inhabitants had been able to escape before the eruption, warned by earth tremors, though they would have been unlikely to survive the subsequent giant tidal wave.

Spyridon Marinatos, who sadly died at the excavation site of Akrotíri just a few years after his discovery, described the culture that had been buried there as: "… the world of the Golden Age of the Aegean. It is alive with an appreciation of stunning colors, with an attraction for geometric beauty, with the delicacy of plants, with the intoxication of flowers, and with the fairy-tale world of the seabed". The beauty of the ancient world was depicted on the magnificent frescoes, which today can be admired at the National Museum in Athens.

especially Mylopotas Beach, approximately 1 km (½ mile) long, and probably one of the most beautiful in the Cyclades. Life is more sedate on the equally long Aghia Theodoti Beach in the north-east of the island, and some other very beautiful beaches can (or could until recently) only be reached via unmade gravel tracks or by boat. The steep mountainous terrain makes it difficult to build roads that access every nook and cranny on the island.

⑪ Santorini (Thíra) This is a landscape that seems to have emerged fully formed from the dreams of a surrealist. Steep crater walls drop down into a wide ocean lagoon that sparkles blue and turquoise in the sunlight and from which emerge several charcoal black islands. This small, circular ring of islands is all that remains of an enormous volcanic explosion in the 16th century BC that buried a flourishing city (see panel, left) and destroyed what was once a single island.

After this catastrophic event, what was left of the island of Thera/Thíra was covered with a layer of tuff and pumice stone, up to 30 m (98 ft) deep. It was not settled again until three centuries later, first by the Phoenicians, and from about 1000 BC also by the Dorian Greeks. Earthquakes have shaken the island (now known as Santorini or Santorin) periodically since then, and even fairly re-

cently. In 1956, a large number of the settlements, as well as the Greek Orthodox cathedral in the island's capital Thíra, were destroyed. Despite this, Santorini has developed from a rural economy of farmers, winegrowers, and fishermen into an important tourist resort, especially attracting visitors cruising around the Aegean. Patient mules tirelessly carry tourists to the upper reaches of the island from the port of Athinios, south of Thíra, or from the quay below the city. The island's capital in particular offers a wide range of accommodation while at Ía, on the northern tip of the island, you can stay in "cave houses" set into the steep cliffs. Ía is renowned for its spectacular sunsets.

One of the best walks in Santorini is along a track that hugs the edge of the caldera, about 12 km

(7½ miles) long (four hours' walk). Looking eastward, you can enjoy views across the plain that slopes down toward the coast, and to the hills in the south-east.

Santorini is the main island in this small group. Viewed from above, it looks like an open mouth, about to gobble up the much smaller island of Thirassia in the west. The archipelago is also something of a work in progress as the small islands of Palea Kameni are relative newcomers. Kameni rose from the sea in 1570 and Nea Kameni in 1707. Other islands and islets have also emerged from the sea and, after some time, have sunk back down again into its depths. Ferries sail to and fro, carrying passengers from island to island. You will find the best beaches on Santorini itself, near Akrotíri in the south and near Kamári in the east, but

Palea Kameni and Thirassia also offer good swimming facilities.

⑫ Anáfi Not many stop at Anáfi, the "shining island" as the name translates, which covers around 38 sq km (15 sq miles). Despite being the most south-easterly of the Cyclades, it is not completely cut off from the rest of the world, but the ferries do not run every day, and sometimes the island is cut off for several days in a row if the weather is bad.

Steep cliff walls rise up directly from the sea, but around the Ormos Katalimatsa in the south of the island, there are also some very good sandy beaches.

(continued p.100)

1 A bell tower in Ía on Santorini.

2 Kokkini Ammos, the Red Sands.

Thíra: a view of the caldera, the crater left behind after the enormous volcanic eruption in the 16th century BC, now flooded with the Agean. Other islands

⑬ Mílos The island of Mílos is much larger than Santorini, and its landscape almost as spectacular. It is also volcanic in origin, and has a large gulf that resembles an inland sea, known as Ormos Milou, but still tourism only plays a fairly minor role here. Visitors do not linger for long in the small modern port of Adámas, but generally move a few miles farther along to Plaka, the island's main village. Set on a rocky outcrop, Plaka is a traditional Cycladic village with narrow streets inaccessible to cars. Climb up through narrow alleyways to the chapel of Mesa Panagia at the top of the Kastro hill, or enjoy the magnificent panoramic views of Plaka and the widely curving caldera bay of Mílos from the ruins of the Venetian fortress. If you tire of the views, you can visit a museum:

the Ethnographic Museum, based in an old house with a weaving room, or the Archaeological Museum, housed in a neoclassical villa. You can also visit Christian catacombs near Plaka and some small fishermen's homes on the coast at Klima, on Ormos Milou. You can even stay in some of the fishermen's huts. However, you cannot, unfortunately, still see the Venus de Milo here. It was discovered in the 19th century in a field by a local farmer. He hid it in his barn for a while, but it was eventually seized and taken to Paris by a French officer, where today it can be admired on display in the Louvre.

A boat tour around the island will enable you to see some of the strange shapes carved out of the volcanic rock by wind and sea. Most of these bizarre shapes can

only be seen from the sea. The formations viewed from the bay of Kleftiko, in the mountainous south-west of the island, are particularly beautiful and in some places minerals have left colorful deposits on the rocks. You can jump into the clear waters and swim through rocky arches. In fact there is no shortage of places to swim: along the south coast, near Pollonia and Filakopi for example, or from the small offshore island of Kímolos.

⑭ Sifnos Ancient legend has it that, thanks to their gold and silver mines, the Sifnians became so rich that they created a magnificent treasury in Delphi where they offered a golden egg to the god Apollo every year. When one year greed led them to offer only a gilded egg, Apollo sent a giant

wave to flood the mines, bringing about the end of their prosperity, hence the origin of Sifnos (meaning "empty") as the island's name. However, Sifnos is certainly not empty of people in the summer! They come to see the island's attractions, which include the typical Cycladic village of Kastro, perched on top of a green mountain peak above the sea, and Moni Chrisopigi, a village set picturesquely on a rocky outcrop and accessible on foot from Faro. It is also known for the pottery that is made in the traditional workshops here.

⑮ Kythnos Oriented from north to south, Kythnos has around 100 km (62 miles) of coastline and over 70 beaches, some of which are inaccessible by car. In the early 19th century,

when the Greeks finally broke free of Turkish rule, the first queen of Greece, Queen Amalia, had the thermal baths built around the healing springs at Loutra. The springs have been in use since ancient times and you can still soak in them today. They are the only natural thermal springs on the Cyclades. Many Greeks visit the island (around 99 sq km/38 sq miles) and have holiday homes here because of its proximity to mainland Greece and the port of Athens at Piraeus, and because of the excellent beaches that can be found north and south of the coastal village of Mérichas. With its red-tiled roofs and wide alleyways, Mérichas is not a typical Cycladic village. If you are in search of something more traditional, visit the main village, known locally as Hora. Perched 160 m (525 ft) above sea level, flowers, ships, fish, and similar folklore motifs are painted in white on the pavements. They are repainted every year at Easter.

1 Comfortable seating in the port of Mérichas on Kythnos.

2 A chapel on Sifnos.

3 Rock formations on the south coast of Milos.

Ándros The most northerly of the Cycladic Islands is surprisingly green. The medieval part of the island's capital is situated on a small headland, at the tip of which stand the ruins of a 13th-century Venetian castle (shown here).

Tínos Rich in valleys and beaches, Tínos also has numerous churches, chapels, and stone towers, once used to keep doves. This view shows Isternia.

Mykonos This "jetset" island is famous for its seemingly endless beaches. Among its other sights are Little Venice, the museums, and Mykonos Town center.

Náxos The capital of the island that bears same name, the largest of the Cyclades, is home to the emblem of Náxos: a temple portal from the sixth century BC.

Amorgós Rising steeply from the sea, the most easterly of the Cyclades has a wild romantic beauty. Especially worth visiting is the Hozoviótissa Monastery.

Kythnos Sometimes also known as Kythnos Thermiá, this island is home to the only natural thermal baths on the Cyclades at Loutra. There are fine swimming beaches, especially near Mérichas.

Mílos Although less well known, Mílos is as spectacular as Santorini. The rock formations, such as the white pumice-stone cliffs seen here, are impressive.

Syros Ermoúpoli, the island's capital, is also the capital of the Cyclades (shown here is the former customs house). The south of the island is green and fertile.

Páros In ancient times, it was the island's famous white marble that brought prosperity to its inhabitants; today it is tourism. The port of Náousa is shown here.

Santorini The half-moon shape of the island is the visible reminder of a powerful volcanic eruption in the 16th century BC. Santorini is known for its white and blue houses, as well as for the breathtaking sunsets at Ía in the north of the island.

Karpathos: A goat looking for its herd near a whitewashed church on Pigadia.

Greece

The Southern Sporades: Lesbos to Rhodes

Mainland Greece makes up only a quarter of Greece's total land area. The rest is a patchwork of islands, split into seven island groups, six of which are in the Aegean Sea. This cruise concentrates on one of these groups: the Southern Sporades, together with excursions to the North Aegean Islands of Lesbos and Chios. It provides an excellent insight into the variety of the Aegean Islands.

On this cruise you travel through many different eras and cultures: Romans, Crusaders, Turks, and Italians all left their mark on the islands. The Sporades are what remains of a chain of mountains which were flooded by the sea some 30 million years ago, leaving only the peaks exposed above the water. The Southern Sporades lie off the coast of Turkey and include the Dodecanese, a group of twelve large and 150 smaller islands. Archaeological evidence has been found showing that they were inhabited as early as 7500 BC, though the majority of the islands are uninhabited today.

The Minoan (3000 BC) and the Mycenaean peoples (2000 BC) were the earliest to inhabit the islands, until around 1000 BC. Then the Dorians arrived, a Hellenic people who had settled in ancient Greece around 1100 BC. Their era was followed by the Roman, Byzantine, and Venetian, each leaving their mark, whether as occupying forces or merely inhabitants.

Geometric decoration on the front of houses is typical of the charming village of Pyrgi on Chios.

A twilight view toward the island of Halki, from the ruins of a castle built by the Knights Hospitaller in Kritinia on the west coast of Rhodes.

Lesbos: The port town of Mithimna, built against the cliffs, is listed as a historic site.

The Knights Hospitaller (also known as the Order of St John) also settled here, making Rhodes their new homeland after defeat in Acre (Palestine). The crusaders left a considerable legacy of buildings and castles, but they too were eventually superseded and their place taken by the expanding Ottoman Empire. The later cultures made frequent use of the islands' ancient temples and palaces as their bases. The islands are full of prime archeological sites, where history and myth intertwine. The Heraion, the temple dedicated to the goddess Hera, on Sámos is glorious, while the Asclepieion on Kos, dedicated to Asclepius, the healing god, is the most important archaeological site in the Aegean. The physician Hippocrates is said to have been born on Kos and his oath is still sworn by doctors all over the world today. The mathematician, scientist, and philosopher Pythagoras was born on Sámos, and Chios is the birthplace of Homer, the author of the *Iliad* and the *Odyssey*. At Pátmos, the world-famous Monastery of St John the Theologian is where St John had his vision. Lesbos is forever associated with Sappho, the ancient Greek lyric poet; and Ikaria is home to the legend of Icarus, the young man who flew too close to the sun.

The landscape of the islands is frequently wild and dramatic, such as the volcanic landscape of Nissyros, while Kálimnos is a diver's paradise. Culturally Karpathos has retained many of its traditional Greek roots, and the medieval old town of Rhodes is a World Heritage site.

Our journey begins on the island of Lesbos. One of the sunniest and most verdant of the Greek islands, it is steeped in history and popular with tourists.

Priests in the Monastery of St John the Theologian on Pátmos, where St John had his vision.

This island-hopping cruise route around the Southern Sporades runs from north to south. It begins in Lesbos, the third largest Greek island (1,630 sq km/629 sq miles). The landscape on Lesbos is dominated by olive groves, so it is not surprising that it is Greece's second most important exporter of olives.

1 Mytilíni, Lesbos More than a third of the island's 90,000 population live in Mytilíni, which is the capital of Lesbos. The poet Alkaios was born here (620 BC), as was the important modern Greek painter, Theophilos (1868–1934) in the nearby village of Vareia. In the fourth century BC, Aristotle taught at the school of philosophy here. The town has an oriental feel because Lesbos belonged to Turkey until 1912, which accounts for the mosques and other buildings in the same architectural style.

Mytilíni has two lively ports, though the north of the town still has the feel and appearance of an ancient town. The remains of a third-century theater are nearby, which is thought to have held up to fifteen thousand people. A narrow road leads north through mountainous, fertile countryside, often hugging the east coast, to Molivos, 56 km (35 miles) away.

2 Míthimna, Lesbos Also known as Molivos (its Turkish name), this historic town and port with a population of just under two thousand lies at the foot of Lepetymnos mountain, which towers some 968 m (3,176 ft) above. Míthimna is a center for local painters and attracts many tourists with its romantic cobblestone streets and quirky little houses. It is built around a cliff and, since the 14th century, has been dominated by an impressive Genoese castle. The port is full of brightly painted wooden boats, and is a lovely spot in which to while away the hours, sitting at one of the many traditional quayside tavernas while enjoying the typically Greek scene.

3 Petra, Lesbos Just 7 km (4 miles) to the south of Míthimna is the village of Petra, built right on the coast. It is particularly well known for its churches, the most important of which is the convent church and place of pilgrimage, Panagia Glykofiloussa. Built in 1747, the church dominates the village from its high position. To reach it you have to climb 114 steps carved out of the rock. There is another pilgrimage church to see, this time in the town center, the 15th-century Agios Nikolaos church. As the route now continues west the landscape changes and becomes more barren. After 42 km (26 miles), you reach Eressós.

4 Eressós, Lesbos The lyric poet Sappho was born here

Travel information

Route profile
Length: 1,630 km (1,012 miles), of which 800 km (497 miles) is by sea
Duration: approx. 4 weeks
Itinerary (main locations): Lesbos, Chios, Sámos, Ikaraa, Pátmos, Léros, Kálimnos, Kos, Nissiros, Tílos, Rhodes, Karpathos, Rhodes.
NB The spelling of place names varies, and some have several different names.

Travel tips
Scooters, motorbikes, and

cars can be hired on virtually every island. Car ferries run between the islands.

When to go
April–June or September–October

Tourist Information
Greek National Tourist Office
7. Tsoha, 11521 Athens
Tel. +30 210 8707000
www.gnto.gr
www.greeka.com
www.travel-greece.org
www.greece.travelmall.com

The Néa Moni Monastery

The world-famous Néa Moni monastery, near the village of Karyes, was built in 1042 by Emperor Constantin IX on the place where, according to legend, three monks found an icon of the Virgin Mary. The monastery is well known for its Byzantine sacred art and architecture.

In the 19th century, the monastery was sacked and looted by the Ottomans during the Greek War of Independence and suffered further damage

around 610 BC. Some of her poetry describes love and passion for women. It is this aspect of her work, coupled with her association with the girls to whom she taught music, that has given rise to the term "lesbian" for same-sex female partnerships, and similarly the term "sapphic" even though it is not known whether her poetry is autobiographical. The philosopher Theophrastus (372 BC) was also born here.

Eressós is also used as a starting point for a trek through the mountains to the petrified forest on the western tip of the island, where the remains of trees that are at least a million years old can be seen.

The Skala Eressou Beach near Eressós is one of the most beautiful on Lesbos. The drive back across the island to Mytilíni, where the ferry to Chios awaits, is around 77 km (48 miles).

5 Chios Town, Chios Chios Town is the capital of the fifth largest of all the Greek islands at 842 sq km (325 sq miles). It was the birthplace of Homer, the most important epic poet of ancient history. The historic Kastro quarter with its 10th-century remains is well worth a visit. Chios Town is also a good

base from which to explore the world-famous Néa Moni Monastery, which lies some 15 km (9 miles) away.

6 Mestá, Chios Chios is known for its aromatic mastic gum, made from the resin tapped from the mastic tree. It was once an indispensible product used in industry, but nowadays is mainly used to perfume and flavor food. There were twenty-one so-called mastic villages in the Middle Ages. Nowadays, the best preserved of these is Mestá, 34 km (21 miles) south of Chios Town. Mestá's narrow lanes and inviting tavernas make

it an interesting place to stop before heading back to Chios Town and the ferry to Sámos.

1 A fisherman pulls in his net in Míthimna port on Lesbos.

2 In autumn, the moorlands of Lesbos take on a different hue.

3 Windmills feature on many holiday postcards from Chios.

4 In Mestá on Chios the houses are built very close together.

5 In springtime, the olive groves of Chios look particularly inviting.

The Néa Moni Monastery stands in a picturesque valley on Chios.

during a devastating earthquake in 1881, but despite this, many of the very fine mosaics survived. It was converted to a convent in 1952.

Sámos and the Sanctum of the Goddess Hera

Sámos lies just 1.3 km (3/4 mile) off the Turkish coast, a stone's throw away from Mykale Mountain and the place where the Persians killed Polycrates, the tyrannical ruler of Sámos, around 500 BC. But the island is better known for the philosopher Aristarchos, who influenced Galileo's world view in 300 BC; or indeed for Pythagoras (around 580–496 BC), the great natural philosopher and mathematician who founded the philosophical order of the Pythagoreans. However, the one name that is most closely connected to ancient Sámos is that of the goddess Hera, wife of Zeus, mother of Area, Hebe, and Hephaistos. This important ancient excavation site, on the east coast of the island near Iréo, dates back to 2500 BC. According to legend, it was here that in 1000 BC, Ionian

The Heraion on Sámos was one of the most important ancient temples dedicated to the goddess Hera.

immigrants found a lygos bush, which they believed to be a sanctum of Hera (the goddess was said to have been born under a lygos bush). They dedicated the site to her and in the eighth century BC, the Heraion was erected here in her name. Two centuries later, the architects Theodoros and Rhoikos built a new temple for her, twelve times larger and the largest in Greece at the time. Polycrates, the tyrant who ruled Sámos in the sixth century BC, planned to build an even larger temple, but the Heraion never regained its former glory and nowadays only one of the columns is still standing, though you can still see its extensive floor plan from the foundations.

❼ Sámos Town, Sámos Also known as Vathy, this town has been the capital of the island since 1832. At first glance, it appears small and peaceful, with just 10,000 inhabitants, but it is a different matter in summer when the tourists arrive. Sámos Town is one of two large settlements on the island, whose 473 sq km (183 sq miles) of fertile mountain landscape also make it a paradise for nature lovers. The town is split into the "new" town, with its waterside promenade and main street, and the "upper" town, Ano Vathy, with its village feel. Perched on the hill above the port, it was originally built here in an attempt to protect it from pirates. The Agios Niklaos Church (18th C.), the town's principal church, is worth visiting, but the town's real "must-see" is the Archeological Museum. It houses pieces

excavated from the Heraion on Sámos, the temple dedicated to Hera, assembled by archeologists over the last ninety-five years. The statue of a *kouros*, almost 5 m/16 ft tall (*kouros* is Greek for "young boy"), is the most important of its kind in the whole of Greece.

The route now leaves town on the Sofouli Road (No. 62), and follows the island road for 11 km (7 miles) southward. After driving through hilly landscape for about a quarter of an hour, you reach Pithagóreion.

❽ Pythagoreión, Sámos This modern port town is one of the most picturesque in the Sporades. It has around 1,700 residents and is built on the site of ancient Sámos, which according to legend was a thriving city of some 25,000 inhabitants. Parts of the town walls, which were

originally 7 km (4 miles) long, date back to this period (6 BC). The town was previously called Tigani, meaning "frying pan" after the shape of the port. Although some still cling to this old name, it was changed in 1955 in recognition of the town's most famous son, the philosopher and mathematician Pythagoras (580 BC). There is a triangular monument in the

port dedicated to his theory $a^2 + b^2 = c^2$. Pythagoras was also responsible for the building here of the first man-made port basin in the Mediterranean. A technical masterpiece well worth seeing is the aqueduct built in the sixth century BC, named the Tunnel of Eupalinos after its designer. It runs underground through a mountain and is 1,036 m (1,133 yards) long.

The town's emblem is the castle that stands on the cliffs above the sea.

9 Iréo, Sámos On leaving Pythagoreión head for Chora, then after 3 km (2 miles) turn left by the airport. After an 11-km (7-mile) drive through the picturesque island interior, you reach Iréo. Pythagoreión and Iréo were both designated UNESCO World Heritage Sites in 1992. Meaning "the place that belongs to the goddess Hera" Iréo is the nearest settlement to the "Heraion" (see panel, left). It also makes a perfect base from which to explore the incredible stone tower of Pyrgos Sarakinis (16th C.) and the Agios Ioannis Church (17th C.), which both belong to the Monastery of Saint John the Theologian on Pátmos. In the opposite direction is Agios Nikolaos. If you

have the time, it is worth venturing a little way inland to visit some of the nearby villages, which are idyllic. Back on the route, the drive north-west across the island, through Myli, Pyrgos, and Platanos is beautiful.

10 Karlovássi, Sámos After almost 40 km (25 miles) of roads that wind through pine and olive woods, with fantastic views glimpsed through gaps in the trees, you reach Karlovássi, the second largest town on Sámos (6,000 inhabitants). The great economic importance that the town enjoyed in the 19th century has now largely been lost, and its many factory buildings now stand abandoned. The town was established after several smaller settlements banded together in 1958, with the result that it now covers quite a large

area, stretching both along the coast and inland. It has many villas dating from the 19th century, with the Agias Trias Church also providing a point of interest. The oldest part of town, Paleo Karlovássi, extends down from the church. The port in Karlovássi is just as important as that in Vathy, and from here the ferry makes the crossing to Foúrni.

11 Foúrni Foúrni is a group of around twenty small islands, which are still far off the beaten track as far as many visitors are concerned. Virtually all of the island's 2,000 inhabitants live in the main town of Foúrni, but around four hundred fishermen live in the village of Chrysomilia and on the island of Thymaina. Despite its small population, Foúrni is a bustling town with plenty to offer in terms of nightlife. Two good roads lead north to Chrysomilia (15 km/ 9 miles) and south to the Agios Ioannis Monastery, on a tiny island. The commercial center of Foúrni is the port, from where you cross to Ikaría.

12 Ikaría This 255-sq km (98-sq mile) island takes its name from Icarus, the son of of Daedalus, who fell into the sea nearby according to Greek mythology. The Atheras Mountains (1,033 m/ 3,389 ft) split the island across its

40-km (25-mile) diameter between the fertile north and the rocky south. The largest town and administrative capital of Ikaría is Agios Kírikos, which has a monument to Icarus. Nearby is the spa resort of Therma. The winding island road leads northward out of town, passing the Theoktisti Monastery, built below two large rocks in a forest. In the coastal town of Nas, the remains of the Artemis Temple are worth a visit. Near Kampos, you can see the ruins of ancient Oenoe, at one time the most important town on the island. The ferry to Pátmos leaves from Agios Kírikos.

1 The port town of Pythagoreión is located on the site of the ancient town of Sámos, on the island of Sámos.

2 Karlovássi port on Sámos nestles against a hilly landscape.

3 Motorboats bob up and down gently on the turquoise water around Sámos' stony coast.

4 Low-growing bushes form the only vegetation on Foúrni.

5 The church belonging to the Theoktisti Monastery in the northwest of Ikaría.

Icarus

According to Greek mythology, both Daedalus and his son Icarus were held captive on Crete, imprisoned in the labyrinth that Daedalus himself had created to contain the man-eating Minotaur. In order to escape, Daedalus built a pair of wings for himself and his son made of feathers and wax. Enjoy-

A relief depicting Icarus' flight on Ikaría.

ing the feeling of soaring through the sky, Icarus ignored his father's warnings and flew higher and higher. When he flew too close to the sun, the wings melted and Icarus fell into the ocean and drowned. Daedalus then named the island after his son: Ikaría.

The Holy Island of Pátmos and the Monastery of St John the Theologian

For the Greek Orthodox church, the 12-km (7-mile) long island of Pátmos is one of the most important islands in the Aegean because of its sacred sites. The Cave of the Apocalypse where St John the Theologian had a revelation, and its dedicated monastery, have made Pátmos a popular place of pilgrimage. John the Apostle spent two years in exile on Pátmos from AD 95. The Greek government declared the whole island a holy site in 1983. The Monastery of St John the Theologian

Top: The Monastery of St John the Theologian was founded in the 11th century on Pátmos.
Bottom: A monk pauses for a moment in the courtyard of the Monastery of St John the Theologian.

was founded in 1088 by the monk Christodolous. Looking rather like a castle, it sits on the rocks high above the town and the sea. It has been altered and rebuilt continually over the centuries. The treasury still houses priceless artifacts, such as the mosaic throne of the holy Nikolaus from the 11th century, sacred and secular art from the 17th century, and valuable texts. The monastery library contains a hand-written copy of the Book of Job. The courtyard with its ancient frescos is unique and the main church, the Katholikon, date from 1090. The nearby Cave of the Apocalypse, is said to be where John of Pátmos saw the visions that he recorded in the Book of Revelation. The monastery and the Cave of the Apocalypse have been designated a World Heritage Site.

13 Skála, Pátmos Pátmos is the most northerly of the Dodecanese ("twelve islands"), a group that consists of twelve larger and around 150 smaller islands in the eastern Aegean. Cruise ships and ferries are frequent visitors to Skála's port. You can still see the Venetian influences in the architecture of the buildings that line the quayside. The town acquired its name from the Greek word for stairs as an imposing stairway leads up to one of the most important sites in the Greek Orthodox church, the Monastery of St John the Theologian (see panel, left), which, along with the Cave of the Apocalypse is one of the main tourist attractions on the island.

14 Pátmos Town, Pátmos Around 4 km (2½ miles) from Skála is the 12th-century Pátmos Town, the island's main settlement, which is a good base from which to explore the sacred sites that are located between Skála and Pátmos. Thanks to its monasteries, churches, and religious sites, some of which are mentioned in the Bible, Pátmos was formally declared a Holy Island in 1983 by the Greek government. But this is not the only reason for Pátmos Town's popularity with tourists. They also enjoy the medieval ambience of the ancient streets, centuries-old villas, and the beautiful panoramic views out over the surrounding countryside. The historic town center has been declared a World Heritage Site by UNESCO. The Simandiri House is a typical mansion dating from 1625, which once belonged to a captain. Not far from there is the idyllic convent of Zoodohou Pigis.

15 Grikos, Pátmos Follow the road that winds down (2 km/11/4 miles) toward Grikos bay and the picturesque fishing village of the same name. Grikos village is popular with visitors during the summer, though it is still quieter than some of the tourist spots. In the south of Pátmos, the beautiful beach of Psili Amos with its fine golden sand shaded by tamarisk trees sweeps out in a 200-m (656-ft) wide isthmus. The caves in the imposing Kalikatsou cliff to the south of the town were once inhabited and have steps carved into the rock. The route then follows another road 4 km (2½ miles) back to Skála for the crossing to Lipsi.

16 Lipsi This tiny island (17 sq km/6 sq miles), just 277 m (745 ft) at its highest point, is said to have been inhabited since prehistoric times. The first records of

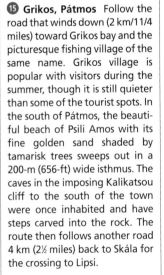

the island, however, date from the 13th century, when it was said to belong to the Monastery of St John on Pátmos. The ancestors of today's inhabitants came to the island in the 17th century. There are almost as many churches, hermitages, and monasteries as there are resident families on Lipsi. The landscape is rocky and hilly, with several small valleys that are fertile, though water is fairly scarce here. The pilgrimage church Miropolis, with its Panagia ti Mavri ("black Virgin") and Panaghia tou Harou ("goddess of death") icons, is well worth a visit. From the large port at Lipsi, the route continues by ferry to Léros.

17 Léros The ferry docks at the port of Agia Marina. The town of Platanos lies just above, but the two have now virtually

Sponges

People have dived for sponges for thousands of years. In the 19th century, this dangerous industry was centered in the Dodecanese, in particular on Kálimnos. Sponges are marine creatures that live at great depths. Divers dig them from the sea bed at depths of up to 90 m (295 ft) with a specially designed fork. The sponges are then laid out to dry or hung from the walls of houses. Only the black and brown part of the sponge skeleton is used, which then takes on the characteristic yellow after washing and chemical treatment. The number of sponges has

A merchant selling sponges on Kálimnos.

now fallen sharply and only around a dozen or so divers are able to make a living from sponge fishing. The island's sponge-fishing fleet now operates near the coast of Africa.

---

merged into one. The town is dominated by the imposing medieval castle of the Knights Hospitaller and the Pagaia tou Kastrou monastery on the cliffs above the town.

Covering an area of 54 sq km/ 21 sq miles, Léros has been governed by various occupying forces over the years. During World War II, it was used as a prison island; during the Greek Civil War (1945–1949) it was a re-education center for displaced children; and when the Greek Military Junta was in power (1967–1974) more than three thousand political prisoners were held here. You can see wall paintings by prisoners in the Agia Matrona Kioura Church in the north of the island, physical evidence of this dark chapter in its history. The route leaves Léros via Xirokambos in the south of the island, from where ferries

leave for Kálimnos. Nearby on the coast is the small cave church of Panagia Kavouradena where a fisherman found an icon of the Virgin.

18 Kálimnos Kálimnos (109 sq km/42 sq miles) is famous for its sponge fishing and is home to the only sponge-fishing fleet in Greece, though the industry is currently facing problems due to a disease that is killing off the sponges. Fortunately, the island also has other sources of income such as conventional fishing and citrus fruit cultivation, as well as a growing tourist trade.

The beautiful villas in the capital Kálimnos, where most of the island's inhabitants live, date back to the golden age of sponge diving. You can visit a sponge factory, learn about the life cycle of the sponge and find out how they become the yellow sponges

that are a familiar item in every bathroom. The town's nautical museum has memorabilia of the golden age of sponge fishing, as well as a collection of local art. The town of Vathys is also well worth a visit, nestling at the end of a deep bay, as is the ninth-century castle above the town of Chorio, once the island's capital. The castle was built to defend the town against pirates. There are also caves, and grottoes to see and at Therma, just over half a mile south of Kálimnos there is a healing spring. If you have time to spare, visit the nearby island of Telendos, which was separated from Kálimnos around 600 BC by an earthquake. There are a number of lovely beaches there. From Kálimnos, the route continues on to Kos by ferry.

19 Kós Town, Kós Supposedly the birthplace of Hippocrates,

Kós is the third largest island in the Dodecanese (290 sq km/112 sq miles). Bearing the same name as the island, the capital was already a bustling trading

1 The island's capital, Pátmos Town, enjoys wonderful views over the natural port of Skála.

2 Grikos bay on Pátmos is extremely popular with tourists.

3 A ship docking on the tiny island of Lipsi.

4 Kálimnos is famous for its sponge fishermen. They have to sail far offshore in search of sponges.

5 The Knights Hospitaller left a legacy of castles on Kálimnos.

6 Ágia Marina port is one of the most beautiful places on Léros.

Kós and the Asclepieion of Hippocrates

Kós first gained importance in the sixth and fifth centuries BC with the cult of Asclepios and the teaching and practice of the physican Hippocrates (c. 460–377 BC) who was born on the island. Known as the "father of medicine" he is said to have written the hypocratic oath relating to the ethical practice of medicine that all doctors have to swear. In ancient times, an asclepieion was a sanctuary dedicated to the god of healing, Asclepios. In the second century BC, the Asclepieion at Kós was the largest of the holy

Top: The remains of the Asclepieion in a sun-drenched Mediterranean landscape.
Bottom: The reconstruction of Apollo's temple in the Asclepieion.

temples dedicated to Asclepios. Today its ruins are considered some of the most important in the Aegean. The Asclepieion was both a temple and a spa, but was not constructed until after Hippocrates' death (between fourth and second centuries BC), though he is still thought of as being linked to the site. The remains include three terraces: the lowest contains a Roman spa and fountain, the middle terrace contains a temple area dedicated to Asclepios and Apollo, with a sacrificial altar and treasury, while from the top terrace, reached by a stairway, there are fantastic views over the coastal landscape.

port in 400 BC and nowadays has a population of around eighteen thousand people. The ancient Mandraki port still exists, though it is now mostly only used as a base for excursions as most private yachts and catamarans dock farther east. Between the two ports lies the imposing Neratzia Castle, built on the foundations of a Byzantine fortress in the 15th century by the Knights Hospitaller to protect the port of Kós.

Directly behind the castle, the Hadji-Hassan-Pascha Mosque (built in 1786) marks the edge of the ancient Agora (marketplace) dating from around 400 BC. Next to the mosque's minaret is an ancient plane tree, under which Hippocrates and Paul the Apostle are said to have studied. Botanists dispute this and estimate the age of the tree to be more like five hundred years. The Aesclepion where Hippocrates is said to have practiced and taught medicine is the main tourist attraction in Kós. It is located some 3 km (2 miles) south-west of town toward Platani (turn right after 2.5 km/ 1½ miles).

20 Antimáhia, Kós Remaining on the same road, the route continues 29 km (18 miles) to the village of Antimáhia, located 140 m (459 miles) above sea level on a rugged plateau. The settlement here dates back to ancient times. The name derives from Andimachos, son of the mythical Greek hero Heracles. The largest castle ruin on the island, Palea Antimáhia, was built in the 13th century by Venetians and enlarged a hundred years later by the Knights Hospitaller. Two churches within the castle walls display sacred art. Also worth seeing in the town are the 260-year-old windmill and traditional stone farmhouse. These have survived even though the town has been hit a number of times by powerful earthquakes. The route leaves Antimáhia to the south-west and skirts round the nearby airport; then the main road on the island leads across an isthmus to Kéfalos, 15 km (9 miles) away.

21 Kéfalos, Kós The town is situated on the Kéfalos peninsula, and was the first to bring mass tourism to the island. In ancient times Kéfalos was the island's capital, but it was destroyed by an earthquake in 412 BC and never regained its former importance. The monasteries of Agios Ioannis Thimianos and Agios Theologos are well worth a visit, as is the early Christian basilica of Agios Stefanos. There are several other churches and chapels to visit in the area surrounding Kéfalos, as well as a medieval castle and a Hellenistic theater dating from 200 BC. Kéfalos is also a good base from which to explore Níssiros Island, 44 km (27 miles) away.

22 Níssiros Though relatively modest in size (42 sq km/16 sq miles), this island seems much larger because of its arid craterous moonscape. According to Greek mythology, the sea god Poseidon broke off a piece of Kós to hurl at his adversaries,

3

4

Níssiros volcano

The almost perfectly circular volcanic island of Níssiros to the south of Kós was created around 50 million years ago by earthquakes and volcanic eruptions, and successive eruptions that took place up to 15,000 BC. The volcano is a magnet for tourists. Although it is still active, the last real eruption was more than five million years ago. Since then, it has occasionally released hot steam and small quantities of ash, sometimes leading to earthquakes. In actual fact, the whole island is a volcano, a 698-m (2,290-ft) high mountain of lava. The main crater is 3.5 km (2 miles) long, 1.5 km (1 mile) wide,

Top: The volcano on Nissiros is like a desert landscape.
Bottom: Various walks take in the volcano's crater.

and almost 500 m (1,640 ft) deep and contains five smaller, sub-craters. Two villages are built around the edge of the crater.

Around half of the island is covered with vegetation, with fruit and vegetables flourishing in the fertile volcanic soil, while the other half is a barren desert of lava. There are plenty of walks that enable you to look down into the crater where the temperature is 45°C (113°F), and water boils and bubbles, and steam shoots out of small fissures at temperatures of up to 100°C (212°F). The smell of sulfur is everywhere on the island.

24 Rhodos Town, Rhodos Also known as Rhodes Town, on Rhodes Island. The "Sun Island" is the largest of the Dodecanese covering 1,398 sq km (540 sq miles) and is the fourth largest Greek island. It lies just 18 km (11 miles) off the Turkish coast. Rhodes Town (65,000 inhabitants) on the north-east tip of the island, is the capital of both the island and the island group. It was first established in 408 BC by the architect Hippodamos of Milet.

The medieval old town has been a UNESCO World Heritage Site since 1988. The 4-km (2½-mile) long walls, up to 12 m (39 ft) thick in places, including towers and seven gates, encircle and dominate the old town. From the Amboise Gate, you can climb up onto the walls and take a stroll above the rooftops taking in the town with a bird's eye view. The Knights Hospitaller left a legacy of impressive buildings including the large Palace

1 The ancient market place in Kós, with the Hadji-Hassan-Pascha Mosque in the background.

2 Dusk descends over the waterfront promenade in Kós town.

3 An isolated rocky bay near Koutroulaki on Tílos.

4 The new Taxiarchis Michail Church in Megálo Horío on Tilos.

which is how Níssiros was created. Over 100,000 tourists make the day trip from Kós, "the mother land" every year, to see the crater on Níssiros. During the summer months, they vastly outnumber the 1,600 inhabitants. The capital of the island and port is Mandráki on the north coast. Attractions include the Panagia Spiliani Monastery (18th C.), which offers wonderful views and has a Byzantine cave church, and the ruins of the Knights Hospitaller Castle, at 140 m (459 ft) above sea level. From Mandráki, the ferry leaves for Tílos.

23 Tílos This 63-sq km (24-sq mile), rugged and mountainous island (highest point: Profitis Ilias at 651 m/2,136 ft) is sparsely populated. Currently there are around five hundred inhabitants living in the island's two settlements, Megálo Horío and Livádia, and the village of Mikro Horío is a ghost town that has been deserted since 1967. In the center of the island (16 km/10 miles long) is the Charkadió cave, where the skeleton of a dwarf elephant *Palaeoloxodon antiquus falceroni*, extinct since 4500 BC, was discovered in 1978. All the archeological finds, well

over two thousand, are documented in the Megálo Horío museum. The island boasts many interesting buildings including several castles built by the Knights Hospitaller dating from the 14th and 15th centuries, the Ágios Pandeleimon Monastery (14th–18th C.), and both the old (16th C.) and new (19th C.) Taxiarchis Michail Church in Megálo Horío, which contains valuable icons and a carved wooden iconostasis and pulpit. Beaches of rock, pebble, and sand line the island's bays. From the small, hidden port town of Livádia, we leave Tílos for Rhodes.

Rhodes Town and The Avenue of the Knights

Nowhere are the Middle Ages so alive as in the Avenue of the Knights (Odós Ippotón) in Rhodes' old town. Built in the 15th and 16th centuries by the Knights Hospitaller, the buildings have been well preserved. Also known by several other names, including the Knights of St John or the Knights Templar, the order was established around 1080 to care for sick and poor pilgrims to the Holy Land. Following the Christian conquest of Jerusalem during the First Crusade, the order's mission was to defend the Holy Land against the

Top: The Amboise Gate leads to the Palace of the Grand Master.
Bottom: The medieval Avenue of the Knights was constructed by the Knights Hospitaller.

Muslims. When the Holy Land was lost after the Siege of Acre (1291), the crusaders retreated to Cypress and then to Rhodes. Led by Grand Master Fulko of Villaret, they conquered the island and built a fortress in Rhodes Town and the famous Avenue of the Knights, divided into different sections according to the native languages spoken by the knights. The French group dominated and as a result the most beautiful building is the Auberge de France (built 1492–1507). All "tongues" chose a grand master, who was the representative of each order for life. The Palace of the Grand Master (14th C.), reconstructed in 1940, is one of Rhodes' most popular attractions. When the Ottoman Emperor Suleiman the Magnificent conquered Rhodes in 1523, the palace was used as a prison and later Turkish merchants occupied the palace and buildings of the now homeless crusaders.

of the Grand Master, dating from the 14th century and The Avenue of the Knights. The Colossus of Rhodes, a statue of the sun god Helios, was one of the Seven Wonders of the Ancient World. It towered approximately 42 m (138 ft) high above the entrance to the port of Mandraki until around 226 BC when it was destroyed by an earthquake. The remains lay on the ground for some 800 years, but were eventually broken up and sold as scrap metal. The port still exists however. Its entrance guarded by two pillars carrying the two symbols of the island, the stag and the doe, must be the most well-known picture postcard view on the island.

Ialysos, Rhodos The route leaves Rhodes Town to the west and hugs the coast until it reaches Trianda, or Ialysos, after 10 km (6 miles). It is said to be the oldest Mycenaean settle-

ment on Rhodes, dating back to around 1450 BC. When the Dorians settled on the island in 1000 BC, Ialysos was declared one of three independent town states. One of its most famous sons was Diagoras who became three-time Olympic champion in the fifth century BC. Outside the town, you can see the late Classical and early Hellenistic remains

of the Acropolis of Ialysos that once stood on the 267-m (876-ft) high Filerimos Mountain ("friend of loneliness").

Kámiros Skala, Rhodos The route continues along the coastal road for another 40 km (25 miles) until it reaches Kámiros Skala and the archeological excavations to the north

at the ancient town of Kámiros. A flourishing town in the sixth century BC. this was the smallest of the three Dorian town states. The remains of many of the buildings can still clearly be seen, from residential buildings to the bath house and its water supply system. At the center was the Agora with a temple (3rd C. BC) dedicated to Apollo. Today

The island of Rhodes and the Acropolis of Lindos

The ancient Acropolis of Lindos, one of the most important historical sites on the island of Rhodes, stands high above the sea, close to a castle built by the medieval Knights Hospitaller. The main part is the temple dedicated to the goddess of Lindos, Athena Lindia. The Dorians erected an altar in her name in the seventh century BC, which was then enlarged by the tyrannical Kleoboulus to form a lavish temple following a fire in 342 BC. Inside the temple was a statue of the goddess made out of gold, marble, and ivory. The crusaders recognized the strategic importance of the temple's position 120 m (394 ft) above sea level and built a castle adjacent to it in the 15th century, accessible via over three hundred steps. Other historical remains include the ruins of a Roman temple (AD 200), a Byzantine tower, a Knights Hospitaller church (13th C.), the remains of an ancient water system, and the

Top: A beautiful view of the town and the hilly landscape from the Acropolis on Lindos.
Bottom: The Athena-Lindia temple in the centre of the Acropolis in Lindos.

natural anchorage on Rhodes, and is a National Historic Landmark. Founded in the 10th century BC, Lindos was the most powerful of the three Dorian town states, laying claim to more than half of the island. The 17th-century houses below the Acropolis that belonged to the well-to-do still stand out clearly in the townscape. The architecture has obvious Arabian, Byzantine, and Aegean influences. The route now leads 55 km (34 miles) back to Rhodes Town via Archangelos.

(continued p.116)

architectural centerpiece, an Ionian portico dating from the second century AD. At 87 m (285 ft), it was as wide as the whole Acropolis. Of the original forty-two columns, there are twenty still standing today.

Kámiros Skala is a small fishing village and ferry port. The castle of Kritinia offers wonderful views over to Hálki island.

27 **Apolakkia, Rhodos** A chain of mountains with peaks up to 1,215 m (3,986 ft) high and slopes covered with forests of pine occupies the interior of Rhodes Island. You will have

good views of the mountainous landscape on the continuing journey south. After Kámiros Skala, the road leads inland to a beautiful viewpoint at Móno-lithos and then on to Apolakkia. Look out for a Byzantine castle on the way, set high up on the cliffs. The Agia Irini Basilica and the somewhat remote but idyllic Agios Georgios o Vardas

Chapel (dating from around 1250) are well worth a stop on the way. The winding road cuts directly across the island to the east, where it joins the coastal road that leads to Lindos.

28 **Lindos, Rhodos** After 41 km (25 miles) you reach Lindos, the largest town on the island (see panel, right). It has the only

1 Mandraki Port on Rhodes has been preserved since ancient times.

2 Buildings and walls from the Middle Ages dominate the main port of Rhodes.

3 A hill near Lindos offers a panorama over the bay of Lindos and the east coast of Rhodes.

Nowhere else in the Sporades is Easter celebrated as vividly and traditionally as it is in the village of Ólymbos on Kárpathos. Icons are taken in procession to the cemetery for the dead, and the resurrection of Jesus is celebrated in a joyful

procession with traditional lyre music and the traditional drink ouzo. The women wear bright traditional dress, with long, heavy chains laden with gold coins and jewelry around their necks, and scarves and ornaments in their hair. The celebrations and dancing go on into the night.

29 Kárpathos Town, Kárpathos Lying to the south-west of Rhodes, Kárpathos (301 sq km/116 sq miles) is reached by ferry in 4 to 6 hours. It is the second largest island in the Dodecanese and one of the earliest to be settled: the towns of Arkesia, Thoantion, Vrykos, and Poseidion sprang up here around 1000 BC. Nowadays Kárpathos Town, also known as Pigadia, stands on the site of Poseidion. Situated on an almost circular bay, it is the island's capital and most important port. The main tourist attraction is the early Christian Basilica of Ágia Fotini. It was erected in the sixth century in remembrance of Fotini the Martyr and is now largely in ruins, though half a dozen columns are still standing, and there is a hand-carved rood screen with reliefs. A hill behind the town would have been the obvious place for an Acropolis, but there is nothing to be seen there. Instead there are plenty of ancient remains at Arkássa, which lies south on the west coast. To get there, take the main road across the island.

30 Arkássa, Kárpathos After 16 km (10 miles), the road reaches Arkássa. There is plenty here to please lovers of history,

but its beaches are also popular with swimmers and sunbathers. Among the remains are traces of the ancient capital Arkesia on the headland, and the early Christian church of Agia Anastasia dating back to the fourth to sixth centuries. A Dorian Acropolis stood on the rocks above the village, as did a Venetian-Turkish fort. Arkássa is also fortunate in being set in the most attractive part of the island's coastline. Just a short walk west of the town center, the bay of Agios Nikolaos contains the most popular beach on Kárpathos. To the north, a modern memorial remembers the seven local residents who went for help in a tiny boat after the island's occupation in autumn 1944. Past the memorial, the route leaves town on the coastal road, which leads 50 km (31 miles) north to Ólymbos. On the way, it passes Kali Limni (1,215-m/3,986 ft), the highest mountain in the Dodecanese. Winding its way through the mountain landscape, the road offers spectacular views.

31 Ólymbos, Kárpathos As you continue along the road, houses in white and pastel shades start to appear, and churches and windmills hug the steep hillside. They belong to

the most picturesque mountain town in Greece. Ólymbos was founded in 1420 by the inhabitants of the now deserted island of Saria and ancient Vrykos, who went in search of a safe place out of reach of pirates. Thanks to the fact that the town was cut off until the 1980s when a road was finally built to connect it to the rest of the island, Olymbos is like a living museum with its original culture still virtually intact. Houses are built in the traditional style,

the old Dorian dialect is still spoken, and older women wear their traditional dress every day, not just on special occasions. Bread is still baked in stone ovens outside and its centuries-old traditions are maintained, admittedly now partly to please the tourists. The port of Ólymbos is Diafáni (18th C.), around 10 km (6 miles) away on the east coast. Ferries have only been calling here since 1975. Many visitors take a day trip over to the island of Saria (16 sq km/

6 sq miles), just 100 m (109 yds) off the coast. The ferry back to Rhodes then brings the cruise to an end.

1 Children play in the sea in Pigadia, the main town on the island of Kárpathos.

2 The houses and churches of the traditional mountain village of Ólymbos nestle on the side of Profitis Ilias mountain on Kárpathos.

Lesbos The 1,630-sq km (629-sq mile) island of Lesbos lies in the north-east Aegean. The picturesque port of Míthimna, in the north of the island, is shown here.

Chios The ubiquitous windmills are a popular symbol of the island and the Néa Moni Monastery (11th C.) attracts many tourists.

Sámos The island was home to Pythagoras, in recognition of whom the town of Tigani was renamed Pythagoreión (shown here).

Pátmos The most northerly Dodecanese island. Its most important site is the Monastery of St John the Theologian (1088).

Foúrni Still relatively untouched by tourism until now and perfect for nature lovers. Nearly all the island's inhabitants live in the main town of the same name.

Kós The island is just a stone's throw off the Turkish coast. The main town has a lively port. The ancient physician Hippocrates was born here.

Kalímnos Picturesque ruins left behind by the Knights Hospitaller on the island famous for its sponge divers.

Kárpathos The second largest island in the Dodecanese is still very traditional. The island's main source of income, aside from cattle rearing, is tourism.

Tílos The mountainous slopes of this island are dominated by castles, a legacy of the Knights Hospitaller. Hidden bays form inviting places to swim.

Rhodos The old town has been a UNESCO World Heritage Site since 1988. The town walls, built by the Knights Hospitaller, are up to 12 m (39 ft) thick in places. Mandraki port dates back to ancient times.

The pyramids at Giza are the only wonder of the ancient world still standing today.

Egypt
A journey through the land of the pharaohs

The ancient pyramids of Giza are the most iconic sight in Egypt. The pharaohs for whom they were built in their quest for immortality were treated like living gods. The highly developed culture of the ancient Egyptians, who lived in the fertile Nile valley thousands of years ago, has left behind a host of impressive architectural relics, making this cruise a unique and unforgettable experience.

In the north-east of the great continent of Africa, but with a "toe" in both Asia and Europe, Egypt is a true crossroads of cultures. Its history offers an insight into a strange world. The rule of the pharaohs began over five thousand years ago, but still fascinates visitors today with its strange rituals, monumental tombs and temples, and the potent imagery of its hieroglyphic script. The majority of monuments from the times of the pharaohs are located near or on the banks of the Nile.

With the exception of the bustling city of Cairo, the 300-km (186-mile) long stretch of the Nile Valley between Luxor and Aswan contains the most interesting ancient sites, while the Valley of the Kings, the mighty Temple of Karnak, and the Mortuary Temple of Queen Hatshepsut are the main attractions at Luxor itself. Farther south, the temples of Edfu and Kôm Ombo show that the conquering Greeks and Romans were also fascinated by the pharaohs. In Aswan, in the 1960s,

The gold mask of the boy king Tutankhamen.

the very old met the very new when the construction of a huge dam threatened to flood ancient temples such as those at Abu Simbel. The answer was simple: they would have to be moved, resulting in an international rescue operation.

Around 95 percent of the total surface area of Egypt (well over 1,000,000 sq km/ 386,000 sq miles) is desert. As a result, most of Egypt's 75 million people live in settlements hugging the Nile, while relatively few live elsewhere: in the oases of the Western Desert, on the banks of the Red Sea, or near Mt Sinai. Along with the Egyptians, who are descended from the Ancient Egyptians, there are also minority populations of Syrians, Bedouin, Berbers, Palestinians, Beja, Nubians, and Europeans. The majority of Egyptians are Muslim, with some Greek Orthodox, Catholics and Protestants, and Copts.

The four colossal figures of Pharaoh Ramses II stand 20 m (66 ft) high in front of the great temple at Abu Simbel.

In the evening light, the long avenues guarded by sphinxes in front of the temple to the god Amun in Luxor look particularly impressive.

In the fifth century BC, the Greek historian Herodotus wrote "Egypt is a gift from the Nile" and so it seems today. The annual summer floods, nowadays controlled by the dam in Aswan, coupled with the hot climate mean the *fellahin* (farmers) can enjoy two to four harvests per year, depending on the crop, ensuring that the growing population has a steady supply of food.

In ancient times, five major branches of the River Nile spread across the delta area in the north of Egypt, irrigating the fertile alluvial plain, but over the centuries the landscape has changed and today, there are just two. The 24,000-sq km (9.264-sq mile) Nile Delta is Egypt's most important farming area, where grain, vegetables, and fruit are grown, and cotton is also cultivated. The river is also used to transport freight, aided by a well-developed canal network. Alexandria benefited enormously from the export of cotton, or "white gold" as it was known in the 19th century, and developed into a major modern city and port on the Mediterranean. Cairo lies at the southern edge of the Nile Delta and connects Upper and Lower Egypt. Everything is on a large scale in Egypt's bustling capital: the population, the traffic chaos, and the treasures of its fabulous ancient history housed in the National Museum. At Giza, at the western edge of the city, the famous pyramids point to the stars and stand guard over modern Egypt. In the center of the city, minarets, church towers, and appartment blocks also reach into the sky. People meet in cafés, shop in the markets, and stroll along the banks of the river in the cool of the evening. A host of cultures converge here in Egypt's capital city.

Minarets appear as silhouettes in the evening sky at Cairo.

Copts

Egyptian Christians have been called Copts since the seventh century, though the term was originally used to describe all Egyptians. It was only after the expansion of Islam that it became confined to the Christian inhabitants of the Nile Valley.

Christianity established itself in Alexandria in the first century, from where it spread quickly to the rest of the country in the decades that followed. This had terrible consequences in the third century, when Roman rulers killed and tortured thousands of people for their beliefs. The Coptic church still remembers the particularly terrible Christian persecution under Roman Emperor Diocletian in its calen-

Top: Coptic monastery in Wadi el-Natrun.
Bottom: Coptic monks celebrating Christmas.

dar. Coptic years are counted from AD 284, the year Diocletian became Emperor, which counts as their year 0 Anno Martyrii (year of the martyrs). Just 200 years later, in-fighting among Christians led to further persecution of the Copts and their church. To this day, the Copts do not recognize the Pope in Rome as their head, but follow their own patriarch, the Pope of Alexandria. Copts represent between 8 and 14 percent of the Egyptian population, a percentage that is often contested as it has a bearing on how many ministerial posts are allocated to Copts in the government.

Ancient and modern meet on this journey from the Mediterranean to Lake Nasser in the arid south, following the River Nile. But before taking to the river, you head east from Alexandria along the coast of the Mediterranean, then down the Suez Canal to Ismailia (Ismâilîya), from where you travel by road to Cairo and then on to Luxor, where the Nile cruise finally begins.

① Alexandria Named after its founder Alexander the Great, the city dates back to 332 BC. It became Egypt's capital under the Ptolemaic dynasty (323–330 BC), and achieved great fame as a center for science. The Serapeum (a temple dedicated to Serapis, the protector of the city), the library, and the lighthouse (one of the Seven Wonders of the Ancient World) all have become symbols of Alexandria.

After the city was conquered by the Romans, its ancient monuments began to crumble and decay and it was not until the rule of Mohammed Ali (1805–1849) that Alexandria started to undergo a resurgence. Urban renovation and the marine excavation of the port that began in 1994 and is still ongoing have helped attract interest, putting the city back in the news again. It made the headlines worldwide when relics from the time of Cleopatra, the last Egyptian queen, were discovered in the port basin.

Alexandria now has almost five million inhabitants, making it the second largest city in Egypt. Its narrow beaches become very crowded in summer. In the east, the outskirts of the town extend almost as far as Rashid (Rosetta), home to the famous Rosetta Stone, discovered by French archaeologists in the 19th century and today housed in the British Museum in London. Containing three different translations of the same text, its discovery was hugely instrumental in helping to decipher ancient Egyptian hieroglyphics.

The ship departs Alexandria and follows the coast to the east until it reaches the mouth of the Suez Canal.

② Port Said Port Said is the second largest port in Egypt, after Alexandria. It takes its name from Said Pasha, who approved the ambitious plan of Ferdinand de Lesseps to build a canal between the Red Sea and the Mediterranean. Several buildings dating from the 19th

Travel information

Route profile
Length: approx. 1,400 km (870 miles) (without excursions)
Duration: min. 14–20 days
Start: Alexandria
End: Abu Simbel
Itinerary (main locations): Alexandria, Port Said, Cairo, Luxor, Edfu, Aswan, Abu Simbel
NB The spelling of Egyptian names (places, people, gods) varies, and some have several different names.

Important note
The route between the Suez Canal and Cairo, and between Cairo and Luxor, has to be made by road or rail. Nile cruises are only available between Luxor and Aswan, and from Lake Nasser to Abu Simbel. A police escort is required for trips outside Cairo, Luxor, and Aswan.

Transport tips
The Egyptian style of driving can be erratic, so take care to avoid accidents. It is recommended that you do not travel in private or hired cars after dark.

When to go
October–May

Tourist information
www.touregypt.net
Cruise operators
The Egyptian Tourist Office website has information on Nile cruises, including a list of tour companies *www.touregypt.net/ egyptnilecruises.htm*

3

4

Suez Canal

The long-held dream to connect the Mediterranean with the Red Sea finally became a reality in the middle of the 19th century. Even in ancient times there had been attempts to establish a shipping route using the Nile Valley; but it was not until the Austrian engineer Alois von Negrelli drew up plans confirming it was possible to construct a direct waterway between Port Said in the north and Suez in the south without the need for locks, that the canal became a real possibility. French developer Ferdinand de Lesseps finally convinced Ismail Pasha to build the canal, which would shorten trade routes between Europe

The Suez Canal: unusual because it has no locks.

and Asia by 85 percent. In 1858, the Compagnie universelle du Canal de Suez was founded. Egypt attempted to raise funds for the project by selling shares in the canal; but a lack of interest in Europe meant that many shares went unsold, loading Egypt with enormous national debt. Despite this, eleven years later on the project's completion in 1869, Ismail made sure its opening was an occasion never to be forgotten and guests from around the world were invited to Cairo. In 1875, Great Britain bought a large number of shares, acquiring 44 percent of the Suez Canal Company and as a result, together with France, was able to exercise considerable control over Egyptian affairs. In 1956, President Nasser nationalized the canal but paid the price with the resulting Suez War. The canal was closed by Egypt during the 1967 Arab-Israeli War and not reopened again until 1975, depriving Egypt of a great deal of revenue from canal fees. Now ships of up to 136,364 tonnes (150,000 tons) carry freight up and down the 191-km (119-mile) long waterway every day. The canal fees are one of the most important sources of income for the country.

Cairo, 120 km (75 miles) away, and then on to Luxor.

4 Cairo See also pages 122–3. Egypt's capital (Cairo means "the vanquisher") is the most densely populated metropolitan area in Africa. Around twenty million people live here, and the number is increasing all the time. In the time of the pharaohs, there was no city where Cairo now stands.

The district now called Old Cairo is where the Persians, who conquered Egypt in 525 BC, established a fortress. The old town is a haphazard network of narrow alleyways, tenement buildings, and mosques, while hotels with glass façades, offices, and shopping malls characterize the city's newer (continued p.124)

century remain and hint at the town's former elegance and standing.

After suffering heavy destruction during the 1956 Suez War and 1973 Arab-Israeli War, Port Said was rebuilt in the modern style and is quickly developing into Egypt's most popular domestic holiday resort, due not least to the creation of a free trade area. The boat departs from the port and is piloted through a 15-hour navigation of the Suez Canal. Lake Timsah lies almost halfway down the canal.

3 Ismailia (Ismâilîya) The west shore of the lake was used as a base for engineers working on the canal. The town was named after Khedive Ismail ("Khedive" was a term used for the rulers of Egypt and the Sudan). It was during Ismail's rule that the canal project became a reality. It was inaugurated in 1869 but by the end of the 19th century its cost had driven Egypt to bankruptcy.

The "pearl of the canal" as Ismailia is sometimes known, is nowadays popular with summer visitors because of its beau-

tiful parks and the leisure activities offered on Lake Timsah. The university and the Suez Canal management service are important employers in the region. A small museum, built in a neo-pharaonic style, exhibits relics from ancient times, among them a sphinx and a Roman floor mosaic. A folklore festival takes place at the end of August, and music and dance groups from all over the world perform there.

Sandwiched between fertile farmland and desert, the route now continues by car or bus to

1 Alexandria stretches out for miles along the Mediterranean coast.

2 The citadel of Qait Bey in Alexandria was built in 1477.

3 The Sultan Hassan Mosque in Cairo (pictured left) serves as a house of worship, a mausoleum, and a place of teaching; right, the Ar Rifa'i Mosque.

4 The commander of the Mamluke Army, Emir Sarghatmish, had a mosque built next to the old Ibn Tulun Mosque in Cairo in 1356.

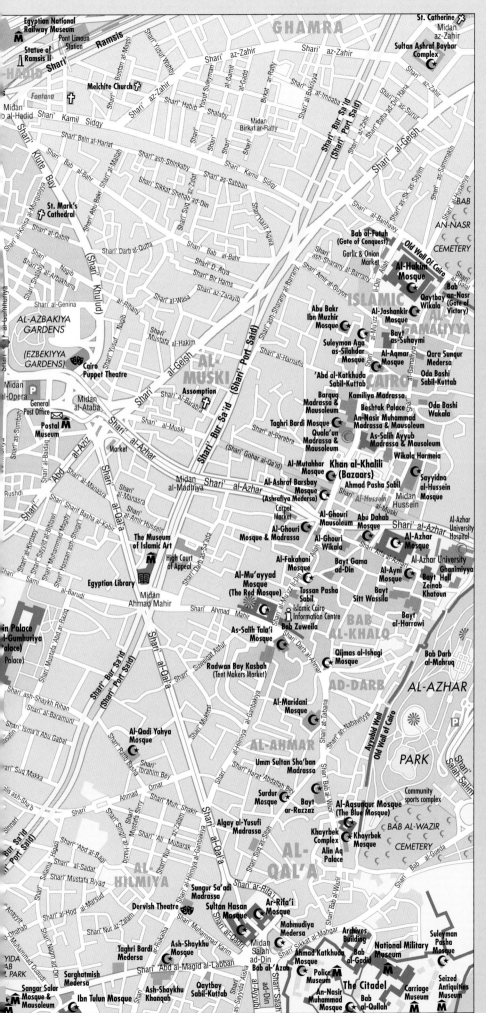

Cairo

Looking west from the Citadel, a landmark on Cairo's eastern skyline, on a clear day you can see over the minarets to the silhouettes of the pyramids at Giza, but the view over the city is often hazy: humidity from the river, sand storms, and pollution from the busy city center all sometimes contribute to obscuring what should be a stunning view.

On the southern tip of Roda (Al-Rawda) Island, a Nilometer testifies to the age of the Egyptian capital. In the 10th century, long before the city became known as Cairo, priests built devices for measuring the height of the Nile flood up and down the river, which also enabled them to calculate the amount of tax the *fellahin* should pay: the higher the flood, the more fertile the soil and so the more tax due.

Opposite the island is one of the most important inland ports in the country, Per Hapi en Junu. The Romans fortified the port and the early Christians built their first church here. In the Candle Quarter next to the Mari Girgis metro station, the university, make it one of the most important Muslim institutions in the world. The area between the town gates of Bab el-Futug and Bab en-Nasr in the north and Bab es-Suweila in the south contains some beautiful Muslim architecture. The Selijuks, Mamluks, and Ottomans all built mosques, palaces, commercial buildings, fountains, and schools in the city over a period of 600 years. Although Salah ed-Din, who came to power in 1171, had his residence in the Citadel, the lively center of town remained Al-Qahira. The bazaar of Khan el-Khalili still captivates visitors to this day.

Town planning was once again put on the agenda in the 19th century under Mohammed Ali, who wanted

Top: The skyline at twilight.
Middle: View of the city with the Nile.
Bottom: The Muezzin reciting the call to prayer at the Bussra Mosque.

Mamluk Church for the Virgin Mary stands on the foundations of the Roman fort. The Ben Ezra Synagogue in the old town is the oldest in Cairo and is famous because, according to legend, it stands on the place where the pharaoh's daughter found Moses in the river. Just a few hundred yards to the north is the oldest mosque in Africa, which has recently been renovated. It was built on the orders of Amr Ibn el-As in 642 when the city was still known as Fustat. Commissioned by the Abbasids, the governer Ibn Tulun, declared de facto independence on the Nile 235 years later. His residence must have once been beautiful and opulent, but the huge mosque (876–879) is the only building that remains from this period. It is one of the largest mosques in the world with a surface area of almost 2.5 ha (6 acres).

Just under a hundred years later, the country had new rulers. Naturally, the Shiite Fatimas also needed a mighty residence. Surrounded by well-fortified walls, they occupied the palaces of Al-Qahira. Its Friday mosque, built in 969, and its Muslim

to turn Cairo into a modern European-style metropolis. Some beautiful art nouveau façades can be seen in the area between Midan el-Opera and Midan Talaat Harb. From here it's just a stone's throw back to the present at Midan et-Tahrir, where the first metro station was built, where the Arabic League has its offices, and where the National Museum is based, with its numerous treasures from the time of the pharaohs.

1

districts. The commercial and residential buildings lining the Nile tower twenty to thirty floors high, and properties here are expensive. Beyond the busy center lie greener suburbs such as Heliopolis or Maadi.

⑤ Giza Located on the west bank of the Nile, the city of Cairo has crept ever further south until it now extends almost as far as the town of Giza. The three huge pyramids of the Pharaohs Khufu, Khafre, and Menkaure sit on a chalk plateau above the town. Erected as tombs in the third century BC, they were built to last for eternity.

The blocks that make up Khufu's colossal Great Pyramid (the oldest and largest of the pyramids located here) weigh an average of 1.8 tonnes (2 tons) each. Originally 147 m (482 ft) high, the pyramid is nowadays 10 m (33 ft) shorter than it once was as in the Middle Ages, the people of Cairo found it a useful supply of stone to build their houses. Nothing remains of the polished stone casing that once covered the exterior, but part of the façade of the adjacent Khafre Pyramid (Khufu's son) is still intact.

At 65.5 m (215 ft) the tomb of Menkaure (believed to be Khafre's son) seems quite small in comparison. The imposing sphinx watches over the pyramids from the east. Carved out of the surrounding bedrock, its face is believed to be that of Khafre attached to the body of a lion. Next to it is Khafre's valley temple built of rose granite and alabaster.

⑥ Memphis The first capital of ancient Egypt, Memphis was the kingdom's administrative centre, its largest garrison town, and a centre of worship for the god Ptah. Today there is little physical evidence that this mighty city once stood on the west bank of the Nile. Its palaces and grand residences have long disappeared and the land has now returned to fertile pasture. Only a few traces remain, including a large statue of Ramses II and an alabaster sphinx. These are on display between the palm trees in an open-air museum in the village of Mitrahina on the southwestern edge of Giza.

⑦ Sakkara Around 20 km (12 miles) south of Giza, a vast ancient burial ground, the

2

largest in Egypt, stretches out into the desert. It was an important site for cult ceremonies and minor burials for some 3,000 years. The site became important when the first pharaoh of the third dynasty, Djoser, had a step pyramid built here (around 2750 BC). Its architect, Imhotep, used stone as a building material for the first time and in so doing set the prece-

dent for the next 3,000 years. There are sixteen other pyramids built on the site. Among the largest and most beautiful of the tombs dating from the Old Kingdom is that of Ti, which features some wonderful carved reliefs of the pharoah hunting. Around one thousand years later, General Haremhab also had a tomb built here, before he became pharaoh in 1320 BC and

ordered another, more magnificent tomb to be constructed in the Valley of the Kings.

The next pyramid site is reached 10 km (6 miles) farther south, at Dahshûr.

⑧ Dahshûr The Bent Pyramid (so-called because of its unusual shape) and the Red Pyramid (named after the red limestone used) were built here during the

reign of Snofru, the father of the pharaoh Khufu. Snofru's architects were cautious after a previous project, a mile or so to the south, encountered serious construction problems; it suffered internal cracking, and on completion was found to be leaning. The Bent Pyramid's shape may be the result of reducing the angle after signs of instability appeared during construction.

Farther south, the uneven silhouette of Amenemhet III's Black Pyramid is visible on the horizon.

It was built in 1800 BC using a completely different method. A huge mountain of clay bricks was built up over its limestone center. The road runs parallel to the Nile and reaches the turn-off for Meidum after 45 km (28 miles).

9 Meidum Snofru was also active here, on the edge of the fertile valley of Faijûm. The pyramid attributed to him is in the form of a stepped tower and rises up from the desert like a gigantic sandcastle. The adjacent tombs contain many famous wall paintings. The Geese of Meidum panel is now a prized exhibit in the National Museum in Cairo.

Back on the road, the route continues south through small towns until it arrives at the provincial town of Beni Suêf after 42 km (26 miles). It is recommended that you cross the Nile here onto its eastern bank, where a faster road south makes for an easier journey down to El-Minia.

10 El-Minia With around 250,000 inhabitants, El-Minia is one of the liveliest towns in central Egypt. As an administrative center, university town, and center for industry, it provides employment for many locals, while visitors use the town as a base for exploring the surrounding area. The town is characterized by its large number of churches. Minia has a higher than average percentage of Copts.

11 Beni Hassan From the west bank of the Nile, around 25 km (16 miles) south of El-Minia, take a boat to the tombs of the Beni Hassan princes, which are cut into the rock. The site dates back to the 11th and 12th dynasties (between 2000 and 1755 BC). The wall paintings depict many fascinating scenes from everyday life: children dan-

cing and playing with a ball, craftsmen, and Egyptian soldiers wrestling each other in combat training. The subject matter of the paintings is an indication of the confident and relaxed mood of the society at that time.

12 Ashmunein/Hermopolis The ruins of Ashmunein lie on the west bank of the Nile, 8 km (5 miles) north of Mallawî. The god of wisdom, Thot, was worshipped here. He is depicted in the form of two giant statues of baboons, one of his sacred animals. In Christian times, a basilica was built on top of the remains of the Ptolemaic temple.

13 Tuna el-Gebel Ashumein's burial ground lies on the edge of the Western Desert. It is unusual for its catacombs (underground tombs) containing animals sacred to the god

1 An atmospheric scene in front of the Pyramids at Giza.

2 The step pyramids of the Pharaoh Djoser in Sakkara.

3 Water wheels are only rarely seen on the Nile nowadays.

Thot, such as ibis and baboons, though a variety of other species, from crocodiles to fish, have also been found. The temple's priests were also laid to rest here. The tomb of the high priest Petosiris, from the early Ptolemaic period, contains a mix of ancient Greek and Egyptian decoration.

The route then continues through Mallawî to the south and leads back to the Nile on a narrow road via the village of Deir Mawas. The boat crosses back over the river, from where you can take an all-terrain vehicle to visit local attractions.

14 Tell el-Amârna Pharoah Akhenaten founded his new city, Achetaten, here in 1350 BC. He attempted to change religious practice in Egypt by introducing the worship of only one god, Aten. He built temples to Aten here, as well as palaces and residences, but the town was abandoned after his death. Despite the fact that later pharaohs attempted to destroy much of Akhenaten's legacy, dismantling his temples and removing his name, excavations in the early 20th century still uncovered a number of unique artifacts from the period. The famous bust of Akhenaten's wife Nefertiti (today in the Egyptian Museum in Berlin) was discovered in 1912.

15 Assiût After around 75 km (47 miles), passing through a number of villages and small towns on the banks of the Nile, the route reaches the next provincial town of Assiût. Here, the long desert road to the

oases of Kharga and Dakhla branches off into the sands. At the end of the 19th century, a dam was built here to control the level of the Nile. Cross the river to the quieter east bank for the onward journey.

16 Sohâg/Akhmîm The sister towns of Sohâg and Akhmîm, 120 km (75 miles) south of Assiût, are connected by a strange bridge over the Nile. On the west bank outside Sohâg, ruins of the fourth-century Deir el-Abjad ("white monastery") remain as evidence of Egypt's early Christian history. Many of the blocks used in the buildings date back to the age of the pharaohs. In its heyday, the monastery had up to four thousand resident monks under the abbot Schenute (348–466). He is the father of Coptic literature and was a fierce opponent of ancient Egyptian cults and traditions.

The route continues on the west bank along the main road. After a good 50 km (31 miles), a sign in the town of Balyana indicates the turn-off to Abydos.

17 Abydos One of Upper Egypt's most important ancient sites, the sacred city of Abydos is also a burial place of kings and princes. Its tombs, mortuary temples, and gravestones all testify to the ancient Egyptians' belief in life after death. It was also a center for worship of the god Osiris and became a place of pilgrimage. As ruler of the afterlife, Osiris also symbolized hope of resurrection. The funeral temple of Sethos I

(1290–1279 BC), with its detailed carved reliefs, is particularly impressive.

Continue for another 35 km (22 miles) past the town of Nag Hammâdi, and the main road returns to the east bank of the river. The route along the west bank leads through numerous villages and fields. It then follows the Nile as it curves to the east and reaches the turn-off for the temple of Hathor in Dendera after 60 km (37 miles).

18 Dendera (Dandarah) In a rather isolated location on the edge of the desert, south of the town of Dendera, lies the Dendera Temple Complex enclosed by mud brick walls and

containing the Temple of Hathor. The Egyptian goddess of love and fertility, she was a popular deity and pilgrims flocked to her temple. The maternal aspect of the goddess is represented by her sacred animal, the cow, and for this reason Hathor was often depicted with a cow's head or with cow's horns. The most interesting detail from the Ptolemaic-Roman temple is the Dendera Zodiac, a circular relief depicting what could be an astrological chart. The relief displayed in the temple is a copy as the original is now in the Louvre in Paris.

From Dendera, the route crosses to the east bank and Qena, a provincial capital and

prosperous town on the road to Luxor, around 60 km (37 miles) away, where the Nile cruise will begin.

19 Luxor One of the main destinations for visitors to Egypt is Luxor, served by road, rail, and an international airport. Tourism is vital to the local economy here and accommodation is available at all price levels. Luxor (ancient Thebes) is a popular base from which to visit the surrounding area, but also boasts Luxor Temple itself and the impressive temple complex of Karnak, situated just outside the town. Built during the reigns of Amenophis III (1390–1353 BC) and Ramses II

(1279–1213 BC), Karnak's reliefs are brought to life in the light of the evening sun. An avenue of sphinxes guards the way to the massive pylon (monumental gateway, 24 m/79 ft) built by Ramses II, decorated with scenes from his battles. There follows a series of shrines, statues, courtyards, columns, chambers, and a sacred lake. The roof of the Great Hypostyle Hall has now collapsed but it was supported by 134 enormous columns 24 m (80 ft) high that are still standing today. The whole complex was built over a period of almost two thousand years. Numerous artifacts are displayed in the Luxor Museum, including large blocks from a

temple to Aten dating back to the rule of the heretic pharaoh Akhenaten. The museum also houses statues from the reigns of Amenophis III and Haremhab, discovered in Luxor as recently as 1989. The small mummification museum, which is located underground next to the river on the east bank, exhibits mummies and embalming tools, and explains the mummification process.

⑳ Western Thebes Across from Luxor, on the opposite (western) bank of the river lies the world famous Valley of the Kings, where the pharaohs of the New Kingdom (1540–1075 BC) were buried. The area shot to fame in

1922 when Howard Carter discovered the unplundered grave of the young King Tutankhamen. Today the treasures of his tomb are displayed in the National Museum in Cairo. Several of the tombs, including Tutankhamen's, can be entered and the beautiful wall paintings depicting the pharaohs' journey to the afterlife seen at first hand. The Valley of the Kings contains over 60 known tombs, including those of Thutmosis I and Rameses II and III, with more still to be discovered. The nearby Valley of the Queens contains the tombs of the wives of the pharaohs, including Nefertari, wife of Ramses II, which has been restored, and

many princes and princesses. One of the most impressive buildings is the mortuary temple of the female pharaoh Queen Hatshepsut (1479–1458). Consisting of three long terraces on successive levels, connected by ramps, the temple is carved into the cliff at Deir el-Bahari. The Valley of the Workers at Deir el-Medina is also worth seeing. It is the site of the village where the builders and craftsmen who worked on the tombs of the pharaohs lived with their families. The workers also built their own tombs here and decorated them with wall paintings depicting scenes from everyday life. The pictures are charming, showing the workers enjoying festivals with their family and friends, as well as showing the different stages in their careers.

㉑ Esna (Isna) Around 60 km (37 miles) south of Luxor, you reach one of the few locks in the Nile near Esna. It is closed twice a year for maintenance. From where the ships dock, a busy bazaar can be reached in no time. The remains of a Roman temple for the creator god Chnum can be found well below street level. Only the entrance hall and its columns are visible nowadays; all other parts of the temple have been built over in modern times.

㉒ El Kab Some 35 km (22 miles) farther to the south is El Kab, on the west bank of the Nile, where the stone tombs in the east face of the mountains are worth a visit. El Kab gained importance early on as a sacred

place for the Upper Egyptian goddess Nechbet. Two tombs are of particular interest: Ahmose Sa Ibana was fleet commandant under Pharaoh Ahmose (1539–1514 BC) and helped drive out the occupying Hyksos, as inscribed on the tombs. As teacher to the princes, Ahmose's grandson Paheri received the highest accolade under Pharaoh Thutmosis III, being depicted together with the king's son in his tomb. The Wadi Hilal is located to the south, its entry marked with small temple buildings.

㉓ Edfu On the edge of the lively town of Edfu, 30 km (19 miles) farther south on the west bank of the Nile, is one of the best preserved sacred sites in Egypt, the Ptolemaic Temple of Horus, and an ancient settlement. Depicted as a hawk, Horus was a multi-tasking god, he
(continued p.130)

❶ Restoration work has given the terrace temple of Hatshepsut a new lease of life.

❷ The monumental figures of Amenophis III, located on the western bank of the Nile opposite Luxor are known as the Colossi of Memnon.

❸ In the second court of the mortuary temple of Ramses III in Medînet Habu, a few miles from the Valley of the Kings, reliefs depict a procession for Min, the god of fertility.

❹ Some parts of Ramses III's temple have maintained their original vivid decoration.

Today, there is only one obelisk outside the pylon of the Amun temple in Luxor. Its twin was given as a gift to Paris by the Francophile Muhammad Ali in 1836,

Top: The Amun temple in Luxor bathed in twilight. The sphinx-lined avenue leads up to the colossal pylon, which is now guarded by just one of the two original obelisks. Bottom: At the back of the temple, mighty papyrus capital columns are still standing from the time of Amenophis III.

protected the kingdom and was god of war and the law, among other things. He was worshipped widely throughout Egypt. The son of Osiris, murdered by Set, Horus was tasked with avenging his father's death, which led to his becoming patron of law and justice. Paintings in the temple at Edfu show the annual battle between Horus and his father's murderer. The inscriptions on the walls of the temple proved very useful for understanding more about ancient Egyptian culture, since they show detail of the rituals for celebrations and contain instructions for priests.

24 Gebel el-Silsila Close to the banks of the Nile, around 40 km (25 miles) south of Edfu, shrines are cut into the sandstone at Gebel el-Silsila. Sandstone was quarried from the banks on both sides of the river here for building work during the time of the pharaohs. Farther south, the valley opens into a fertile landscape with a backdrop of mountains in the distance. The main crop farmed near this part of the river is sugar cane, which

is also refined locally. This region became the new home of many Nubians, displaced by the building of the Aswan Dam.

25 Kôm Ombo The picturesque remains of the unusual double temple lie here on the banks of the Nile at Kôm Ombo, built in the Ptolemaic-Roman period. One side is dedicated to the falcon-headed Aroeres, worshipped during Greek and Roman times, and the other to the crocodile-headed god Sobek, god of fertility and creator of the world. The depiction of the Roman emperor Trajan with medical equipment is one of the unusual details of this site. Various other crocodile artifacts (mummies and sarcophagi) from nearby sites can also be seen here.

26 Aswan Situated at the first cataract of the Nile, Aswan is another busy tourist center. It is one of the driest inhabited places in the world, receiving very little rainfall. Some of the rooms in the houses in the nearby Nubian villages do not even have roofs. This is where

the larger boats on the Nile are forced to stop as the river becomes shallow, its surface frequently broken by rocks on the river bed interspersed with small rapids. However, a trip in a traditional *felucca* (sailing boat) is a must, and is particularly peaceful and atmospheric at dusk. A short way downstream from the first cataract in the center of the river is Elephantine Island, at the border between Egypt and Nubia. On its southern tip, you can see the excavations of the ancient Egyptian settlement Aby ("ivory") where archeologists discovered the oldest shrine in Egypt, dedicated to the goddess Satet, which developed into an impressive temple over the course of centuries. Toward the end of the Old Kingdom the rulers of the border town were buried in the mountainside on the west bank. Steep paths lead up to the tombs. The ruins of the monastery of St Simeon are located on the west bank, which was home to a large number of monks between the 7th and 13th centuries. On a nearby hill, a mausoleum to

Aga Khan III (1877–1957) was built in the style of a Fatimid mosque.

To the south of the town, two vast dams control the flow of the Nile, which would otherwise flood each year. The older

Aswan Low Dam was built between 1898 and 1902, while the new Aswan High Dam was built between 1960 and 1971, creating the 500-km (311-mile) long Lake Nasser. The new dam had considerable economic,

too was destined to be flooded with the construction of the new High Dam and so a nearby, but higher island called Agilkai was modified to take the temple, which was dismantled and reassembled in its new home. The island and temple are only accessible by boat, but it is well worth the trip to see the temple in its new peaceful and romantic location.

28 Kalabsha The port serving ships on Lake Nasser is to the south-east of the dam. From there, you can take a boat to the west bank to see another temple complex, this time comprising four temples that had to be rescued from the rising waters of the Nile. While excavating the Kalabsha Temple, archeologists found blocks of stone from walls that belonged to an even older temple; these blocks are now housed in the Egyptian museum in Berlin and are known as the Kalabsha Door. This temple, from the Roman period, was built for the god Mandulis, a Nubian variant of the Egyptian falcon-headed god Horus. On its south side,

there are stone carvings from prehistoric times depicting giraffes and elephants, proving that the climate here was much more humid around 5000 BC. The columns and statues from the temple of Gerf Hussein, built during the reign of Pharaoh Ramses II, create a weighty impression. The reliefs in the stone temple of Beit el-Wali, built around the same time, are much more detailed, and were relocated to a site 100 m (109 yds) west of the Kalabsha Temple. The graceful Kiosk in the quarry area of Kertassi was dedicated to Isis and offered the workers holy protection.

1 A peaceful scene near Aswan where the river is no longer navigable to large boats, but is full of rocks and pools, and bird life thrives.

2 The columns of the temple to Horus in Edfu have huge dimensions.

3 The temple dedicated to Isis at Philae was rebuilt on an adjacent island to protect it from flooding.

social, political consequences. Britain and the USA were originally intended to help finance the project, but then cancelled their aid. In response Egypt's President Nasser nationalized the Suez Canal resulting in the

Suez Crisis. In 1958, the Soviet Union stepped in and construction was able to begin. Many artifacts and ancient sites and over 90,000 Nubian people had to be moved to new areas in Egypt and the Sudan when Lake

Nasser was created. The Nubian Museum that opened in 1997 in Aswan tells their story.

27 Philae Philae Temple, dedicated to the goddess Isis is no longer on its original island. It

Lake Nasser

Lake Nasser is ten times bigger than Lake Constance. Two-thirds of the lake's 5,000 sq km (1,930 sq miles) belong to Egypt, a third to Sudan. As a reservoir for controlling the Nile flood, the lake has great importance for Egypt and its economy. It has helped to improve agriculture in the region and

The rock temple of Ramses II, Abu Simbel.

generates power for Upper Egypt. Its hydroelectric power plant can produce up to 10 billion kWh a year. But the project also has negative aspects, including the accumulation upstream behind the dam of the silt that used to flow down to enrich the Nile Delta, the erosion of the Delta and adjacent area by the Mediterranean, and the increased use of chemical fertilizers.

A boat trip on Lake Nasser brings with it a sense of time-lessness and tranquility. Rich in fish, the lake has a growing crocodile population, though they normally shy away from passing boats. The wardens warn of huge crocs, while at the same time presenting baby crocodiles for tourist photos.

29 New-Sebua Wadi es-Sebua meaning "Valley of the Lions" was given its name thanks to the sphinxes that once lined the avenue leading to the first of the two temples here. The largest structures are the pylons. Ramses II is depicted in confident poses on the temple walls and also inside sitting next to the gods.
The temple of ed-Dakke is dedicated to Thot, the god of wisdom. Thot journeyed to the Nubian region as a messenger of the gods, in order to bring Tefnut, the daughter of Re the sun god, to Egypt. One of the scenes, showing an ape dancing in front of a lion, relates to this legend. The chapel of el-Maharraka is small and was never completed. In Roman times, it marked the border between the Roman Empire and the Meroitic Empire, whose

capital was excavated to the north of Khartoum.

30 New Amada Egypt extended its territory further south during the reign of Thutmosis III (1479–1426 BC). The Egyptians built a temple dedicated to Amun-Re and Re-Harachte here as a symbol of the power of their gods. In the 20th century, the temple had to be dragged on runners onto higher ground.
The adjacent temple of ed-Derr, built by Ramses II, is largely carved into the rock. The hypostyle hall is particularly beautiful. The third monument in New Amada is the small stone tomb of Pennut, who enjoyed prominent social standing as an administrator in the conquered province.

31 Qasr Ibrim Only the tip of this once mighty cliff-top fortress can still be seen poking above the waters of the Nile today. There was once a basilica here that served as the bishop's residence for the Nubian Christian kingdom. Before that, both the Romans and the Pharaohs built castles here to secure the southern borders of their empires.

32 Abu Simbel The monumental temples at Abu Simbel hit the headlines in the 1960s when they too had to be moved to avoid the Nile. The whole temple complex was cut out of the rock and dismantled block by block at great expense and taken to a location 64 m (210 ft) higher, well above the water level. Four colossal statues of

Pharaoh Ramses II guard the façade of the larger temple. The interior features images of historic battles and scenes of ritual carved in relief on the walls. The smaller temple is dedicated to the god Hathor and his wife Nefertari. The statues of Ramses II wear the double crown (symbolizing his rule of upper and lower Egypt), and the characteristic Nemes head cloth. On his forehead, the royal Uraeus, protects him against all evil.

1 The temple of Wadi es-Sebua is one of many buildings commissioned by Ramses II in the Nubian region.

2 The southernmost destination for most visitors to Egypt is the famous rock temple of Ramses II in Abu Simbel.

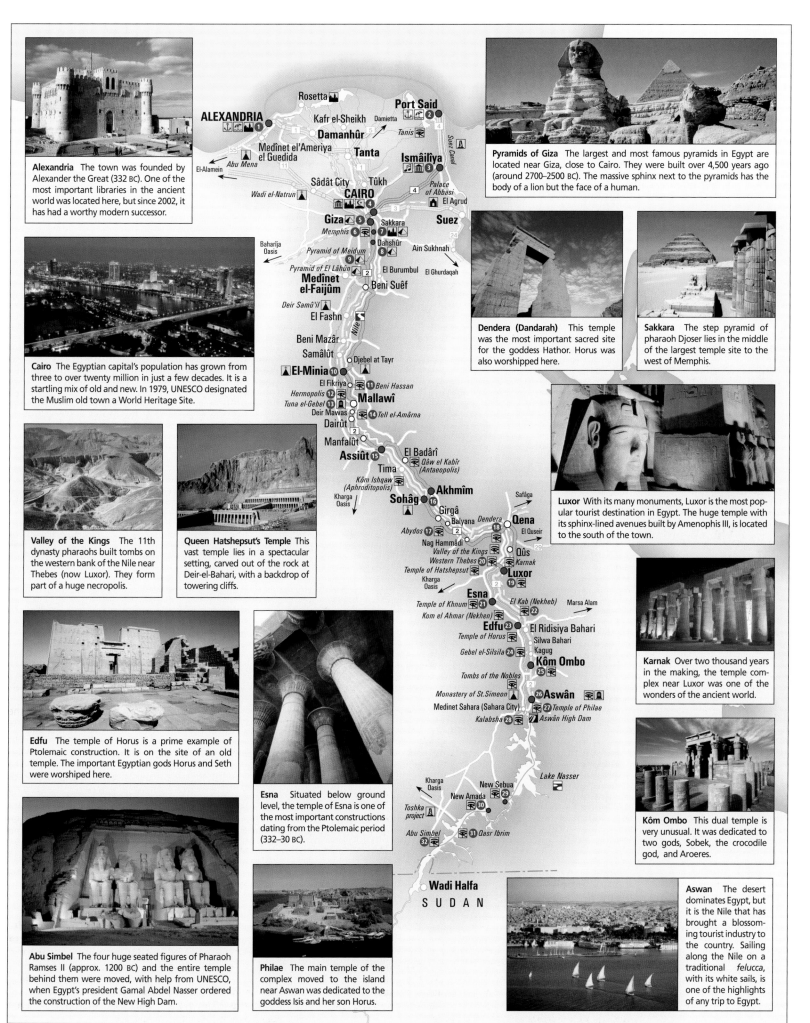

Alexandria The town was founded by Alexander the Great (332 BC). One of the most important libraries in the ancient world was located here, but since 2002, it has had a worthy modern successor.

Pyramids of Giza The largest and most famous pyramids in Egypt are located near Giza, close to Cairo. They were built over 4,500 years ago (around 2700–2500 BC). The massive sphinx next to the pyramids has the body of a lion but the face of a human.

Cairo The Egyptian capital's population has grown from three to over twenty million in just a few decades. It is a startling mix of old and new. In 1979, UNESCO designated the Muslim old town a World Heritage Site.

Dendera (Dandarah) This temple was the most important sacred site for the goddess Hathor. Horus was also worshipped here.

Sakkara The step pyramid of pharaoh Djoser lies in the middle of the largest temple site to the west of Memphis.

Valley of the Kings The 11th dynasty pharaohs built tombs on the western bank of the Nile near Thebes (now Luxor). They form part of a huge necropolis.

Queen Hatshepsut's Temple This vast temple lies in a spectacular setting, carved out of the rock at Deir-el-Bahari, with a backdrop of towering cliffs.

Luxor With its many monuments, Luxor is the most popular tourist destination in Egypt. The huge temple with its sphinx-lined avenues built by Amenophis III, is located to the south of the town.

Edfu The temple of Horus is a prime example of Ptolemaic construction. It is on the site of an old temple. The important Egyptian gods Horus and Seth were worshiped here.

Esna Situated below ground level, the temple of Esna is one of the most important constructions dating from the Ptolemaic period (332–30 BC).

Karnak Over two thousand years in the making, the temple complex near Luxor was one of the wonders of the ancient world.

Kôm Ombo This dual temple is very unusual. It was dedicated to two gods, Sobek, the crocodile god, and Aroeres.

Abu Simbel The four huge seated figures of Pharaoh Ramses II (approx. 1200 BC) and the entire temple behind them were moved, with help from UNESCO, when Egypt's president Gamal Abdel Nasser ordered the construction of the New High Dam.

Philae The main temple of the complex moved to the island near Aswan was dedicated to the goddess Isis and her son Horus.

Aswan The desert dominates Egypt, but it is the Nile that has brought a blossoming tourist industry to the country. Sailing along the Nile on a traditional *felucca*, with its white sails, is one of the highlights of any trip to Egypt.

The surf on the beaches of the Canaries can often be quite strong, as shown here near Playa Blanca in the south of Lanzarote.

Spain

The Canaries: the mountains of the moon

Despite their location off the coast of Africa, the group of islands known as the Canary Islands belong to Spain. The Spanish influence is evident in their architecture, culture, and way of life. However, their geographical proximity to the African mainland has also had an influence on the islands' flora and fauna. There are many exotic plants and impressive natural phenomena point to the islands' volcanic origins.

The Canary Islands are an autonomous province of Spain. The archipelago includes the seven main islands Lanzarote, Fuerteventura, Gran Canaria, Tenerife, La Gomera, El Hierro, and La Palma and several smaller secondary islands. The route winds its way between the islands by ferry and continues by (rented) car to explore each of the islands. Over millions of years, volcanic activity has created bizarre landscapes formed of vol-

Bird-of-paradise flowers.

canoes and calderas (large volcanic craters formed by collapsed volcanoes). Parts of the islands' coastlines are lined with beaches, many of which have black sand, while others have more typical white or golden sand. The striking landscape and the mild climate that prevails almost all year round have ensured that the islands are a popular holiday destination.

Each island has its own special character that makes it unique. Lanzarote has magical volcanic scenery and several beautiful beaches. Gran Canaria has the largest of the island's cities in Las Palmas de Gran Canaria, and so attracts visitors who revel in the nightlife along with nature lovers. On the largest of the islands, Tenerife, the town of Santa Cruz de Tenerife draws the crowds with its cultural history, and the Pico de Teide, Spain's the highest mountain. La Gomera has an impressive selec-

tion of plants and offers great walks for ramblers. El Hierro is the smallest and most remote island in the Canaries and has a natural peaceful charm. La Palma is the greenest of the islands, with a fascinating volcanic landscape.

The archipelago has always been a focal point for Europeans because of the strategic importance it acquired following the discovery of America by Christopher Columbus. From 1600 onward, almost every ship heading into the Atlantic stopped at the Canaries in order to stock up on supplies. Though a great deal of the islands' trading was legal, much of it was illegal too, and the Canaries were an ideal hideout for smugglers and pirates. The islands were colonized by Spain during the expansion of the Spanish Empire, beginning with the 1402 expedition to Lanzarote led by

The Pico de Teide above the Lake of Clouds on Tenerife. The mighty peak with its huge craters is the highest mountain in Spain.

Las Palmas de Gran Canaria: the Santa Ana Cathedral in the Plaza Santa Ana, lined by palm trees.

Jean de Béthencourt. Eventually, the Guanches, the island's original inhabitants, almost completely died out. The islands' current inhabitants are Spanish citizens, though, being far from Madrid and the seat of the Spanish central government, they are sometimes critical of Spain.

Famous for their very diverse vegetation, some parts of the Canary Islands are covered in dense rainforest with a rich variety of flora, while other parts have a volcanic landscape, but this too contains its own plant life, though sparse. Some of the more interesting types of vegetation include a species of dragon tree with its stout trunk and broad canopy, which can grow up to 20 m (66 feet) in height and apart from the Canaries, only grows in the Azores and Madeira; and forests of laurel trees, though these have become smaller in size over the past hundred years or so. Cacti and succulents such as *Aeonium* and the candelabra tree with its toxic sap grow in the driest parts. Some areas are protected within national parks and reserves.

After tourism, agriculture forms the most important source of income for the people of the Canaries. The volcanic soil is very fertile and the land is irrigated extensively due to the low level of annual rainfall. Some of the steep slopes have been terraced in order to provide level areas on which to farm. Fruit (including bananas, citrus fruits, and wine grapes) and vegetables (mainly tomatoes) are cultivated on plantations, some of which are very large. Fishing also plays an important economic role. Many of the local crafts are still traditional and you can learn more about them in the islands' museums.

The Canaries are ideal for sailing thanks to the lively trade winds.

La Geria: wine from a volcano

La Geria, the largest winegrowing region in the Canary Islands, covers the middle of Lanzarote between the towns of Uga and San Bartolomé. The Lanzaroteños have managed to transform the black lava landscape into cultivated vineyards, but it has taken a great deal of hard work. They are planted in individual craters to protect them from the strong winds and are also shielded by low semi-circular stone walls called *zocos*. A thick layer of porous lava granules (*lapilli*) is laid

Top and bottom: In the winegrowing district of La Geria, the grapevines thrive despite the low rainfall.

on the ground as a mulch, reducing the evaporation of water from the soil. The lava also cools quickly at night, producing moisture caused by rapid condensation that sinks into the soil to be absorbed by the vines' roots. From a distance, the vineyards look like miles of tiny green oases in the middle of a black desert. A well-used road crosses the region from La Geria, where several *bodegas* are open for wine-tasting along the way.

The route through the Canary Islands begins in the north-east on Lanzarote and travels through Fuerteventura, Gran Canaria, Tenerife, La Gomera, and El Hierro to La Palma in the north-west. Each of these seven main Canary Islands is a worthwhile travel destination in its own right. There is evidence of the archipelago's volcanic past on all the islands. The scenery varies from sandy beaches to thick forests, and mountainous regions bordered by fertile lowlands. There are obvious similarities between the islands, yet each has its own individual character too.

❶ Arrecife The capital city of Lanzarote is a transport hub with an airport and ferry terminal, that has developed considerably over the past few years. The Avenida La Marina, lined with beautiful gardens, runs through the heart of Arrecife where there is a busy market popular with tourists. Among the sights worth seeing are the

Travel information

Route profile
Length: approx. 1,100 km (684 miles) (including travel connections/flights between the individual islands)
Duration: at least 3 weeks
Start: Arrecife (Lanzarote)
End: Fuencaliente (La Palma)
Itinerary (main locations): Lanzarote, Fuerteventura, Gran Canaria, Tenerife, La Gomera, El Hierro, La Palma

Travel tips
Several sections of the route (e.g. to the Playas del Papagayo on Lanzarote or up to

the Cañadas del Teide on Tenerife) involve traveling along unpaved roads. The order of the route may be changed according to the available ferry connections. Heavy rainfall may cause rockslides on mountain roads. People who want to do water sports should take extra care due to the strong surf and currents.

Tourist information
More information about the Canary Islands is available from:

Tourist Information of Spain
Kurfürstendamm 63
10707 Berlin
Tel. (030) 882 65 43
berlin@tourspain. es

Spanish Tourism Board
Calle Jorge Juan, 35
28001 Madrid
Tel. (34) 914261516
www.spain.info

Canary Islands Tourist Office
Plaze de España
1 – 38002 Santa Cruz de Tenerife
Tel. (34) 922239811
www.spain.info

3

4

Iglesia de San Ginés, the Castillo de San José, and the Castillo de San Gabriel.

2 Cueva de los Verdes and Jameos del Agua To the north of Lanzarote lie some strange caves, which are part of a 7-km (4-mile) long tunnel through the volcanic rock, created over 3,500 years ago. Some 1,000 m (3,281 ft) of the Cueva de los Verdes is accessible to visitors. Accompanied by the echoing sound of music, a guided tour takes you through various lava formations. The two caves known as the Jameos del Agua are volcanic caves with collapsed roofs. The local artist César Manrique has helped to create a unique world here, skillfully combining nature

and clever lighting to turn the caves into an nightclub with swimming pool, gardens, and a bar and restaurant.

3 Timanfaya National Park/La Geria Driving onward through the middle of Lanzarote to the west, you will pass Haria and Teguise before entering the volcanic landscape known as the Montañas del Fuego (Fire Mountains) of Timanfaya. Established in 1954, the national park contains a variety of volcanic phenomena including deep black lava fields, craters, and startling volcanic cones. This fascinating moonscape was formed by volcanic eruptions that took place between 1730 and 1736. It is not

possible to wander freely around the park, but a coach trip is included in the entry fee. You will see just how hot it is just below the surface when your guide throws dry leaves or water into a hole in the ground as the leaves either catch fire immediately or the water shoots back out in the form of steam. Adjacent to the park sprawls the wine growing district La Geria (see panel, opposite).

4 Playas del Papagayo The tourist resort of Playa Blanca lies on the southern tip of Lanzarote, famous for its beach promenade lined with bars, *bodegas*, and restaurants. From here, you can take the car over some bumpy terrain to the Pla-

yas del Papagayo, a series of beautiful sandy bays surrounded by rocky cliffs and one of the most popular destinations on the island for swimmers. From the port of Playa Blanca, ferries make trips to Corralejo on the island Fuerteventura.

5 Corralejo In just a few years, this former fishing village at the northernmost point of Fuerteventuras has developed into one of the most important tourist centers of the islands. It now contains hotels and souvenir shops and many visitors also come here to enjoy the sandy beaches. There are long stretches of dunes, including the famous dunes of El Jable where it is like stepping into the Sahara, and the blue Atlantic creates an impressive backdrop. The next stop on the journey is to the west, past La Oliva.

6 El Cotillo In comparison to Corralejo, El Cotillo is something of a well-kept secret. The Playas de Cotillo is a surfing hotspot. The most remarkable building here is Castillo de Tostón, a tower made out of volcanic rock. It was built in the 18th century to defend the port, which was repeatedly attacked by pirates. Return to the main road heading south and shortly after Lllanos de la Concepción, you reach Betancuria.

7 Betancuria Situated in a picturesque valley in the interior of the island, this town is named after the French explorer Jean de Béthencourt who led an expedition to the Canaries in 1402. As the oldest settlement and former capital city of Fuerteventura, it has a fascinating history. Its many interesting buildings include the Iglesia Nuestra Señora de la Concepción, which once served as a place of refuge during pirate attacks, and the Convento de San Buenaventura. From Betancuria the road leads to the south, past the Punta de Guadelupe to the peninsula Jandía, to the south of which is Morro Jable.

8 Morro Jable A major tourist destination built around a headland at the southern tip of

1 The Montañas del Fuego (Fire Mountain) volcano in the Timanfaya National Park on Lanzarote.

2 A sailing ship off the coast near the Playa del Papagayo on Lanzarote.

3 An atmospheric evening on the beach at Morro Jable on Fuerteventura.

4 The port of El Cotillo with the Castillo de Tostón, Fuerteventura.

Fuerteventura, Morro Jable is especially popular with German visitors. A lively mix of old and new, it is known for its architecture and water sports. The long promenade by the old fishing port, lined with bars and restaurants, is a lively meeting-point for tourists and locals. Fishing boats land their catch in the early afternoon at the port, where you can also hire boats for pleasure trips, or take the ferry over to Gran Canaria.

9 Las Palmas de Gran Canaria The island's capital city is flanked by two magnificent beaches, the Playa de las Alcaravaneras in the south-east and the Playa de las Canteras to the north-east. Las Palmas is a bustling place with plenty of Spanish flair. Founded in 1478, the town developed from a small anchorage for fishing boats into a thriving economic center following the construction of the port. The largest and certainly the liveliest town in the Canary Islands has a number of buildings that document its evolution from a small trading center to one of the most important Spanish seaports. A variety of different architectural styles are on show in its

buildings built between the 15th and 19th centuries. A visit to the Museo Canario will give you a good overview of the history of the island, and includes many artefacts from pre-Hispanic times. The cityscape of Las Palmas is characterized by sweeping squares and broad streets. The Plaza Santa Ana in the old town district is surrounded by attractive villas, which are splendidly decorated with flowers on festive occasions. Just a few miles south-west of Las Palmas is the Jardín Botánico, one of Spain's most impressive botanical gardens. One of the garden's prize exhibits is its comprehensive cactus collection.

10 Arucas Situated slightly farther inland, to the west of Las Palmas, this town is where Canary rum was first made. The native laurel plants that grew here were cut down in the 16th century to make room for sugar cane plantations and distilleries provided jobs for many locals in the surrounding area. Later on, banana production also became important, bringing more prosperity to Arucas. The plantations close to the town's suburbs still exist. You can take a tour round a rum factory (Fábrica y Museo del Ron) with sample included! Grand residences several stories high, with a maze of steep alleyways in

between, dominate the old town. The most striking architecture can be seen at the Iglesia de San Juan Bautista, which is built from black basalt. Its church tower (60 m/197 ft) is the highest on the Canary Islands. From a distance it looks like a Gothic masterpiece that is out of proportion with the rest of the town. The neo-Gothic church, built 1909–1977, has impressive rose windows.
Returning to the coastal highway, the route heads to the north along a road that widens to four lanes in places. At Santa María de Guía you reach Cenobio de Valerón, a network of galleries of small caves, many of which were used by the Guanches as granaries.

11 Puerto de las Nieves At the small town of Agaete, famous for its many art galleries, a road heads off along the coast to Puerto de las Nieves, Agaete's port. Fishing was once the most important source of income for the community here, but tourism has now arrived and makes an important economic contribution, particularly since the ferry connection to Santa Cruz de Tenerife was established. The Paseo de los Poetas, the promenade along the shoreline, is lined with fish restaurants and bars. A popular photo

opportunity is the Dedo de Dios (Finger of God), a rocky structure that rises up out of the ocean like a threatening and accusing finger. Hurricanes have repeatedly caused damage to the basalt rock here.

The Parque Natural Tamadaba, a nature reserve containing the most extensive pine forests in Gran Canaria, lies to the north of Puerto de las Nieves.

The journey continues along the coast, following its many twists and turns, some very tight in places. Several lookout points serve as ideal places in which to take a break along the way. The town of San Nicolás de Tolentino, lies between groves of bamboo and tomato plantations in the region's agricultural district. The road now heads past Mogán and the modern holiday resort of Puerto Rico toward the southernmost point of the island.

⑫ Maspalomas This fairly upmarket resort on the southern coast is well known for the extensive, undulating sand dunes nearby, which cover some 400 ha (1,708 acres) and reach 1,500 m (4,922 feet) inland. Designated a protected natural area, the dunes shelter some rare animal and plant species, and are also popular with naturalists. There are several golf courses nearby. The dunes separate the peaceful Playa de Maspalomas, from the much busier the Playa del Inglés to the east and the large and hectic tourist resort of the same name. Enjoying plenty of sunshine (most of the rain falls to the north of the island) and excellent conditions for water sports such as windsurfing, it is a magnet for the young and active.

⑬ Cumbre From the south, the route leads into the mountainous interior of the island. In the Barranco de Fataga, one of several deep canyons in the region, you will discover picturesque villages such as Fataga and San Bartolomé de Tirajana. The fruit trees are gradually being taken over by pine trees and holm oaks. Make your way along the serpentine roads to the striking Roque Nublo (1,803 m /5,916 ft), with an 80-m (262-ft) finger of rock protruding from its tip. You can enjoy the wonderful view over Gran Canaria from a viewing platform.

A narrow road leads farther east to Pico de las Nieves. The peak of this mountain (1,949 m/6,395 ft) is often covered in clouds, but on clear days you can see Tenerife. To the north-west of the central mountain is Tejeda, one of the most beautiful towns on the island, a cluster of whitewashed houses with green shutters and wooden balconies set in a fertile valley.

⑭ Teror After the Cruz de Tejeda, a huge stone cross set in the side of the mountain pass at 1,600 m (5,250 ft), you reach Teror, a town with both historic and religious importance. The Basílica de Nuestra Señora del Pino (18th C.), a well-known pilgrimage destination, contains a statue of the Virgin Mary and opulently gilded baroque altars. A large market is held beside the church every Sunday morning,

1 Twilight descends over the dunes of Maspalomas on Gran Canaria.

2 Misty clouds obscure the Pico de las Nieves in Santa Lucia, the highest mountain on Gran Canaria.

3 Restaurants at the Placa Cairasco in the old town of Las Palmas.

4 The Tamadaba Nature Park on the west coast of Gran Canaria.

5 Puerto de las Nieves on Gran Canaria.

6 Iglesia de San Juan Bautista in Arucas on Gran Canaria.

La Laguna

Splendid churches and residential buildings with wooden balconies characterize the former capital city of Tenerife. The university town La Laguna, its full name is San Cristobal de la

The inner courtyard of a house in La Laguna.

Lagun, was designated a World Heritage Site by UNESCO in 1999. Particularly worth seeing are the Plaza de Adelantado with its convent and the Catedral de los Remedios.

where local traders sell food and crafts, and this otherwise peaceful town comes to life.

⑮ Santa Cruz de Tenerife The capital city of Tenerife is cosmopolitan yet quiet, and commercial yet charming. Container ships, luxury liners, yachts, and foot passenger ferries land at the port, which is an important transport hub for Europe, Africa, and America. From here it is not far to Plaza de España, the central town square. Prestigious buildings surround the plaza, which is the pulsing heart of Santa Cruz and a good place to watch the glitzy local carnival. Nearby is the Iglesia de Nuestra Señora de la Concepción, built in 1502, the most important church in the city with a six-story bell tower which can be seen from a distance. The Calle Castillo, with its exclusive stores, is an ideal place for a shopping trip. There are many cafés and bars at the Plaza de la Candelaria, providing a good place to take a break. But despite these more commercial distractions, the town also has several places of cultural interest, including the Museo de la Naturaleza y el Hombre, with exhibits explaining the nature

and ethnology of Tenerife, and the Museo de Bellas Artes with paintings by European artists. From Santa Cruz the journey continues in a westerly direction to the north coast.

⑯ La Laguna The former political and spiritual center of the island is very close to Santa Cruz (see panel, left).

⑰ La Orotava/Los Realejos The route now leads past vast banana plantations to Orotava, a picturesque little town by the Puerto de la Cruz, one of the most popular tourist spots in Tenerife thanks to its wide beaches. La Orotava has a beautiful historic town center with the Plaza de la Constitución and charming gardens, and look out

for the Casa de los Balcones, a magnificent 17th-century mansion. The town holds the most dazzling of the island's Corpus Christi festivals, during which the streets are decorated with carpets of flowers in beautiful patterns. The diversity of the vegetation on the island is represented, along with many other species, among the 3,000 or so

3

tropical and sub-tropical species grown in the botanical gardens. A few miles to the west lies the village of Los Realejos. The view from Mirador de la Corona above the village, across the Orotava valley to the coast, is stunning.

18 Cañadas del Teide Continuing through the Orotava valley

toward the north, you reach the Cañadas del Teide. You certainly won't be able to miss the huge volcanic cone of the Pico del Teide, which seems to be visible from just about everywhere. It is set in a strange-looking landscape that was formed over millions of years as a result of countless volcanic eruptions. The whole area has been protected since 1954 as the Las Cañadas del Teide National Park, and was designated a World Heritage Site by UNESCO in 2007. The park is approximately 2,000 m (6,562 ft) above sea level and looks like a moon landscape in parts, although the plant life is well-developed and diverse. A type of *Echium wildpretii* native to Tenerife grows here, up to 3 m (10 ft) tall with spires of red or blue flowers. Car parks have been built near some of the most spectacular rock formations. Los Roques is a group of needles or fingers of rock standing some 30 m (98 ft) high. A path leading from them takes you past lava formations of different shades, ranging from black to brown and blue-green.

19 Pico de Teide At 3,718 m (12,199 ft), this is the highest mountain not just in the Cana-

ries, but in the whole of the Spanish mainland. The base of the mountain has a diameter of around 17 km (11 miles). It is possible to climb it on foot, however making the trip by cable car is a lot easier. It takes you to approximately 200 m (656 ft) below the peak. Access to the summit is restricted, so if you want to climb to the top you have first to obtain a permit from the National Parks office in Santa Cruz. Having been inactive for many years, there is now just the smell of sulfur to remind you of its violent past. In winter, the peak is covered in snow.

20 Los Gigantes After crossing the Las Cañadas del Teide National Park in a westerly direction, turn north toward Santiago del Teide. One of the most striking sections of coast in Tenerife awaits you at Puerto de Santiago: the cliffs of Los Gigantes, which are over 500 m (1,640 ft) in height. They are a stunning sight from land or sea, but you will see them best from the water, and a boat trip is recommended to see their full extent; you will then understand why the people who lived here used to believe the cliffs marked the end of the world. On the other side of the

bay is the beach of Los Gigantes, which you can reach on foot.

21 Los Cristianos and Playa de las Américas The journey continues to the south of the island to take in two major tourist resorts. The island enjoys over three hundred days of sun a year so it is not surprising that many visitors head straight for the beach and the water. Excursions on glass-bottom boats are available from the port of Los Cristianos, which is also a good location for diving and fishing. You can catch a connecting ferry to La Gomera from here. The Playa de los Cristianos is right by the port and is pretty busy, but the Playa de las Américas is even livelier and offers a wide range of sports and nightlife. Surfers and windsurfers, however, tend to head for the beach at El Médano at the southern tip of

1 Tall cacti on the rocky coast of Los Gigantes on Tenerife.

2 A heavy storm on the volcanic coast near Los Realejos on Tenerife.

3 Volcanic landscape at the 3,718-m (12,199-ft) high Pico de Teide.

The carnival in Santa Cruz

Each year in February, carnival is celebrated in spectacular fashion in the main city of Tenerife. It is one of the most impressive in Spain. Rio comes to Santa Cruz! Imaginative costumes and

A carnival dancer.

booming rhythms create a vibrant and exciting atmosphere, and performances by Musgas singing groups add to the all-night partying.

Tenerife, where conditions for catching a wave are ideal. From here the costal road leads back to Santa Cruz de Tenerife.

22 San Sebastián de la Gomera This small town's charm is evident as soon as you reach the port of La Gomera. Yachts and fishing boats anchored here bob up and down on the waves and look like bright specks of paint from a distance. For many visitors, San Sebastián is no more than a place to pass through, but it does have sights to see, such as the Torre del Conde, a 16-m (52-ft) fortress tower (15th C.) that once acted as a temporary storehouse for shipping freight. From here you head along the Carretera del Norte to the northern coast, passing through Hermigua along the way. Its landmark, the twin peaks Roques de San Pedro, can be seen from a distance.

23 Agulo The north of La Gomera is dominated by thick vegetation, dotted with pretty towns. A typical example is Agulo on the northern coast, a small village with a labyrinth of alleyways and elegant houses that are typical of traditional

Gomeran architecture. The parish church San Marcos, with its statue of Christ made by sculptor Pérez Donis, attracts many visitors. Banana fields stretch down to the sea. If you are here at Easter, watch out for the traditional local spectacle of young men jumping through hoops of fire as part of a huge festival.

24 Garajonay National Park A good starting point to your visit is the Juego de Bolas Visitors Centre in the north near Las Rosas. Situated in the center of the island, and covering an area of around 4,000 ha (9,885 acres), the area has been a national

park since 1981, and a World Heritage Site since 1986. It has some of the most beautiful laurel tree forests in the Canary Islands. The trade winds from the north bring the humidity needed to keep the vegetation healthy and there is an almost permanent mist over the peaks. Walking trails are marked, branching out from Laguna Grande (where there are car parks), and maps are available. You can also climb The Alto de Garajonay, the highest mountain on La Gomera at 1,487 m (4,879 ft).

25 Valle Gran Rey This broad valley is easily accessible from the mountainous inner region of

the island. The "great king" (*gran rey*) referred to in the valley's name is Hupalupa, a Guanche chief who once lived here. Groves of palms and lush fields characterize the area. The town of Valle Gran Rey lies at the bottom of a steep ravine. On the waterfront, Vuelta and the La Playa area are lively and the beaches are the best in the region, stretching all the way to La Puntilla.

You can book boat trips to Los Órganos from Vuelta and guided walks into the forests. People who want a quieter time might prefer to stay at the upper end of the valley at El Hornillo.

26 Valverde Many visitors to El Hierro will also make their way to Valverde, the small capital of this, the smallest of the Canary Islands. Set slightly inland and in an elevated position, it is the only island capital not located on the coast. It is accessible from the island airport and from the ferry port Puerto de la Estaca. The most noteworthy buildings are the church of Santa María de la Concepción (18th C.), which features a statue of the Madonna, an ornate altar, and a beautiful wooden ceiling; and the town hall, a striking secular building, built in 1940 in a traditional Canary Islands style.

27 El Golfo From Valverde, the route heads past San Andrés, climbing to a height of around 1,300 m (4,265 ft). Stop at Mirador del Golfo, for a spectacular view of the island, and then continue through Frontera, and its church Nuestra Señora de la Candelaria, and down into the semicircular cove of El Golfo. Finally, you reach the small town of Las Puntas on the rugged coast, one of the most popular destinations on the island.

28 Santa Cruz de la Palma At one time trade with overseas made the capital of La Palma very wealthy and you can still see many houses with elegant balconies as proof of the town's former glory. Its importance diminished when the port of Santa Cruz de Tenerife was built. Take a stroll beside the sea along the Avenida Marítima, lined on one side with street cafés and magnificent and much-photographed residences such as the Casa de los Balcones, or follow the Calle Reale from the port to the naval museum, past the triangular Plaza de España on the way. It is one of the most beautiful squares in the Canaries and contains one of the most magnificent Renais-

sance buildings in Spain, which houses the Town Hall.

29 Roque de los Muchachos The highest point of La Palma (2,426 m/7,960 ft) can be reached either directly from Santa Cruz de la Palma or by taking the longer route from the capital northward and then west to Santo Domingo de Garafía. A detour to the north leads to El Tablado, famous for several gnarled old dragon trees. From Santo Domingo de Garafía the road winds up to the Roque de los Muchachos. It is only a short climb of a few minutes from the car park to the peak. The view takes in the Caldera de Taburiente, a vast volcanic crater around 7 km (4 miles) wide and up to 2,000 m (6,562 ft) deep. One of the biggest reflecting telescopes in the world was installed near the peak in 1985.

30 Puerto Naos Back in Santo Domingo de Garafía the route leads along the western coast in a southerly direction. Form Los Llanos de Ariadne you continue south to Todoque, where a narrow road passes through banana plantations to Puerto Naos on the west coast. This small tourist resort has the most beautiful

beach on the island, a black lava beach lined with palm trees.

31 Fuencaliente This southernmost town on Las Palmas is known for its wine. The vineyards grow right up to the edge of the town and you can visit the wine cellars and taste the wines. Nearby, the mountain of San Antonio (657m /2,156 ft) dominates the horizon. A tour around its crater is one of the Canary Islands' classic excursions.

1 Agulo is surrounded by banana plantations in the north of the island of La Gomera.

2 The Garajonay National Park with its unique laurel tree forests (*laurisilva*) covers around 10 percent of the island's land area and is a UNESCO World Heritage Site.

3 Valle Gran Rey on La Gomera.

4 A row of historic houses in the Avenida Marítima at the port of Santa Cruz de la Palma.

5 Surf on the east coast of El Hierro.

6 A dragon tree stands tall at El Tablado on La Palma.

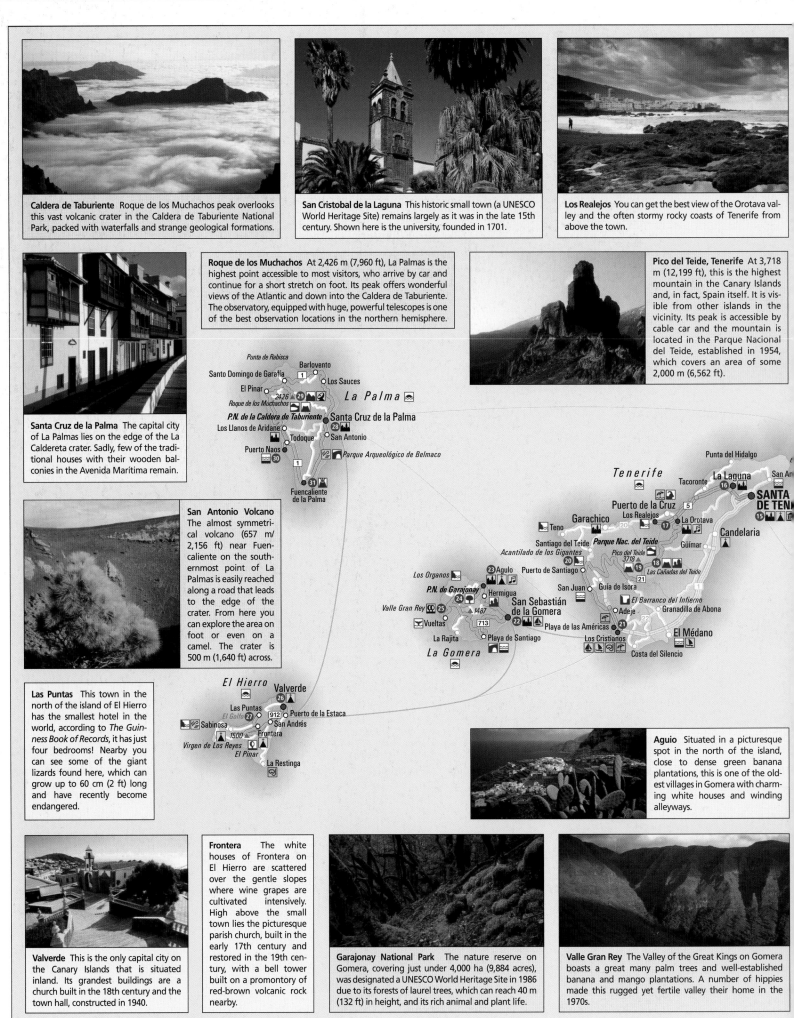

Caldera de Taburiente Roque de los Muchachos peak overlooks this vast volcanic crater in the Caldera de Taburiente National Park, packed with waterfalls and strange geological formations.

San Cristobal de la Laguna This historic small town (a UNESCO World Heritage Site) remains largely as it was in the late 15th century. Shown here is the university, founded in 1701.

Los Realejos You can get the best view of the Orotava valley and the often stormy rocky coasts of Tenerife from above the town.

Roque de los Muchachos At 2,426 m (7,960 ft), La Palmas is the highest point accessible to most visitors, who arrive by car and continue for a short stretch on foot. Its peak offers wonderful views of the Atlantic and down into the Caldera de Taburiente. The observatory, equipped with huge, powerful telescopes is one of the best observation locations in the northern hemisphere.

Pico del Teide, Tenerife At 3,718 m (12,199 ft), this is the highest mountain in the Canary Islands and, in fact, Spain itself. It is visible from other islands in the vicinity. Its peak is accessible by cable car and the mountain is located in the Parque Nacional del Teide, established in 1954, which covers an area of some 2,000 m (6,562 ft).

Santa Cruz de la Palma The capital city of La Palmas lies on the edge of the La Caldereta crater. Sadly, few of the traditional houses with their wooden balconies in the Avenida Marítima remain.

San Antonio Volcano The almost symmetrical volcano (657 m/ 2,156 ft) near Fuencaliente on the southernmost point of La Palmas is easily reached along a road that leads to the edge of the crater. From here you can explore the area on foot or even on a camel. The crater is 500 m (1,640 ft) across.

Las Puntas This town in the north of the island of El Hierro has the smallest hotel in the world, according to *The Guinness Book of Records*, it has just four bedrooms! Nearby you can see some of the giant lizards found here, which can grow up to 60 cm (2 ft) long and have recently become endangered.

Aguio Situated in a picturesque spot in the north of the island, close to dense green banana plantations, this is one of the oldest villages in Gomera with charming white houses and winding alleyways.

Valverde This is the only capital city on the Canary Islands that is situated inland. Its grandest buildings are a church built in the 18th century and the town hall, constructed in 1940.

Frontera The white houses of Frontera on El Hierro are scattered over the gentle slopes where wine grapes are cultivated intensively. High above the small town lies the picturesque parish church, built in the early 17th century and restored in the 19th century, with a bell tower built on a promontory of red-brown volcanic rock nearby.

Garajonay National Park The nature reserve on Gomera, covering just under 4,000 ha (9,884 acres), was designated a UNESCO World Heritage Site in 1986 due to its forests of laurel trees, which can reach 40 m (132 ft) in height, and its rich animal and plant life.

Valle Gran Rey The Valley of the Great Kings on Gomera boasts a great many palm trees and well-established banana and mango plantations. A number of hippies made this rugged yet fertile valley their home in the 1970s.

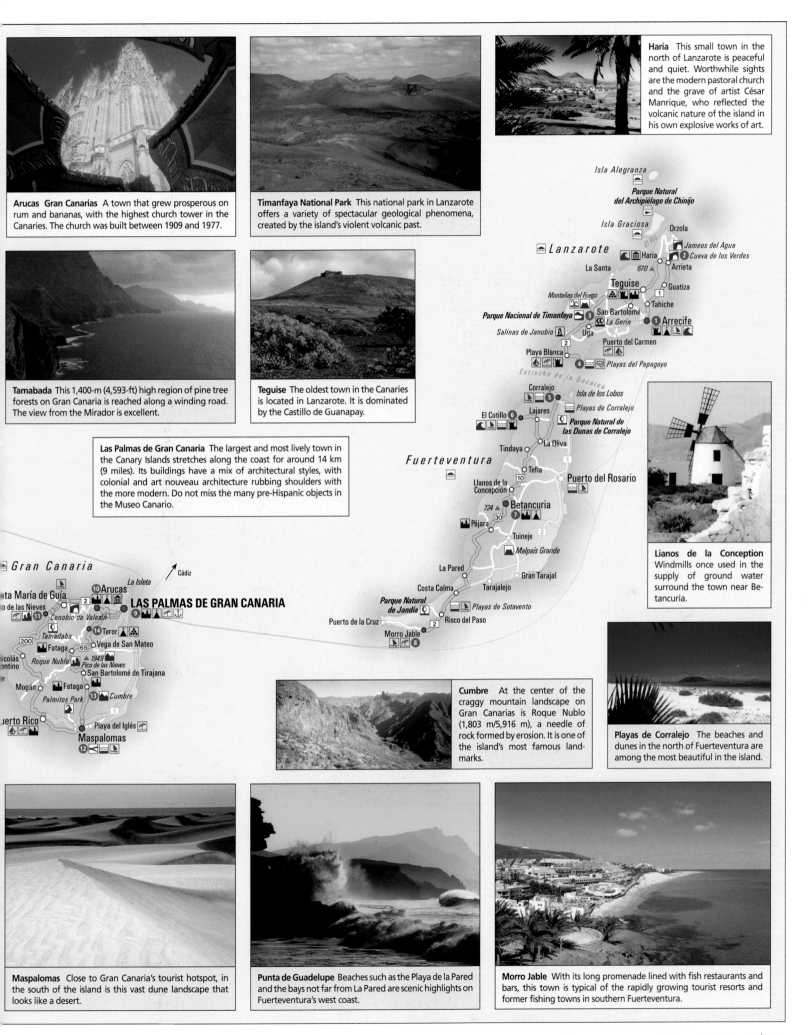

Arucas Gran Canarias A town that grew prosperous on rum and bananas, with the highest church tower in the Canaries. The church was built between 1909 and 1977.

Timanfaya National Park This national park in Lanzarote offers a variety of spectacular geological phenomena, created by the island's violent volcanic past.

Haria This small town in the north of Lanzarote is peaceful and quiet. Worthwhile sights are the modern pastoral church and the grave of artist César Manrique, who reflected the volcanic nature of the island in his own explosive works of art.

Tamabada This 1,400-m (4,593-ft) high region of pine tree forests on Gran Canaria is reached along a winding road. The view from the Mirador is excellent.

Teguise The oldest town in the Canaries is located in Lanzarote. It is dominated by the Castillo de Guanapay.

Las Palmas de Gran Canaria The largest and most lively town in the Canary Islands stretches along the coast for around 14 km (9 miles). Its buildings have a mix of architectural styles, with colonial and art nouveau architecture rubbing shoulders with the more modern. Do not miss the many pre-Hispanic objects in the Museo Canario.

Lianos de la Conception Windmills once used in the supply of ground water surround the town near Betancuria.

Cumbre At the center of the craggy mountain landscape on Gran Canarias is Roque Nublo (1,803 m/5,916 m), a needle of rock formed by erosion. It is one of the island's most famous landmarks.

Playas de Corralejo The beaches and dunes in the north of Fuerteventura are among the most beautiful in the island.

Maspalomas Close to Gran Canaria's tourist hotspot, in the south of the island is this vast dune landscape that looks like a desert.

Punta de Guadelupe Beaches such as the Playa de la Pared and the bays not far from La Pared are scenic highlights on Fuerteventura's west coast.

Morro Jable With its long promenade lined with fish restaurants and bars, this town is typical of the rapidly growing tourist resorts and former fishing towns in southern Fuerteventura.

The Bahamas

A Caribbean paradise

Tropical sun, white sandy beaches, rustling palms, and the blue ocean make the Bahamas one of the most popular vacation destinations in the world. In Nassau and Freeport, you can enjoy both fun activities and relaxing luxury, while the Family Islands offer seclusion and peace.

"It's better in the Bahamas" was the advertising slogan that was used by the islands' tourist board for many years. The islands are still the perfect place to leave everyday life behind on white sandy beaches beneath rustling palms, and to wash your troubles away in the warmth of the ocean. Pastel houses in brilliant sunshine, bright coral, and turquoise water… it really is a tropical paradise. The Bahamas are made up of around 700 islands and have been independent since 1973. They are also part of the British Commonwealth and the British influence is still in evidence everywhere. The best

known islands are New Providence Island with the capital city of Nassau, Paradise Island, and Grand Bahama with Freeport, the economic center of the islands and the home of numerous casinos. The Family or Out Islands, as the Bahamas excluding New Providence, Grand Bahama, and Paradise Island are known, are also a magnet for tourists in search of seclusion and a place to chill out. The people are warm and friendly, the water is crystal clear, and the coral reefs are some of the most beautiful in the world.

The original inhabitants, known as the Lucayans, lived undisturbed on the islands

Young girl from Cat Island in the south-east of the Bahamas.

A yacht anchors near the Abacos Islands. Out at sea it is still possible to enjoy peaceful isolation, unlike on those islands overrun by large numbers of tourists.

A fantastic sunset on Andros, the largest island of the archipelago and still largely untouched.

until the 15th century. On October 12, 1492, Columbus anchored off the shore of the island now known as San Salvador, and is said to have uttered the words *baja mar* (shallow sea), which eventually became the name Bahamas. Over the next century, the Lucayans who lived there were either killed or enslaved by the Europeans. The first permanent settlers were Puritans from Bermuda who had been religiously persecuted and so took up residence on one of the larger islands, naming it Eleuthera after the Greek word for freedom.

During the 18th century, Nassau developed into an important refuge for pirates. The infamous Blackbeard and over a thousand of his compatriots hid in the many coves and caves and attacked European trading ships as they sailed the Caribbean Sea. Some of the galleons that were sunk here still lie on the ocean floor today and treasure hunters search for valuable hoards of gold in the wrecks. The British crown finally brought the reign of the pirates to an end when it gained control of the Bahamas in 1717. The statue that stands outside the Hilton Hotel in Nassau is a monument to the most successful bounty hunter, Captain Woodes Rogers. Until slavery was abolished in 1834, the islands formed an important hub for the slave trade. In the Bahamas themselves, however, plantation owners had little success farming the dry ground and so set most of their slaves free. During the American Civil War, the English set up a base in the Bahamas to provide the Southern States with war supplies, and during the 1920s Prohibition era rum-runners smuggled illicit alcohol from the Bahamas into the USA.

Dolphins: these intelligent sea mammals, are sometimes seen in the waters around the Bahamas.

Fish market in Nassau

On Potter's Cay, beneath the bridge to Potter's Island, the lively fish market attracts visitors with its wide variety of stalls and snack bars and vibrant mix of people. Visitors and locals meet for a grouper sandwich, a hot conch salad, and a cool beer, which must be sipped out of a brown paper bag due to its high alcohol content. The fish is sent

Above: A stallholder with a pile of red snapper.
Below: A cage full of crabs.

straight from the fishing boats to the window displays: fresh grouper (sea perch), red snapper, tuna, mahi-mahi, crabs, lobsters (with no claws in the Bahamas), and of course the tough conch snails with their white and pink shells, which are made into salads and the spicy soup called conch chowder.

1

Nassau in New Providence is both the starting point and destination of the Bahamas round trip. Many islands lie on the route in between, such as Grand Bahama, Bimini, Harbour Island, and Andros.

❶ Nassau (New Providence)
The round trip begins in Nassau, the administrative capital of the Bahamas on New Providence Island. Over half of the population in the Bahamas lives on this island, although it is significantly smaller than Andros and Grand Bahama.
Nassau was founded in 1656 by English settlers, who named it Charlestown; it was renamed in 1689 for the English king William III from the Dutch house of Orange-Nassau. The legendary Cable Beach was first named in 1907 after the transatlantic cable that was laid under the sea at the turn of the century between Jupiter, Florida, and Nassau.
The city center of Nassau has a fascinating Caribbean charm and contains reminders of the eventful colonial era in its houses, Victorian villas, and fortifications. Trade is brisk at the numerous markets and in the boutiques and shops selling crafts and expensive jewelry.

Luxurious hotels, huge casinos, and the marinas make Nassau an upmarket, fashionable destination for tourists.
A relic of British colonial times is Parliament Square, situated in the middle of the town with
(continued p.150)

1 A typical scene: Fishing boats are moored next to cruise ships in the port of Nassau.

2 The Columbus statue outside the seat of government in Nassau is a reminder that the explorer first set foot in the New World on one of the Bahamian Islands in 1492.

Travel information

Route profile
Length: approx. 1,600 km (1,000 miles)
Duration: 14 days
Start and end: Nassau
Itinerary (main locations): Nassau (New Providence), Paradise Island (New Providence), Abaco, Freeport (Grand Bahama), West End (Grand Bahama), Bimini, Eleuthera, Harbour Island, Cat Island, Long Island, Great Exuma, Andros Town (Andros), Nichol's Town (Andros)

Travel tips
Major travel agents offer attractive package tours in the Bahamas. Once you are there, it's possible to arrange interesting excursions at short notice, such as to Harbour Island.

Tourist information
Bahamas Ministry of Tourism, P.O. Box N-3701, Nassau, Bahamas
Tel. 242-302-2000
Fax. 242-302-2098
www.bahamas.com

Dinghies jostle for position along the coast of New Providence, where radiant sunshine and stiff breezes offer ideal conditions for offshore sailors. Many yachts sailed past Nassau during the World Championship Regatta 2001.

Paradise Island

Atlantis comes to Paradise Island! The island is home to the Atlantis Resort, a complex of hotels and Disneyesque attractions with the theme of Altantis, the legendary underwater city. The hotel complex has the world's largest open-air aquarium, the biggest casino in the Caribbean, and the "ruins" of Atlantis. There are five water slides at the Mayan Temple attraction, including the Leap of Faith, which is followed by a walk along a transparent acrylic tunnel through a lagoon teeming with sharks.

Pleasure-seeking guests have a choice of 2,300 rooms in the colossal hotel towers. In contrast, the other luxury

Above: Slot machines in the casino. Below: A tunnel through shark-infested water!

hotels on the island seem a bit of a comedown, although they are situated at the edge of the sea and offer every comfort imaginable. The former Hog Island was renamed Paradise Island with good reason. It was developed exclusively for tourists and attracts visitors with many restaurants, stores, boutiques, and boat tours to the diving paradise off the coast. Adventure-seeking hotel guests shoot across the water out into the open sea on speedboats.

Although Paradise Island is somewhat reminiscent of Las Vegas and has developed into a huge entertainment center, you can escape to isolated natural surroundings only a short distance away on the Family Islands.

imposing governmental buildings. The Houses of Parliament, the old Colonial Secretary's Office, the Supreme Court, and buildings in soft, pastel shades surround the imposing marble statue of Queen Victoria. The Public Library in Shirley Street was once a prison. Opposite stand the ruins of the Royal Victoria Hotel, the first hotel in Nassau, surrounded by gloriously blooming gardens.

The 66 steps of the Queen's Staircase connect Fort Fincastle to the Princess Margaret Hospital. They are thought to have been carved out of the hard limestone by slaves between 1793 and 1794 and were named for Queen Victoria. The view of the city is stunning from Fort Fincastle on Bennet Hill; it was designed in the shape of a ship's bow and built in 1793. Fort Montagu was completed in July 1742 and is famous for its terrace-shaped cistern, which collects the rain that falls in the fort and drains off the excess. Fort Charlotte, the largest fort in Nassau, was built between 1787 and 1789 and was named after the wife of King George III. However, no shot has ever been fired from the fort, which is protected by a moat, high walls, and a drawbridge.

The pink Government House is located in Parliament Street and was constructed in 1801. The Royal Bahamian Police Force Band plays in front of the statue of Columbus every Saturday to mark the changing of the guard. The late 18th-century Pompey Museum building was a trans-shipment center for slaves and goods before being converted into a museum. The exhibitions show what life used to be like for African slaves in the Bahamas.

The straw market on Bay Street, which has been held since the 1940s and has become a tradition in New Providence, is rather more cheerful.

It arose when the sponge industry collapsed, and many women started to weave baskets, bags, hats, dolls, and other souvenirs from palm fronds and sisal leaves and would sell them at the markets in Nassau, on Cable Beach, and on Paradise Island. Today the straw market is one of the most popular attractions in the Bahamas.

Worthwhile excursions lead to quiet locations such as Coral Harbour and Adelaide and to Lynford Cay with its idyllic residential areas. All of the beaches have enticing white sand.

2 Paradise Island (New Providence) Walk across the bridge from Nassau and you'll find yourself on the luxury resort of Paradise Island, with its casinos, bars, and vibrant nightlife. Until tourism developers rediscovered it, the former Hog Island was for the most part unknown.

However, once the first hotels and casinos had been set up, the island grew into a tourist playground and its character gradually began to change. Since millionaires such as Howard Hughes and the Shah of Persia moved here in the 1950s, it has become a very ex-

Wreck-diving

The Bahamas are a paradise for divers. The excellent underwater visibility is due to the Gulf Stream, which begins south of Florida and protects the islands from unwanted rainfall and keeps the water pure. As a result, the water is turquoise and crystal clear beneath the surface, and even the coral reefs are in good condition, an extra bonus for wreck divers, who have a particularly large area to explore in the Bahamas. Over a thousand wrecks are thought to lie on the ocean floor, mainly galleons and trading ships from the great era of sailing ships, when Spanish and Portuguese gold was transported across the ocean via Florida and the Caribbean, and hundreds of pirates made the waters a dangerous place. Unimaginable gold treasures are thought to remain hidden beneath the waves. Treasure-seekers continue to search desperately for ships laden with gold, which are believed to have sunk off the coast of Great Inagua, and for the Santa Cruz, which sank in 1694 with gold on board that was worth three

Divers by the wreck of the Willaurie.

million dollars. Near Bimini, the legendary city of Atlantis is said to be awaiting discovery at the bottom of the ocean. The diving expeditions to the known wrecks, organized by many diving companies in the Bahamas, are a truly exciting experience. Coral and fungi cover the skeletons of the rotting ships, schools of vivid fish swim through the thick growth, moray eels, ferocious if provoked, and harmless wobbegong sharks sleep in the dark water of the wrecks, and barracudas search for prey. But be careful, other, more dangerous sharks have also discovered that the ships make good hunting grounds.

ists, who enjoy swimming and exploring underwater, fishing, and sailing in the surrounding ocean. There are more boat mooring points than hotel rooms on the island.

Abaco Island is particularly popular among sailors and yacht owners because of its proximity to other islands. The same is true for divers, who can explore the phenomenal "blue holes" off the coast. These are underwater cave systems entered via what, when viewed from above, appear to be "holes" in the ocean surrounded by rocks or reefs. Wreck divers can search for sunken treasure in more than five hundred galleons on the ocean floor. Equally exciting are the underwater caves and coral reefs at the Pelican Cays Land & Sea

(continued p.154)

1 The lighthouse at Hope Town on Abaco.

2 Treasure Cay, an exclusive tourist resort on the Abaco Islands.

3 Abaco, known for its palm-lined beaches.

4 Diving with sharks.

clusive place in which to live (see panel, left).

3 Abaco The first European settlers on the Abaco Islands were supporters of the English King George III. They arrived in 1783, having fled to the Caribbean during the American War of Independence when they realized they were on the losing side. They were farmers originally but soon realized that they would only be able to survive on the Abaco Islands as fishermen. A number of tiny islands and the third-largest barrier reef in the world are located off the coast of the main island. Today the inhabitants of Abaco still live off the sea, their tiny villages clustered along the craggy shores, but tourism has now become an important source of income in addition to fishing. The wonderful water attracts the tour-

Sunken wrecks are common in the waters off the coast of the Bahama Islands, and attract huge schools of fish. These are welcome prey for predators such as sharks and barracudas. White sharks are only dangerous to humans if they panic or are injured or bleeding. Sharks do not usually attack humans of their own accord.

flesh. Many only attack when provoked or when they confuse a diver, surfer, or swimmer with their prey, particularly in those areas of the sea where they hunt.

Lucayan National Park

Around 40 km (25 miles) east of Freeport is the Lucayan National Park, where you can see an untamed wilderness not normally depicted on postcards of the Bahamas. Tangled mangroves and thick clusters of palm trees cover the land right down to one of the most beautiful and remote beaches in the islands. You can only reach the sandy dunes beside the turquoise sea by following a narrow path down to the beach.

The coral reef off the coast here is magnificent and conditions are ideal for snokeling or diving.

An agave in the Lucayan National Park.

In the forest, you can see rare and magical flowers and ferns. One of the largest underwater cave systems is accessible by land and sea; here, acidic water has been eating away at the walls of the limestone tunnels over millions of years. Gold Rock Creek, a small creek in the national park, is fed with water from these caves. There are believed to be around 36,000 entrances to the caves, two of which you can see from the land. Around 2 m (6 ft) of fresh water accumulates and floats on top of the heavier salt water in the caves. Wooden spiral stairs lead down to the pools, from which the Lucayan Indians used to provide the fishermen with drinking water.

Park near Great Abaco. Abaco National Park was founded in 1994 in order to protect the endangered Bahama parrot, a subspecies of the Cuban Amazon parrot that is native to this region. The major attractions on this island are the villages founded by the loyalists, which are similar to those of New England.

Marsh Harbour is the island's commercial center. Half of the 15,000 inhabitants live in the small town, which has only one traffic light. There are a number of banks, insurance companies, supermarkets, and offices in the quite drab town center. The Marina District is rather more romantic, with restaurants and boutiques largely suitable for the more wealthy tourists. Many boats and yachts bob on the water. North of Marsh Harbour is Treasure Cay, a tourist paradise with luxury hotels, villas, 18-hole golf courses, and a huge marina. Before Captain Leonard Thompson recognized the potential of the peninsula and built the first hotels here with US backing, Treasure Cay was known as Sand Bank Cay. South of Treasure Cay lies the Leisure Lee, a quiet community of residential property and protected canals. The inhabitants of Casuarina Point and Bahama Palm Shores to the south are less affluent. Hundreds of coconut palms border the long sandy beach. Nearby is the Cherokee Sound, a sleepy fishing village that provided

protection for the fleeing supporters of George III after the American War of Independence was over, which is in stark contrast to the Abaco Club and its luxurious golf course. Crossing Rock in the south of the island is a popular fishing spot.

The capital city Hope Town, one of the most famous tourist destinations in Abaco, is located in the Outer Cays.

Hope Town's protected port is set in a picturesque cove. Its red and white striped lighthouse is the island's landmark and offers great views over the port. Ironically, the inhabitants of Hope Town protested loudly against the construction of the lighthouse when the English were drawing up their plans in 1860. Today they are proud of the distinctive landmark. Since Elbow Cay, the smaller island, was

opened up for tourism, the area around the port has been booming. New hotels and apartment blocks appear nearly every day. The nearby Lubber's Quarters, with its tangled thick mangroves, and the large boat-building yard in Man-O-War Cay offer a nicely contrasting atmosphere.

Great Guana Cay ("the sleeping giant") is an island 11 km (7 miles) long, which really came to life when tourists discovered the lively Nippers Beach Bar and made it their meeting point. Increasing numbers of visitors took the ferry to the island for the weekly pig roast. Small hotels and villas started appearing. The spectacular Nippers Beach used to be an insiders' secret. Green Turtle Cay, a tiny island also populated by loyalist settlers, has met the

same fate. The island's name comes from the turtle trading that once took place on its shores. Nowadays, lobster-catching is the island's most important source of income.

4 Freeport (Grand Bahama)
From Abaco, the journey continues toward Freeport, the legendary entertainment center on Grand Bahama. The Spanish explorer Ponce de León anchored on the shores of the island back in 1513. However, it was not well known until the 1950s when Wallace Groves,
(continued p.156)

1 An exclusive sports car outside a jeweler's boutique in Freeport.

2 The red and white striped lighthouse on Grand Bahama.

Hot sauces and herbs, such as this selection from the Captain's Charthouse Restaurant (top), are part of the Caribbean cuisine common in the Bahamas. Fresh

Coral

Off the coasts of the Bahamas, the many coral reefs are a popular attraction for divers and underwater explorers due to their glorious hues and many varieties of fish. Coral may look like a strange underwater forest, but it is actually formed by the limestone secretions of living marine organisms found in shallow, tropical seas. The organisms feed off plank-

The fantastic diversity of the coral: large star coral (above), cup coral (middle), closed brain coral (below).

ton, nutrients, and trace elements filtered from the seawater.
Coral can be categorized as soft and stony. It is the stony coral that builds most of the reefs, while it is the coral polyps (marine organisms) that make the coral look like underwater plants. Small algae often stick to the coral, supplying the polyps with additional oxygen and adding to the intensive hues of the parts of the coral that are alive. Coral reefs support a wide range of marine creatures.

a financier from Virginia, invested in tree-felling on the island and founded the town of Freeport/Lucaya. As a free trade area and popular cruise port, the town has developed into a world-famous entertainment destination with huge casinos, restaurants, boutiques, and bars. Freeport is particularly popular among American cruise ship passengers because of its duty-free shopping. The cash tills ring constantly in the town's large casinos, meanwhile guests are entertained by internationally renowned performers.
Tropical plants grow in the Hydroflora Gardens on East Beach Drive. You can marvel at the exotic flowers and birds in The Garden of Groves, the town's botanical gardens. The Grand Bahama Museum is located in the center of the gardens and has interesting exhibitions about the eventful history of the Bahamas. Shopping is highly recommended at the International Bazaar, a shopping center with over ninety stores from many countries, and the marketplace at Port Lucaya.
From Freeport, you can continue along the costal highway through Hawksbill, a quiet residential area, to Eight Mile Rock, the largest community on the island. The town is made up of a series of individual districts, which have merged together over the years.
Holmes Rock and Seagrape are famous for their unique cave,

which fills with fresh water at low tide and with seawater when the tide rises.
Paradise Cove at Deadman's Reef is one of the best locations for underwater exploration. It is possible to swim out to the brightly colored reef. Nearby, numerous artifacts left behind by 13th-century Lucayans, mainly bones and shards of pottery, have been discovered at one of the most important archeological sites in the Bahamas.

⑤ West End (Grand Bahama)
West End is located at the westernmost point of the island, a peaceful fishing village that played an important role during the 1920s Prohibition in America. At that time it was a busy trans-shipment center for European whisky, which was smuggled into the USA through the Bahamas. The so-called rumrunners built large beer halls and bars where the tough guys could relax after their work. Even Al Capone is believed to have once

visited one of the gin palaces on Waterfront Road. However, these times have long since passed. West End now thrives on tourism and is home to the oldest hotel on the island, the Star Hotel, which was built in 1946. It belongs to the successors of a certain Austin H. Grant, who came from Eight Mile Rock and built the inn for Americans who journeyed over to the Caribbean on boat trips. The hotel was forced to close in 1988, although the restaurant and bar still

Caribbean architecture

The eventful history of the Caribbean is reflected in its architecture. Pastel wooden houses stand next to spectacular hotel complexes and simple huts made from palm wood. Some historic areas, such as the colonial quarter of Santo Dominigo in the Dominican Republic, are now on the list of UNESCO World Heritage Sites.

The simple huts made from clay, straw, and twigs that still exist on many of the islands originate from the days when slaves were transported here and followed their African architectural traditions when building shelters. The colonial buildings in the larger Caribbean towns were, however, built by the Spanish conquerors.

Some say that it was a governor from the island of Curaçao who was first

Brightly painted houses on the shore of New Providence.

remain popular among visitors to the island today. The new Old Bahama Resort has provided some much needed stimulation for the town, which had grown sleepy since the old rumrunning days. Other worthwhile sightseeing opportunities on Grand Bahama are the small town of Freetown, where the first slaves were liberated in 1834, the fishing village Sweeting's Cay, which offers first-class lobster and fresh conches, and the quiet Lightbourne Cay, an ideal place to get away from the hustle and bustle of the cruise metropolis Freeport and enjoy a leisurely picnic.

6 Bimini Since Ernest Hemingway became famous, the romantic islands of North and South Bimini are no longer an insiders' secret. The writer lived at Blue Martin Cottage between 1931 and 1937 and his last novel, *Islands in the Stream*, is also set here. Visitors arrive at Alice Town, the largest town in

North Bimini, which is a collection of stores, restaurants, and bars along King's Highway. South Bimini is barely populated and has just one landing strip for small airplanes and a few hotels.

The Bimini Islands are a paradise for sea-anglers and divers. There are many shipwrecks on the ocean floor off the island's coast, but it is thought that something much more interesting is hidden beneath the deep waters: the lost city of Atlantis. In September 1968 divers found blocks of stone under the water off Paradise Point, the so-called Bimini Road. Some archeologists are convinced that the stones form an ancient road or some other manmade structure left behind by a lost civilization. Another legend associated with the island is the Fountain of Youth, which Spanish explorer Ponce de León claimed was in Florida, but some parascientists actually believe is located on Bimini.

7 Harbour Island Dunmore Island, the peaceful main city on Harbour Island, can be reached on a small airplane or by boat. The town was named after Lord Dunmore, the island's former governor (1786–1797) and is one of the oldest settlements in the Bahamas. Pastel houses with white picket fences around tiny gardens give the place a contemplative atmosphere. The Hill Steps were carved out of the hill by prisoners and a tunnel leads to Rock House, a nearby resort hotel. Titus Hole, a cave above the port, was used as a prison by the first settlers.

The main attraction on this island is, however, the hue of the sand on the Atlantic shore. The pink sand stretches for miles along the beaches here, the pinkness comes from the ground coral it contains. There are many coral reefs near the island, which provide excellent conditions for divers and underwater explorers.

8 Eleuthera This beach paradise is only 1.5 km (1 mile) wide but 180 km (112 miles) long, and one of the most popular destinations among the Family Islands. Airplanes land in Governor's Harbour, the administrative center of the small island. Before the journey continues

1 The Bahamas are a divers' paradise. Encounters with sharks are very rare.

2 Near the Bimini Islands, mysterious powers are believed to threaten ships.

3 The pink sands of Harbour Island are some of the most beautiful in the Bahamas.

4 Harbour Island settlers were some of the earliest to arrive in the Bahamas.

5 Puritans landed at the beach by Preacher's Cave on Eleuthera in the 17th century and thanked God for rescuing them.

responsible for the pastel shades with which most Caribbean houses were painted. He was particularly sensitive to light and was blinded by the white paint applied to houses at the time, so he ordered his own house walls to be painted in more muted tones. A more likely story is that the people who built the first houses made this decision for themselves.

Many houses are constructed so that as few surfaces as possible are exposed to the sun, and large windows allow a cool breeze to circulate through the rooms.

Many ornaments used to decorate the houses are based on Indian symbols, supposed to keep evil spirits away. Some of the hotel resorts, on the other hand, follow the style of Las Vegas with legendary themes, such as Atlantis.

Columbus

Christopher Columbus is believed to have been born in October 1451 in Genoa and has been celebrated for many centuries as the discoverer of the Americas, although we now know that it was actually discovered by the Vikings, who arrived on these shores long before him. On his first journey, Columbus was the first European to set foot in the Bahamas, on San Salvador. Upon his death, he still believed he had

A white cross marks the place where Christopher Columbus first landed.

found a new route to South-East Asia. He was probably driven both by a spirit of exploration and by the desire to accumulate wealth. He had to wait a long time in order to make his journey to the lucrative trading centers in Asia. It was only after the Spanish victory over the Moors that the Spanish king and queen were willing to finance journeys of this kind.

Columbus' first voyage (1492–1493) led him not only to the Bahamas but also to Cuba and Hispaniola (today the Dominican Republic and Haiti). On the second trip (1493–1496) he discovered Jamaica and Puerto Rico. Against the will of the Spanish crown, he led a campaign of destruction against the indigenous peoples and enslaved around two thousand men, women, and children. The third voyage (1498–1500) took him to Trinidad and Tobago, where the South American continent was visible from the mouth of the Orinoco. On his final journey (1502–1504), Columbus explored the coast from Honduras to Columbia.

to Cat Island, which lies to the south-east of Eleuthera, it is worth stopping over here.

The Arawak Indians who once inhabited this island were either killed or sold as slaves by Spanish conquerors in the 16th century. Puritan settlers arrived at Eleuthera in 1648. Between 1950 and 1980 a number of US industrialists and Hollywood stars such as Robert de Niro stayed here. However, most hotels were closed down when the island was made independent and tourism has only started to pick up again over the past few years.

Among the island's attractions are the Glass Window Bridge, which connects the Atlantic Ocean to the quieter waters of the Exuma Sound and offers a spectacular view of the gloriously blue sea; and Preachers Cave, used as a natural chapel by the first settlers. The huge cave in Hatchet Bay, however, seems more like a cathedral. The shipwreck in Yankee channel, which is around three hundred years old, and a sunken train (that was being transported on a barge) at Devil's Backbone are exciting places for divers to explore.

❾ Cat Island The next stop is Arthur's Town on Cat Island. The famous actor Sidney Poitier (born in 1924) spent his childhood in this small community before heading for Hollywood, where be became one of the first black superstars, starring in

such classic movies as *The Defiant Ones* and *In the Heat of the Night*.

Some believe that the island is named after the English pirate Arthur Catt, who used a cave here as a hideout. Another version of the story is that the island was named after the many feral cats that made life difficult for the first settlers from America. These are descendents of the tame housecats that were brought to the island by the Spanish conquerors. For 400 years, Cat Island was actually known as San Salvador as it was thought to be the San Salvador where, in 1492, Christopher Columbus first set foot in the New World. In 1926 Watlings Island was renamed San Salvador and Cat

Island was given back its original name. A reminder of the loyalists who settled on the island in 1783 is the plantation in Port Howe, a small community founded by Colonel Andrew Deveaux, the man who reconquered Nassau from the Spanish.

Cat Island is only slightly over 60 km (37 miles) long and just over 1.5 km (1 mile) wide, and is one of the most fertile islands in the Bahamas. The first settlers planted mainly cotton and pineapples here and raised cattle. Tropical flowers thrive in the thick grass and bushes. The tranquility of the island and the bright hues of its flora make it the ideal place to escape from civilization and get back to nature. This is what Father

Jerome Hawkes was probably thinking when he built a medieval-style monastery on Mount Alvernia, the highest point on the island (63 m/207 ft). The architect and priest came to the Bahamas to repair Anglican churches on Long Island. There is a breathtaking view of Fine Beach, a 16-km (10-mile) dream beach with pink sand, from his monastery, which is known as The Hermitage.

(continued p.160)

1 Conch snail shells on the coast of Cat Island.

2 Starfish of San Salvador. This is where Christopher Columbus is believed to have made first land fall in 1492.

Before 1900 there were thought to be over 100,000 flamingoes in the Bahamas. Early settlers hunted them for their meat and their numbers fell to 3,000.
Today, over 80,000 Caribbean flamingos once again thrive in the Bahamas, in particular on Great Inagua.

Iguanas

There were once thousands of iguanas in the Bahamas, but they have almost all died out. The best way to see these rare lizards is to visit a national park. Many species of iguana live in North and South America and on the Caribbean islands. Most are 10–30 cm (4–12 in) in size, but some, especially the green iguana, can grow up to 2 m (6 ft) in length. Iguanas have adapted to their environment in amazing ways. The shape of their scales and the length of their tails vary according to the landscape they live in, and their webbed feet help them to travel through water. All iguanas can see well, their sight is their strongest sense, and their hearing is also excellent, but their sense of smell is fairly poor.

Above and below: Allans Cay iguanas.

There are five groups of iguana: the iguanas that live in the Bahamas, basilisks, anoles, tropical thornytail iguanas, and spiny lizards. They can all be identified by their different outer appearances. Iguanas defend themselves against their enemies using their tails and, when fleeing, they usually head for water.

10 Long Island Just a stone's throw away is Clarence Town on Long Island, one of the most charming of the Bahamian islands with grass-green hills, fertile pineapple and banana plantations, and flat salt lakes. On the gulf side perfect white beaches are lined with palm trees, while on the bleaker Atlantic side, the surf crashes against craggy rocks. Long Island is particularly popular among divers due to the thrill of shark-feeding trips offered by local organizers.

A white cross at the northernmost point of the island forms a memorial to Christopher Columbus, the first European visitor. He named the island Fernandina in recognition of his sponsor in Spain. Supporters of the English king George III based in North America followed his footsteps in the late 18th century, and grew cotton on large plantations. Some of their houses are still standing today. Clarence Town and other communities lie along a former coach road built for the farmers.

One of the major events held on the island is the Long Island Sailing Regatta, which takes place in early summer each year. Swimmers and sunseekers can relax at Cape Santa Maria, one of the most beautiful beaches in the world.

From Clarence Town you can enjoy an excursion to Gran Inagua (see panel, right).

11 Great Exuma The journey continues to Georgetown on

Great Exuma, the largest of over 360 mainly tiny islands referred to collectively on maps as Exuma or Exuma Cays. The Tropic of Cancer runs right through the town, which reflects the character of the entire island. There are no mooring points for cruise ships, no tourist traps, and just small hotels. The only concession to tourism is the famous Club Peace and Plenty Hotel in Georgetown. Endless sunshine, turquoise water, and fantastic beaches make Exuma the perfect Caribbean island paradise. Worth seeing in Georgetown are the St Andrew's Anglican Church and Elizabeth Harbour, where the National Family Island Regatta starts each year. Another highlight is the Bahamian Music and Heritage Festi-

val, which also takes place annually.

Exuma was settled in 1783 by royalists from North America, who set up a cotton plantation on the island.

Some settlements on the Exumas are named after Lord John Rolle, one of the most prominent royalists. A section of the beach and a number of caves and coral reefs are contained within the Exuma National Land and Sea Park and are protected sites. Thunderball Grotto was used as a filming location for the 1965 James Bond film *Thunderball*.

12 Andros Town (Andros) Covering an area of around 6,000 sq km (2,316 sq miles), Andros Island is one of the largest but least developed of

the Bahama islands in terms of tourism. When you disembark in Andros Town, the commercial center of the island, you will see only a small town with a few hundred inhabitants and two hotels, mainly used by seaanglers. Andros Island is one of the best fishing locations in the Caribbean, along with the Bimini Islands. It is said to be the bonefish (a premier game fish) capital of the world.

Off the coast of this island is the largest reef in the Bahamas, around 225 km (140 miles) long, an immense habitat for fish, not to mention a paradise for divers and underwater explorers, as most of the coral is only 4 m (13 ft) below the surface of the water. Behind the reef the water depth plunges to 2,000 m (6,562 ft).

Excursion

Inagua National Park

Inagua National Park, founded in 1965, is located on Great Inagua Island, and is a special visitor attraction because of the 60,000, or more, pink flamingos that live there. You can see these graceful birds on the shores of the great Windsor Lake, which is part of the 75,000-ha (185-acre) park.

Caribbean flamingos are the brightest and largest of their species. Their wing covers are red, but their flight feathers are black. Their relatively small heads have curved bills with a black tip. They have a life expectancy of around 40 years, one of the longest of all birds. Their long stilt legs are ideal for wading in shallow water.

Above: Scrubland at Windsor Lake.
Below: Flamingos in the lake.

The birds' characteristic pink hue does not develop until they are one year old, and is caused by their diet of saltwater shrimp. These cousins of the European greater flamingo are found in the Caribbean, parts of Central America, in the north-east of South America, and on the Galapagos Islands. They are most at ease in large colonies such as the one at the Inagua National Park. In addition to the flamingos there is also a variety of other bird species in the nature reserve, including the Bahama parrot, which almost became extinct in recent years.

The Spanish landed on Andros Island in 1550 and enslaved the local Indians. The contagious diseases the Spanish brought with them wiped out the remaining inhabitants. The Spanish named the island Espiritu Santo (Holy Ghost), but the name appears to have been changed later. According to a map made in 1782, it was called San Andreas. It is believed that its modern name was chosen to commemorate Sir Edmund Andros, who led the English forces in Barbados at the end of the 17th century and later made a name for himself as the governor of New York, New England, Maryland, and Guernsey. The name may, however, also come from the inhabitants of St Andro Island (Columbia), who settled on the island in 1787. In the 18th century, many pirates (including the infamous Welsh buccaneer Henry Morgan) took over control of Andros Island, and in the 19th century US settlers arrived on the island, as they did in many places in the Bahamas, and set up plantations worked by slaves.

Andros Island has been able to contain its tourism and preserve the beauty of its landscape. Light pine forests stretch out to the north of the island and over fifty types of orchid grow in the mangrove marshes and rainforests. Wild pigs roam through the scrubland. Two hundred types of bird are native to this island, including the Bahama Yellowthroat, but also two mythical creatures: Lusca is a sea monster said to pull careless divers exploring "blue holes" down into the depths, while the Chickcharnie, a large owl that used to live on Andros but is now extinct, which also gave its name to a mythical bird-like dwarf creature with glowing red eyes, is believed still to be seeking revenge many years after a British famer cut down the trees in which the bird nested.

The island is also blessed with plenty of fresh water, which collects in the many caves and grottos. Even the capital city Nassau lives off water shipped from Andros to New Providence. As fresh water is lighter than salt water, it is possible to separate it from sea- water without a large amount of technical equipment. Andros has seen its share of celebrity visitors. In the 1960s the Rat Pack (Peter Lawford, Sammy Davis Jnr, Frank Sinatra, and Dean Martin), hung out at Fresh Creek, and thanks to its excellent diving conditions, French diver and scientist Jacques Cousteau spent some time exploring its waters

⑬ Nicholl's Town, Andros
Along the coast of the turquoise ocean is Nicholl's Town at the northern point of Andros Island, one of the largest settlements on the island with a population of around six hundred. Most visitors staying at the hotels in Nicholl's Town are anglers looking for bonefish and tarpon off the coast.

However, Andros is also famous for its crafts. Wood carvings and imaginative products made from straw are some of the most attractive souvenirs you can buy here. Many of the craftspeople are descendants of Seminole Indians from Florida. Androsia, the bright material used for clothing in the Bahamas, also comes from Andros Island, where it is manufactured at the Androsia Batik Factory.

This round cruise through the Bahamian islands ends with the return journey to Nassau.

1 The quiet coves of the Exuma Islands are the perfect place to sail and relax.

2 Exuma has wide sandy beaches and the gentle surf provides excellent conditions for swimmers.

A large reef shark makes its way through the banks of coral, searching for prey. A huge school of fish swims past, but this shark is not a threat to them. There are, however, other kinds of shark that would attack schools of fish like this one with their tail fins.

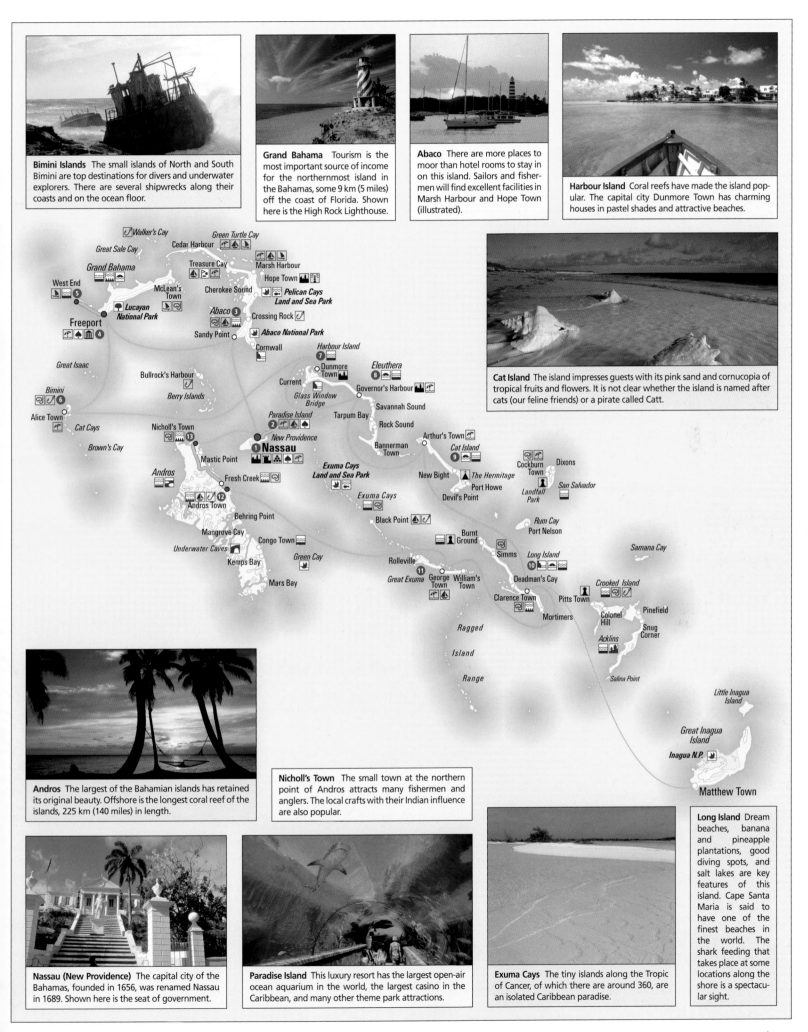

Bimini Islands The small islands of North and South Bimini are top destinations for divers and underwater explorers. There are several shipwrecks along their coasts and on the ocean floor.

Grand Bahama Tourism is the most important source of income for the northernmost island in the Bahamas, some 9 km (5 miles) off the coast of Florida. Shown here is the High Rock Lighthouse.

Abaco There are more places to moor than hotel rooms to stay in on this island. Sailors and fishermen will find excellent facilities in Marsh Harbour and Hope Town (illustrated).

Harbour Island Coral reefs have made the island popular. The capital city Dunmore Town has charming houses in pastel shades and attractive beaches.

Cat Island The island impresses guests with its pink sand and cornucopia of tropical fruits and flowers. It is not clear whether the island is named after cats (our feline friends) or a pirate called Catt.

Andros The largest of the Bahamian islands has retained its original beauty. Offshore is the longest coral reef of the islands, 225 km (140 miles) in length.

Nicholl's Town The small town at the northern point of Andros attracts many fishermen and anglers. The local crafts with their Indian influence are also popular.

Long Island Dream beaches, banana and pineapple plantations, good diving spots, and salt lakes are key features of this island. Cape Santa Maria is said to have one of the finest beaches in the world. The shark feeding that takes place at some locations along the shore is a spectacular sight.

Nassau (New Providence) The capital city of the Bahamas, founded in 1656, was renamed Nassau in 1689. Shown here is the seat of government.

Paradise Island This luxury resort has the largest open-air ocean aquarium in the world, the largest casino in the Caribbean, and many other theme park attractions.

Exuma Cays The tiny islands along the Tropic of Cancer, of which there are around 360, are an isolated Caribbean paradise.

A tributary of the Mississippi flows quietly and languidly by an overgrown riverbank.

Route 11

USA

Mississippi: in the footsteps of Mark Twain

The melodic name of this river is said to originate from the language of the Algonquin Native North American tribe, who called it "misi sipi". Literally translated, "misi" means big and "sipi" means water, but for the Algonquins it meant "Father of Rivers" or "Great River", and rightly so, as the Mississippi is the second longest river in North America. It runs for an impressive 3,778 km (2,348 miles) and flows through ten states. Its major tributary, the Missouri, is even longer at 6,021 km (3,741 miles).

The word "Mississippi" evokes some deep-seated images: a broad, majestic river with grand old paddle steamers making their leisurely way across the water, accompanied by the gentle, melodic strains of the lilting song "Ol' Man River" with which Jerome Kern so entrancingly captured the spirit of the river in his hit musical *Showboat*, and which has almost now become a folk song in the south.

At home in the Mississippi: alligators.

Today, the spirit of the old days can be relived by undertaking a nostalgic cruise on one of the restored old boats that sail from Saint Paul or Minneapolis to New Orleans. The old days were described in great detail by the most famous chronicler of the river, Mark Twain, in his book *Life on the Mississippi*, which describes his experiences of working on the river as a steamboat pilot. The land along the banks of the Mississippi, in particular the middle section of the river, was inhabited long before the arrival of European settlers. Some of the most important archeological discoveries in the USA, such as the Cahokia Mounds and the Effigy Mounds, provide evidence of an ancient Native North American culture that prospered hundreds or even thousands of years ago. Many a local farmer has come across relics, such as arrow-

heads or axe heads while ploughing their fields. The Mississippi river also played an important role in the opening up of the west. Initially forming a barrier that had to be crossed, it later marked the boundary of the land settled by the European immigrants before the hard journey over the prairie began. The town of St Louis, which nowadays has a population of around one million, was originally founded by pioneers, keen to explore the uncharted land to the west. Prospering from its position as the Gateway to the West, St Louis supplied provisions to the many people who set off on wagon trails from here.

From St Louis onward, the Mississippi begins to reflect the romanticism of river travel. Away from the perilous rapids that make navigation difficult in the northern part of the river, riverboats still

The West Bank Expressway crosses the Mississippi on the Greater New Orleans Bridge. In addition to the first bridge, built in 1958, an identical parallel bridge was constructed in 1988.

The approach to the mansion at the Oak Alley Plantation leads through an avenue of spectacular old oak trees.

require pilots (or suitable technical equipment) in places farther south, where the rivers enters shallows. By the time you get to Memphis, the river has truly entered the world of the old south, an area that many still associate with the Civil War era (1861–1865). Most of the war was fought in the south, which suffered greatly as a result. However, some magnificent mansions still survive from the golden age before the Civil War, set in spectacular grounds.

Life was turned upside down in New Orleans on the banks of the Mississippi in August 2005 when Hurricane Katrina struck, causing untold destruction and suffering. Eighty percent of the city was left underwater. Since then, a clean-up program and restoration work has been undertaken, and the returning inhabitants are attempting to restore the city to its former glory. One of the most visited cities in the USA, New Orleans fully justifies its lively reputation. From Bourbon Street with its many bars and restaurants, to the city jazz clubs, many of which are based in the historic French Quarter. It is also home to the Mardi Gras carnival held in February and known all over the world.

The river drifts along lazily on the last part of its journey to the sea, where it spreads out into the Mississippi Delta before emptying into the Gulf of Mexico. Created from the sediment washed down and deposited here by the now slow-moving river, a good deal of the region's shrimp, crab, and crayfish is caught is caught in the Delta. Over the past 5,000 years, the Delta has swollen so that the coastline is now several miles farther out to sea than it once was.

In the evenings, jazz music dominates the streets of the French Quarter in New Orleans.

Saint Paul

Saint Paul's history began with the trappers and missionaries who sought protection in Fort Snelling. In 1841, the same year that a church dedicated to St Paul was built, the settlement, which by then was known as Pig's Eye or Pig's Eye Landing, was renamed Saint Paul. In 1858, Minnesota joined the Union as the 32nd state, with Saint Paul as its capital. It is the second-largest city in Minnesota after its twin town Minneapolis. The Twin Cities did not always coexist as peacefully as they do today; in the past there were frequent conflicts.

An imposing building: the State Capitol of Saint Paul.

The most notable historic building in the city, in addition to the State Capitol building, is the Cathedral of Saint Paul, or more precisely the co-cathedral, as Saint Paul and Minneapolis are joined under one archdiocese. The construction of the church, in French Renaissance style, began in 1904 and was completed in 1917. Chapels are dedicated to patron saints representing the main ethnic groups in the city: Anthony (Italian), John the Baptist (French), Patrick (Irish), Boniface (German), and Cyril and Methodius (Slav). Today, the Fort Snelling State Park stretches out around the restored Fort Snelling down to the banks of the Mississippi, acting as a leisure area and green lung for Saint Paul and and its Twin city Minnneapolis.

The United States of America is a country of highways and cars. But on a Mississippi cruise, it is like stepping back in time to the 19th century. Tourists relax as they watch the countryside drift past and learn about the towns and the people who live there, as the cruise ships make their way sedately downriver.

1 Minneapolis The departure point for the Mississippi cruise is the largest city in the state of Minnesota, which lost its capital city status to its twin city, Saint Paul, in 1858.
Minneapolis is situated near St Anthony Falls, the Mississippi's only waterfall, most of which disappeared during the canalization of the river. If you are interested in culture, you should not miss the Walker Arts Center, which features modern art and particularly impresses its visitors with its extraordinary sculpture garden. The second-largest theater in the USA, the Guthrie Theater, presents many acclaimed productions, from classical literature to new work, but if you want to escape culture for a while, try taking a shopping trip to Bloomington, where one of the country's largest shopping centers, the Mall of America, is located.
There are many lakes in the surrounding area, particularly to the south of the city, including Lake Cedar, Lake Calhoun or Lake Nokomis, or Minnehaha Creek, which connects some of the lakes. It was these lakes that gave the city its nickname City of Lakes.

2 La Crosse La Crosse is located at the point where two rivers, La Crosse and Black River, join the Mississippi. The city, which is in the state of Wisconsin, was founded in the 18th century as a trading post for trappers who sold furs there. Today it is an important economic center with just under 100,000 inhabitants. There are many elevated areas along the river; Grandad Bluff, a scenic viewpoint overlooking the area, is particularly well-known and is also mentioned in Mark Twain's *Life on the Mississippi*. La Crosse is widely known as the City of Beer where brewing is carried out in accordance with German purity laws (concerning standards for the composition of beer), and a big "Oktoberfest" is celebrated each year. If the boat moors at La Crosse for a while, it is worth taking an excursion to see the Effigy Mounds National Monument or Prairie du Chien, both situated about 160 km (100 miles) south of La Crosse.

3 Effigy Mounds National Monument The prehistoric mounds are evidence of the former culture of the forest-

Travel information

Route profile
Length: approx. 3,000 km (1,865 miles)
Duration: around 3–4 weeks
Start: Saint Paul/Minneapolis
End: New Orleans
Itinerary: Minneapolis, La Crosse, Prairie du Chien, Dubuque, Hannibal, St Louis, Memphis, Clarksdale, Vicksburg, Natchez, Baton Rouge, New Orleans

River cruises
The main organizer of Mississippi river cruises is the Majestic America Line
www.majesticamericaline.com
Also: Mississippi River Cruises
www.mississippirivercruises.com
Cruise down the Mississippi between Saint Paul and New Orleans.

Follow in the tracks of Huckleberry Finn, visit plantation houses, Civil War sites, and historic cities, as you take a leisurely trip downriver on one of the beautiful paddle steamers that are so characteristic of the Mississippi.

Travel tips
Smoking is banned in public buildings, stores, and restaurants. The drinking of alcohol is only allowed over the age of 21 and the presentation of a form of identification may be required.

When to go
The best travel seasons are the spring and early summer (April–June), late summer and early fall (September and beginning of October).

Excursion

Madison

James Duane Doty, a former federal judge, founded Madison, the main city of Wisconsin, in an area now known as the Four Lakes Region, in 1836. There are four lakes in this region: Mendota, Monona, Wingra and, a short distance to the south, Waubesa. When Wisconsin joined the Union in 1848, Madison was selected as the capital. The Capitol dominates the inner city. The first state capitol building was completed in 1838 on an isthmus, but the current building dates from 1917 and is only a few feet shorter than the Capitol in Washington DC. The gilded bronze statue called

Inspired by antiquity: the State Capitol in Madison.

"Wisconsin" stands at the very top of the Capitol's granite dome. It is sometimes mistakenly referred to as "Miss Forward" (named after the state's motto, "Forward"). State Street, a lively pedestrian zone with stores and restaurants, starts at the Capitol and leads down to the University of Wisconsin.
Madison is also noted for its association with Frank Lloyd Wright, one of America's most influential architects. Born in Richland Center, in Wisconsin, the Wright family moved to Madison when Frank was still a boy and he spent part of his student days here. He designed Madison's First Unitarian Meeting House, completed in 1951, and Monona Terrace, a convention center, designed in the 1930s but not built until the 1990s.
Art enthusiasts will enjoy the many museums, including the Chazen Museum of Art, belonging to the University of Wisconsin. Children can visit their own museum, the Madison Children's Museum. To end the day in Madison, visit one of the theaters or concert halls in the Overture Center for the Arts.

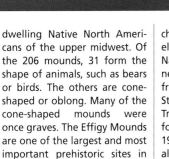

dwelling Native North Americans of the upper midwest. Of the 206 mounds, 31 form the shape of animals, such as bears or birds. The others are cone-shaped or oblong. Many of the cone-shaped mounds were once graves. The Effigy Mounds are one of the largest and most important prehistoric sites in the country.

4 Prairie du Chien The second-oldest city in Wisconsin developed from a 17th-century trading post at the confluence of the Wisconsin and Mississippi rivers. It is named after the chief of the Fox tribe, Alim, which translates as *chien* in French. The first European settlers here were French and so named the site Prarie du Chien (Prairie of the Dog). The Villa Louis was built by art collector Louis Dousman in 1871, the Dousman family having made its money

chiefly in the fur trade. This elegant mansion is now a National Historic Landmark. The nearby Brisbois House dates from 1836 and the Brisbois Store (1852) now houses the Fur Trade Museum. The Fort Crawford Museum includes the fort's 19th-century hospital, which is also a National Historic Landmark.

5 Dubuque Today this town in Iowa, founded by Frenchman Julien Dubuque, is a traffic hub where many highways and railway lines converge. One of the oldest European settlements west of the Mississippi, Dubuque lies at the junction of three states: Iowa, Wisconsin, and Illinois.
Not to be missed is the National Mississippi River Museum & Aquarium. One section is dedicated to the people who relied on the river for their livelihood

and as a source of food; another explores the history of steamboats. In the aquarium, you learn about wildlife living in the Mississippi, such as catfish, sturgeon, stingrays, and alligators. If you wish to view the river from above, you should take a ride up the hill on the Fourth Street Elevator, claimed to be the steepest cable railway in the world. You can also take a walk through the Dubuque Arboretum & Botanical Gardens.
If you are making a longer stopover in Dubuque, you may wish to take an excursion along highways 151 and 18 to Madison, the capital city of Wisconsin (see panel, right).

6 Quincy The next stop is Quincy, a town in western Illinois. It was named in 1825 in recognition of the sixth US president John Quincy Adams, who was born here. There is an open-

air museum on an island in the middle of the Mississippi, Quinsippi Isle, an authentic recreation of a log cabin settlement showing living conditions in the early 18th century. A stroll along Maine Street leads past beautiful houses from Quincy's heyday, the second half of the 19th century. At that time, it was one of the largest towns in Illinois and was an important stopover for escaped slaves on the way to Canada.

1 Minneapolis, together with its twin city Saint Paul, is the first major city along the river on this tour.

2 A view far out across the river at La Crosse, a departure point for popular short steamboat excursions.

3 Bridges over the wide river, like this one at Dubuque, were a huge challenge for engineers.

Mark Twain

Although Mark Twain (Samuel Langhorne Clemens) spent over half his life in the east of the USA, he is remembered as the poet of the Mississippi. He was born in Florida, Missouri in 1835 and spent his childhood in Hannibal, Missouri. Following an apprenticeship as a typesetter, he turned to journalism. From 1857 to 1860 he worked as a steamboat pilot on the Mississippi. This was the origin of his pen name Mark Twain (a term used by steamboat pilots to indicate when the water is two fathoms deep). He used his experiences to describe this time with great insight in his autobiography *Life on the Mississippi.*

Top: Writer Mark Twain.
Bottom: Hannibal characterizes the spirit of Mark Twain.

Following a brief period as a silver miner in the west, he settled in Connecticut in 1871, where he eventually died in 1910. Mark Twain wrote a series of novels and satirical travelogues, but it was the adventures of two scallywags on the Mississippi that made him truly world-famous: *The Adventures of Tom Sawyer* and *The Adventures of Huckleberry Finn.*

7 Hannibal This city in Missouri was founded in 1819, when the first log cabin was built. By 1830, the number of inhabitants had increased to thirty. Hannibal would have remained an inconsequential small town on the banks of the river if Mark Twain had not spent his youth here and had not used it as a location in his stories about Tom Sawyer and Huckleberry Finn. Following in the footsteps of the writer and his heroes is like stepping back into the 19th century. Next door to the house where Mark Twain lived from 1844 to 1853 is a small museum about the life and works of the author. The house where Twain's father worked as a justice of the peace is also open to the public. Another stop on the walk though Hannibal is the house where the girl who inspired Tom Sawyer's beloved Becky Thatcher once lived. Grant's Drugstore-Pilaster House presents a snapshot of life in Hannibal in the 1840s and 50s. To learn more about the life, work, and times of Mark Twain, visit the Interpretive Center and the Museum Gallery.

8 Cahokia Mounds State Historic Site These prehistoric mounds mark the site of what was once the largest American city north of the Aztec settlements in Mexico in pre-Columbian times. Founded in around AD 650, the city reached the height of its importance and development in around 1000 and was abandoned between 1240 and 1400. Archeologists are uncertain as to whether the inhabitants deserted this city because of illness or political unrest. The Native North Americans who built the city raised mounds of earth on which to erect dwellings or to bury the dead. There are approximately one hundred mounds; the chief's residence was built on the highest, which is the largest man-made earthen mound in North America. A video is shown once an hour at the Interpretive Center, explaining the history of the area. Ceramics, stone tools, woodwork, and house construction methods are also displayed at the Center.

The original name of the city is unknown. The modern town of Cahokia is located nearby.

9 St Louis St Louis was founded in 1703 as a missionary base that developed as a French settlement until the Louisiana Purchase of 1803. The town grew prosperous on the success of steamboat travel on the Mississippi, and on the basis of its geographical location as the Gateway to the West, providing a last chance for settlers to stock up on provisions before setting off into the unknown. The year 1904 was an important one for the town, which hosted both a world's fair and the Summer Olympic games.

The town's geographical significance is also evident in its striking architecture. The Gateway Arch, built by Eero Saarinen, is a slender 192-m (630-ft) steel arch. Eads Bridge, which crosses the Mississippi, was the longest arch bridge in the world when it was completed in 1874. It is still used today by cars and trains crossing the river. St Louis also

Elvis Presley

The King of rock 'n' roll was born in 1935 in East Tupelo, Mississippi. After graduating from high school, he worked as a truck driver but recorded a demo acetate in the same year. In the following year he began to attract considerable attention, but his pro-

Graceland, the home of Elvis Presley near Memphis.

has some large churches, such as the Old Cathedral of St Louis, which was constructed in 1834 and is the oldest cathedral west of the Mississippi. Today the new diocesan Cathedral Basilica of Saint Louis is also a bishop's see. Consecrated in 1926, it is a mixture of romantic Byzantine styles and features the world's largest collection of mosaics. Beyond St Louis, the river winds through the countryside in a series of sharp turns.

⑩ New Madrid Situated at the point where the river makes a turn of nearly 360 degrees, known variously the New Madrid Bend, Bessie Bend, or the Kentucky Bend, the town of New Madrid was founded in 1788 by frontiersmen. It lies on the New Madrid Seismic Zone and was shaken by a series of

major earthquakes in 1811–1812. On the site of a former saloon, the New Madrid Historical Museum features Native American artifacts and displays, and many exhibits that record life in the town from the days of the early European settlers. The Higgerson School Historic Site shows how children were educated in the 19th century.

⑪ Memphis Founded in 1819, this town in Tennessee is known to music fans worldwide. Many musicians grew up in this region or began their careers here, including Elvis Presley, Johnny Cash, B.B. King, Aretha Franklin, and "the father of the blues" as W.C. Handy, was often called. He was the composer of the famous "Beale Street Blues" and fans can still wander down this historically significant

street today. However, the main attraction in terms of visitor numbers is Graceland, the preserved home of Elvis Presley. Another place of interest is the Sun Studios (the "birthplace of rock 'n' roll"), where Elvis Presley made his first record; it is also closely connected to Johnny Cash, Roy Orbison, Jerry Lee Lewis, and many others. The National Civil Rights Museum, in the former Lorraine Motel, is an altogether different kind of memorial. It was here that the 39-year-old civil rights activist Martin Luther King Jr was killed by an assassin in 1968.
The next stop is a blues town, Helena, where the King Biscuit Blues Festival takes place once a year. You can make an excursion from here to Clarksdale, which is just a short distance from the Mississippi.

⑫ Clarksdale As befits the official birthplace of the blues, this town has paid tribute to the music genre with its own museum. The Delta Blues Museum is located in an old railway depot. While listening to the (continued p.172)

1 The imposing Gateway Arch, the gateway to the west, soars skyward on the bank of the river in St Louis.

2 The roads in Illinois run for miles through deserted countryside.

3 Memphis is famous for its nightlife and music scene.

4 Parts of the wide Mississippi valley are wildlife protection areas, such as the White River National Wildlife Refuge.

gress was overshadowed by an unsuccessful appearance at the Grand Ole Opry in Nashville. However, Elvis soon became unstoppable and shortly after Bill Haley had helped rock 'n' roll to break though as popular music with "Rock Around the Clock" in 1955, Elvis landed his first number one hit in 1956: "Heartbreak Hotel". His young career was briefly interrupted by military service (1958–1960), after which he made many hit singles and films. When Elvis died in August 1977, millions of fans mourned around the world.

After the introduction of paddle-wheel steamboats, the Mississippi increasingly gained in significance as a transportation route ... until trains and cars took over. Today several steamboats are still employed in river cruises, which are very popular among American tourists and visitors from around the world.

On paddle-wheel steamers such as the *Mississippi Queen*, the *American Queen*, or the *Delta Queen*, which have several decks and luxurious interior decorations, it is possible to escape back to the world of the Old South. They travel along the mighty river and its major tributaries all year round.

1

Mississippi paddle-wheel steamers

The introduction of steamboats revolutionized travel on the Mississippi. Previously, sailing boats (scows) could be used only to travel downstream because of the strong currents. In 1811 the first steamboat, the *New Orleans*,

Steamboats dock at Vicksburg today just as they did 150 years ago.

was launched on the mighty river. The great era of steamboats did not begin, however, until the 1840s. Luxury was common on the boats: chrome lights, carpets, expensive porcelain, precious glass; the passengers must have thought they were in a palace. The boats were also used for freight transportation. Today they are used exclusively for tourism.

sounds of Muddy Waters or John Lee Hooker, you can learn many fascinating facts about the creation and history of the blues through a collection of photographs, musical instruments, and writings.

The Spanish conquistador Hernando de Soto is said to have been the first European to see the Mississippi at a spot not far from Clarksdale. Just past Helena is the White River National Wildlife Refuge, the home of many native wildlife species.

⑬ Vicksburg If you are interested in learning about the American Civil War, you will not want to miss the opportunity of visiting this small town. The Northern states finally gained control of the Mississippi region in the Battle of Vicksburg on July 4, 1863. However, Vicksburg is still highly regarded today among the Southern states, as it surrendered only after a 47-day siege conducted by the troops of General Ullysses S. Grant. The Vicksburg National Military Park, established in 1899, is a memorial to

the events of 1863. Among other military attractions is an iron-clad gunboat that was previously owned by the Union, the USS *Cairo*. Other tourist attractions in Vicksburg include the Catfish Row Art Park, which presents art from the local area. It was in Vicksburg that a local confectioner discovered the recipe for the popular drink Coca-Cola.

⑭ Natchez Natchez is famous for its spectacular houses from the pre-Civil War period, in particular the Melrose Plantation. In its heyday, Natchez was one of the richest towns in the USA. Today its importance has somewhat diminished, but it still acts

as a landing stage for Mississippi steamboats and boasts a row of pleasant restaurants with terraces and a view of the river. You can make an excursion to the Rosemount Plantation in Woodsville from here (see panel, right).

⑮ Baton Rouge The second-largest city in Louisiana, until New Orleans was abandoned by so many of its inhabitants after the havoc wreaked by Hurricane Katrina, Louisiana's capital city has two capitol buildings. The old state capitol was built in the 19th century in the style of a neo-Gothic medieval castle and now serves as a museum, while the new

32-floor building dates from 1932 and was constructed by the controversial Governor Huey Pierce Long. The main employers in Baton Rouge are the huge oil refineries that unfortunately dominate large parts of the cityscape, mainly located along the banks of the Mississippi.

(continued p.174)

1 The Mississippi Trace Bridge near Natchez, leading to Louisiana, is a work of art made of steel.

2 The replica paddle-wheel steamboat *Lady Luck Natchez*, permanently anchored in the river, has been used as a casino for many years.

Excursion

Plantation Houses

The plantation houses epitomize the romanticism associated with the south. This is in part due to two people who did much to define the concept of the "The Old South" for literature and film enthusiasts all over the world: the author Margaret Mitchell with her novel *Gone with the Wind*, and Hollywood producer David O. Selznick, who made the novel into a film; it became one of the all-time great successes of cinematic history.

These elegant houses, with long porches supported by columns, stand resplendent in white at the ends of tree-lined avenues; inside there are polished parquet flooring, thick carpets, glowing chandeliers, and precious porcelain on exquisite tables. It is easy to allow your imagination to run away with you and to conjure up images of Scarlett O'Hara and Rhett Butler on the porch.

In the American south, these great mansions are often referred to as antebellum houses. Meaning houses that date from before the Civil War, this is a term that derives from Latin; "before" translates as *ante* and

"war" as *bellum*. On the other hand, the reconstruction period after the War is sometimes known as *postbellum*. As many owners of these houses made their fortune with the help of slaves, decline set in at the end of the war and particularly after the Emancipation Proclamation, which decreed that all slaves were to be set free from January 1, 1863. In 1865, Congress ratified the Thirteenth Amendment to the Constitution of the United States.

Famous houses that are open to the public for most of the year include Rosemont Plantation, Houmas House Plantation, and, perhaps the most famous of them all, Oak Alley Plantation. Rosemont Plantation is in Woodsville, Mississippi. Jefferson Davis, President of the Confederacy during the Civil War, spent his childhood and early adulthood here. The building is fairly simple in comparison to other plantation houses, but it was built at a time (1810) when the Mississippi still marked the boundary of available land. The house is still authentically furnished today and also displays Jefferson

Davis memorabilia. Some houses that are privately owned are also open to the public occasionally, while others have been converted into hotels or restaurants.

The Houmas House Plantation is in Louisiana. The mansion was built between 1810 and 1840. It is a typical example of the Greek-revival style in radiant white with a spectacular portico. Houmas House is surrounded by magnificent, extensive gardens with seating areas where you can relax and enjoy the scents and beauty of the subtropical vegetation with its year-round growing season.

The Oak Alley Plantation Mansion in Louisiana is likely to fit the image many people have of a plantation house very well. It is partly famous for its impressive setting at the end of an avenue of Oak Trees (hence the name). Surrounded by a colonnade of twenty-eight pillars, it was built in 1841. It was initially called Bon Séjour but visitors soon began to refer to it as Oak Alley and the name stuck.

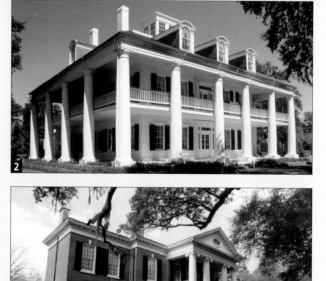

1 The old oak trees of the Oak Alley Plantation appear to form a guard of honor for arriving guests.

2 Houmas House Plantation is a mansion built in the Greek-revival

style, surrounded with balconies supported by imposing pillars.

3 Not all Plantation Houses are a glowing white: Rosalie Mansion is a brick building.

New Orleans: French Quarter

Founded in 1718, the French Quarter (*Vieux Carré* in French) is the district around which the city of New Orleans grew up. It was under Spanish control for some time, and the Spanish influence is evident in the patios, courtyards, and ornate wrought-iron balconies. The golden age of the French Quarter was in the first half of the 19th century, when steamboats brought many visitors to the town. The Civil War and the postwar period led to a decline, but a second golden age was just around the corner with the birth of jazz in nearby Storyville. Many jazz bars began to open their doors to great musicians such as Louis Armstrong and Jelly Roll Morton. Writers also paid tribute to the French

Where night becomes day: the French Quarter in New Orleans.

Quarter, including Tennessee Williams, William Faulkner, Sherwood Anderson, and Truman Capote.

There are many places of interest well worth a visit; its historic buildings have been protected by law since the 1920s. The Old Ursuline Convent, built in 1752, is the oldest building in the Mississippi Delta. St Louis Cathedral was given its cathedral status in 1794, but its current appearance is largely due to the extensive renovation work of 1850. The baroque main altar and the ceiling fresco are well worth seeing. The Cabildo, next to the cathedral, was built to house the Spanish colonial government. Nowadays the building is home to a Mardi Gras museum. A visit to the Jazz Museum in the Old Mint is a must for jazz fans.

The atmosphere of the French Quarter is particularly potent in the evenings when you can stroll from bar to bar, enjoying the sounds of jazz, cajun, zydeco, gospel, soul, and rock.

16 **New Orleans** Until August 29, 2005 and the disastrous Hurricane Katrina, New Orleans was the most highly populated city in Louisiana. No population figures are currently available, as no one knows exactly how many former residents will return once the city has been rebuilt. However, life goes on: Mardi Gras was celebrated in 2006 to show that spirits remain high. Frenchman Jean-Baptiste de Bienville founded the city in 1718 as Nouvelle Orléans. The city changed hands many times: the Spanish took over from the French and then the French returned. It was finally passed to the USA in 1803 as part of the Louisiana Purchase, when a vast swathe of land was purchased from the French.

In 1884 a world's fair, the World Cotton Centennial, was held in New Orleans. It was the hundredth anniversary of the first shipment of cotton from America to England in 1784. By the end of the 19th century, nearly one third of all the cotton produced in the United States passed through New Orleans, also home to the Cotton Exchange.

In the early 20th century, further sections of the land between the Mississippi and Lake Pontchartrain were drained, allowing the city to extend to low-lying ground. Subsequent subsidence during the decades that followed resulted in some of the land lying below sea level, leaving it even more vulnerable to flooding should the levees be breached. However, rebuilding and reconstruction are in full swing, and much of the city will no doubt soon be returned to its former glory.

The Mississippi steamboat cruises end in New Orleans. If you wish to enjoy more of the atmosphere of the Old South, you should visit the Houmas House Plantation and Oak Alley Plantation (see previous page) or head for Lafayette. Jean Mouton founded the town in 1921 as Vermilionville. The town's modern name originates from the Marquis de Lafayette, a hero of the American War of Independence. The culture of the Cajuns dominates the region around Lafayette. These were the successors of the Franco-Canadians who were driven out by the British during the 18th century and moved to Louisiana. Their music, celebrated at many festivals, and the famous cuisine attract many visitors.

1 In the Delta, the Mississippi stretches in all directions, adding to the land mass by depositing silt.

2 Large ships find their way into the port of New Orleans, which was the USA's second most important port before Hurricane Katrina struck.

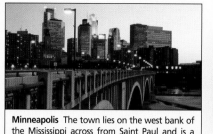

Minneapolis The town lies on the west bank of the Mississippi across from Saint Paul and is a lively economic and industrial center with skyscrapers dominating the skyline.

St Louis The town looks back on a long history as a gateway to the unexplored west, symbolized by the Gateway Arch, designed by the Finnish architect Eero Saarinen. It was built between 1961 and 1966 on the shores of the Mississippi.

White River The National Wildlife Refuge was established in 1935, mainly for the protection of migratory birds. Endangered species of birds and a large variety of mammals, reptiles, and fish inhabit the region, which has many lakes, rivers, and bayous.

Mardi Gras Fat Tuesday is celebrated in wild style in multicultural New Orleans with spectacular parades, bright costumes, and plenty of music. How could it be otherwise in the birthplace of jazz? The celebrations last for two weeks.

Natchez The city's name has its origins in Native North American culture. However, the European settlers also have a long history here, which is closely connected to the Old South. "Antebellum" tours take you to the old mansions that survived the Civil War of the 19th century.

New Orleans The city on the banks of the Mississippi was founded by the French in 1718. The French influence is still evident today in the houses of the French Quarter and in the Cajun culture. The motto here is: *Laissez les bons temps rouler*, Let the good times roll!

Saint Paul Home to the Minnesota State Capitol. It forms the Twin Cities with Minneapolis.

La Crosse The Mississippi viewed from above at La Crosse. Even at the headwaters, the Mississippi is a formidable river, large enough for steamboats.

Dubuque A museum dedicated to the Mississippi explains everything you could want to know about the river, from its natural habitat to its navigation and regulation. The nearby lock has an excellent view over the river.

Memphis This city has Elvis Presley to thank for its fame, with the nearby Graceland estate drawing millions of visitors every year. Many soul and blues stars began their careers in the clubs that line the city's streets.

Vicksburg In 1863, the decisive battle of the Civil War took place here, during which the Southern states were finally defeated. You can visit a museum at the National Military Park and visit the historic battle site accompanied by expert tour guides.

Oak Alley Plantation A view of a bedroom of one of the most spectacular and well-preserved mansions shows how luxuriously and comfortably the masters of large plantations once lived.

Map labels:
Duluth, Hinckley, Fargo, St.Cloud, Minneapolis, St.Paul, River Falls, Eau Claire, Crystal Cave, Minnesota, Mankato, Red Wing, Necedah, Winona, La Crosse, Rochester, Albert Lea, La Crescent, Wisconsin, Sioux Falls, Effigy Mounds N.M., Kickapoo Ind.Caverns, Madison, Des Moines, Iowa, Prairie Du Chien, Dodgeville, Milwaukee, Cedar Falls, Dubuque, Rockford, Cedar Rapids, Crystal Lake Cave, Chicago, Des Moines, Davenport, Dixon, Moline, Bishop Hill S.H.S., Gary, Ottumwa, Burlington, Galesburg, Peoria, Bentonsport, Havana, Bloomington, Keokuk, Lincoln's New Salem S.H.S., Lancaster, Hamilton, Quincy, Springfield, Hannibal, Jacksonville, Mark Twain Birthplace S.H.S., Bowling Green, Illinois, Paris, Alton, Indianapolis, Kansas City, Columbia, Effingham, Cahokia Mounds S.H.S., Missouri, Mount Vernon, Louisville, St.Louis, Ft.de Chartres S.H.S., Jefferson City, Ste.Genevieve, Ft.Kaskaskia S.H.S., Shawneetown S.H.S., Springfield, Kentucky, Ohio, Ft.Davidson S.H.S., Fredericktown, Cape Girardeau, Paducah, Lexington, Nashville, Poplar Bluff, New Madrid, Land Between The Lakes, Paris, Dyersburg, Caruthersville, Jonesboro, Tennessee, Nashville, Arkansas, Brownsville, Oklahoma City, Marion, MEMPHIS, Brinkley, Tupelo, Dallas, Little Rock, Helena, Tunica, Pine Bluff, White River N.W.R., Clarksdale, Cleveland, Winona, Arkansas Post N.M., Lake Village, Greenville, Hamburg, Mississippi, Monroe, Vicksburg, Tuscaloosa, Dallas, Ruins of Windsor, Winnfield, Rosswood Plantation, Shreveport, Natchez, McComb, Tuscaloosa, Rosemont Plantation, Alexandria, St.Francisville, Mobile, Louisiana, Baton Rouge, Biloxi, Lafayette, New Orleans, Houston, Houmas House Plantation, Oak Alley Plantation, Morgan City, Grand Isle, Venice, Port Fourchon, Mississippi Delta

Imposing large yachts in Sir Francis Drake Channel of the British Virgin Islands.

Lesser Antilles

Caribbean cruise: from Puerto Rico to Grenada

Just the name "Caribbean" makes you think of paradise and the sun-blessed islands of the Lesser Antilles don't disappoint with their dazzling sandy beaches, palm trees swaying in the trade winds, lush rainforests, mighty volcanoes, crystal-clear waters, coral reefs, and rich mix of cultures. The music, art, cuisine, and religions of Europe, Africa, America, and Asia all come together here in a heady combination.

On 15th-century maps predating the voyages of Christopher Columbus the long chain of islands to the north of Colombia and Venezuela are called the Antilia Insula. Situated between the South and North American continents and dividing the Caribbean Sea and the Atlantic Ocean, the islands include both the Lesser and Greater Antilles, covering a total area of 236,507 km (146,965 miles). Heading from west to east, the Greater Antilles includes Cuba, Jamaica, Haiti, the Dominican Republic, and Puerto Rico, where our cruise begins. There are over a hundred populated Lesser Antilles islands, ranging from the Virgin Islands in the north to the ABC Islands (Aruba, Bonaire, and Curaçao) near the South American mainland. Depending on their location in relation to the prevailing trade winds that blow east to west, the islands are subdivided into the Windward Islands and Leeward Islands near the South American mainland.

Tobago: Fresh crayfish in the grill.

The Windward Islands were so called because they were situated more windward in relation to ships arriving from the American continent (the prevailing wind came from the side), while the Leeward Islands were in the lee, or downwind, of the prevailing wind.

The Lesser Antilles region is a tropical paradise. The climate remains the same all year round, with average temperatures of 26–30°C (79–86°F) on the coasts. The peak season for the many cruises around this part of the world is from December to April, when the weather is a little cooler and drier. Tourists also avoid the dangerous hurricane season. The shape of the islands and their volcanoes, many of which are still active, is indicative of their position along the boundary of the Caribbean and American tectonic plates.

British Virgin Islands: One of the most beautiful coves in the world is Deadman's Bay on Peter Island, with its long stretch of snow-white sandy beach lined with palm trees.

Cruise ships are a familiar sight in the port of Fort-de-France in Martinique.

But what would the Caribbean be without the appeal and openness of its hospitable inhabitants? The lively mix of people who now live on the islands has developed over many years. The original inhabitants, Carib Amerindians, died out long ago. The European colonizers brought Africans to work on the plantations as slaves. When slavery was abolished at the beginning of the 19th century, workers from Asia also arrived. This created a combination of cultural influences that has nowadays also succumbed to the both the cultural and economic influence of the nearby USA. The islands' languages and dialects, music, art, regional cuisine, and religious beliefs are very diverse.

The gorgeous tropical backdrop, with sun and sea, and the islands' unique atmosphere have all made the Caribbean a top location for the best and most beautiful cruises in the world. A new day means a new island. Cruise passengers aren't limited to life on board, they can also take excursions to the island towns for shopping or sightseeing, or book a tour of the island, go swimming or diving, or can stopover on land (usually in an exclusive hotel). Or they can head for shore independently and find a taxi or one of the local tour guides that are to be found in every port, or plan their own route with a hire car.

The eight sovereign states of Lesser Antilles are: Antigua and Barbuda (Leeward Islands in the north), St Kitts and Nevis, Dominica, St Lucia, Barbados, St Vincent and the Grenadines, Grenada, and Trinidad and Tobago (in the south near Venezuela).

Everyday life in Grenada shows the contrasts in Caribbean culture.

Many Caribbean tours begin in Miami or Lauderdale. An ideal starting point for island-hopping around the Lesser Antilles is the port of San Juan in Puerto Rico, where pelicans fly overhead and luxury sea liners berth. The final destination for the cruise is Grenada.

❶ Puerto Rico The easternmost island of the Greater Antilles was the final bastion of the Spanish in the Caribbean before it was taken over by the USA in 1989. In 1950, the island's inhabitants took part in a referendum to establish whether they would prefer to remain an American colony or become an autonomous US territory. Three-quarters of the population voted for autonomy. Despite the fact that Spanish is the main language, the economy is strongly influenced by the USA. San Juan is one of the largest metropolises in the Caribbean, with over three million inhabitants. Broad streets and high-rise buildings in the new part of town are reminiscent of American skylines.

Before the cruise departs from the port, the picturesque old town of San Juan, with its narrow alleyways and old houses with beautiful wooden balconies, is a must-see. The huge defense fortifications, including the Castillo de San Felipe del Morro, the Fuerte San Cristóbal, and La Fortaleza, are all under the protection of UNESCO. They typify the character of the city and port. Since 1822, La Fortaleza has been used as the headquarters for the Governor

of Puerto Rico and is therefore the oldest government building in the western hemisphere to have been in constant use.

If you do not wish to explore the old Spanish colonial town, you may like to visit Luquillo, a mile of golden beach at the easternmost point of the island, or the Bacardi Rum Distillery and adjoining museum right by the gates to the city.

❷ American Virgin Islands To the east of Puerto Rico and the adjacent Virgin Passage is the series of islands that make up the Virgin Islands. You will head for St Thomas and the port of

Travel information

Route profile
Length: 750 nautical miles (1,389 km/863 miles)
Duration: 10–14 days
Start: San Juan/Puerto Rico
End: St George's/Grenada
Itinerary (main locations): San Juan, Charlotte Amalie, Basseterre, St John's, Point-à-Pitre, Roseau, Fort-de-France, Castries, Bridgetown, St George's

Cruises
There are a number of cruise companies including:

Royal Caribbean Cruises
Tel: 1-888-313-8883 (toll free)
1-727-906-0444 (international)
www.royalcarib.com

Tourist information
www.geographia.com
www.caribbean-on-line.com
www.islandcruises.com
www.onecaribbean.org

Music of the Caribbean

No matter which of the Caribbean islands you find yourself in, you will immediately fall under the spell of the captivating rhythmic music. The infectious calypso, the beat of the steel drums, the cool, relaxed, chugging rhythms of reggae: few people can keep their feet still when the music starts here. Bob Marley's *Soulful Town, Soulful People* can be heard far beyond Jamaica.

The music of the Caribbean is more diverse than almost anywhere else in the world and people are highly creative, making instruments from everything from oil drums and hubcaps to bamboo stalks. The music varies from island to island: Reggae originated in

Above: The steel drum band "The Sulphur Stars" plays in Soufrière, St Lucia.

Below: Steel drums also provide the right atmosphere on the British Virgin Islands.

Jamaica, Soca or Soul-Calypso in Trinidad, Salsa is from Puerto Rico and Cuba, Merengue is the rhythm of the Dominican Republic, Compas is Haiti's pop music, and Zouk originated on the French islands of Guadaloupe and Martinique, but it is the steel bands (known locally as pans) that everyone identifies with the Caribbean. A visit to a pan yard concert is therefore be a must on your travel itinerary.

Charlotte Amalie, landing at the West Indian Company Dock with other cruise ships. The island began to flourish in the 17th century when the Danish West India Company operated a commercial settlement here. It offers excellent views of Margins Bay and the port. The ample shopping for tourists on Main Street, together with a visit to Fort Christian, which also houses the Virgin Island Museum, are both highly recommended.

The adjacent island St John, of which two thirds forms a national park, and the former sugar cane island of Saint Croix

can be seen from a distance. Farther to the east are the British Virgin Islands.

③ British Virgin Islands The islands jut out of the turquoise-blue Caribbean Sea in a series of green forested peaks, the tops of an underwater chain of volcanoes. The two largest islands are Tortola and Virgin Gorda, where only medium-sized cruise ships can dock. Tortola is named after the turtles, of which there are almost 15,000 on this island. The British Virgin Islands are considerably more peaceful than the lively US islands. People spending their vacation

here will stay in one of the attractive beach hotels. The conditions for diving are excellent. The islands are best explored by ferry, or chartered yacht if you can sail. The route now heads for Anguilla.

④ Anguilla It was the Spanish who first discovered the group of small islands in the English-speaking Leeward Islands, including the main island of Anguilla that gives its name to this small group. They did not stay long however, as they found the landscape too flat and dry, but the islands kept
(continued p.182)

1 The fortress of Castillo de San Felipe del Morro, located at the entrance to the port of Puerto Rico's capital city San Juan and surrounded by the sea, was built when the Spanish settled on the island.

2 Luquillo Beach in Puerto Rico is considered to be one of the most beautiful in the world.

3 British Virgin Islands: Rocks on the Virgin Gorda shore.

4 An historic sugar mill is a reminder of the "white gold" era in the Virgin Islands.

5 Anguilla: Work Boat Regatta.

Sheltered bays with crystal-clear water, offshore coral reefs, white sandy beaches with coconut palms, and mountainous inland areas with dense tropical forests characterize the Virgin Islands east of Puerto Rico. The island of St John is part of the American Virgin Islands. Together with Hassel Island, the majority of these

volcanic islands, form the Virgin Islands National Park, which was established in 1956. This protected area provides a habitat for over a hundred species of bird,

Frigate birds

During the mating season, from August to November, the male frigate bird inflates its scarlet red throat pouch in a display to attract females. The bird simultaneously flaps its wings, making a rhythmic drumming sound.

Magnificent frigate birds inflate their throat pouch as part of their mating ceremony.

If the display is successful, the pair will build a nest and wait for their small white chicks to hatch.
Barbuda has the largest nesting colony in the Caribbean. You can learn about them at the Frigate Bird Sanctuary in Barbuda in the Codrington Lagoon, which can only be visited by boat (tickets can be bought at the wharf). Over 2,500 pairs of birds nest in the area. The birds can also be seen at the Frigate Island Nature Reserve on St Lucia.

their original Spanish name (meaning "eel") referring to the shape of the islands.

⑤ St Kitts and Nevis Nevis Peak (985 m/3,232 ft) is a dormant volcano (the last eruption was in prehistoric times) often enveloped in fog, assumed to be *neive* (snow) by Columbus during his voyage, hence the origin of the island's name. Covered in tropical rainforest, the main island, St Kitts, is made up of three mountain ranges. A circular road provides access around the island. The central town of Basseterre, originally founded by the French, was built in the British style. The main square, featuring a photogenic Victorian clock tower, has an easygoing atmosphere.

The route passes through sugar cane fields to Old Road Town, the former capital city of the island, and to the Brimstone Hill Fort with its excellent views. It then follows the shoreline with its numerous hotels. You can reach nearby Nevis, with its mighty lava cone, by boat through The Narrows, a canal about 3 km (2 miles) wide.

⑥ Antigua It is only a short journey to tropical Antigua and the adjacent island of Barbuda. Most of the sugar cane fields have now been abandoned, but the sugar mills, of which there are over two hundred, are a reminder of the past when African slaves worked the fields here in terrible conditions. Due to its sheltered port and

suitable position, the British developed Antigua into one of their most important bases in the Lesser Antilles. The numerous forts and military bases, including Fort James and Fort Barrington, are a reminder of the former economic and strategic significance of the island. At the pier, you find yourself in the typical Caribbean port town of St John's, dominated by its beautiful cathedral with twin towers. You can walk to the many little stores, businesses, bars, and restaurants at Heritage Quay and Redcliffe Quay, eventually arriving at the Museum of Antigua and Barbuda, which explores the history of the island. There are excursions around the island, to Nelson's

Dockyard National Park or Betty's Hope, the oldest plantation on the island, which, for the past fifty years, has been open to tourists. The visitor center explains how sugar was processed and gives an interesting insight into the life and work of the slaves.
Visitors who have the time to stop at Barbuda around 45 km (28 miles) away, will find a large coral atoll and a true paradise for nature lovers with many rare species, including types of lizard, turtles, and birds. A large colony of frigate birds, one of the most interesting species of tropical bird, nest in Codrington Laguna (see panel, right). Passing by Montserrat, the cruise moves on to the next destination, Guadeloupe.

7 Guadeloupe The ship sails overnight and by dawn the largest island of the Lesser Antilles should be looming on the horizon, just as Columbus perhaps once first saw it. He named it Santa María de Guadalupe de Extremadura, after an icon of the Virgin Mary worshipped at a Spanish monastery in Guadalupe, in Extremadura, Spain.

The French took possession of the island in 1635, but it was subsequently seized by the British several times during the ensuing centuries, passing back and forth between the two countries. In 1815 it was acknowledged to be under French control in the Treaty of Vienna and is now an overseas department of France (*départements*

d'outre-mer). As part of France, Guadaloupe is also part of the European Union and the currency is the Euro.

Evidence of its French history and cultural influence are everywhere. French cars dominate the streets, the *tricoleur* waves in the gentle breeze, the police are typical gendarmes, and people chat nonchalantly in cafés and shop in boutiques with a French ambience selling international products. However, the islanders do add a touch of their own lively Caribbean-Creole culture too. When sugar cane was introduced to the area in the late 17th century, it marked the beginning of the islands' great "white gold" era in vast plantations worked by slaves. Slavery

was eventually abolished in 1848 and day-wage workers from India were hired. They left behind a Hindu temple. But things are changing. The distillation plants are now antiquated and rum production is declining. Sugar cane is gradually being replaced by other crops: bananas are now the most important, along with other tropical fruit, vegetables, and flowers.

Guadaloupe comprises five islands, including the two main islands of Basse Terre and Grande-Terre, which are connected by a bridge crossing the Rivière Salée. The butterfly

1 St Kitts and Nevis: A trip to the volcano Nevis Peak on the island of Nevis.

2 At the Antigua Sailing Week.

3 Falmouth Harbour in Antigua.

4 Guadeloupe: View of the densely overgrown mountains Les Mamelles on Basse-Terre.

5 View of the Caribbean from Dickson Bay in Antigua.

6 An alleyway in Basseterre, the main city on the island of St Kitts.

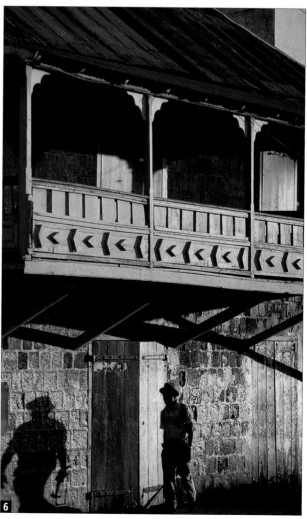

Cockfighting

Cockfighting is as much a tradition on many Caribbean islands as bullfighting in Spain and Portugal. In Puerto Rico, the Dominican Republic, Martinique, and Guadeloupe, it is a national sport. Newspapers give detailed reports of the fights, which often involve high-stake betting. On some islands cockfighting tours are even available for the tourists. The spectacle is not to everyone's taste however, and is best avoided if you are likely to find it upsetting, though the days when the birds would fight to the death are long over. Nowadays, a referee decides

Above and below: Cockfighting in Guadeloupe, Basse Terre.

which bird has won if one can no longer fight or is badly injured. The rules also make sure that the competition is fair. Only cocks of the same weight face each other in the arena. During the fight, which lasts around five to ten minutes, there is a frenzy of activity in the arena, and a great deal of noise from the audience, as people call for the bird they have backed in the betting.

shape of the island's outline is striking. Grande-Terre is smaller and flatter, while Basse Terre has more mountainous terrain, including the 1,467-m (4,813-ft) volcano La Soufrière.

Cruise ships dock at Point-à-Pitre. If you go ashore, you can explore the lively capital city of the island and its Creole markets, such as the Marché Couvert, and the shops along Rue Frébault and in the port area.

Don't miss the opportunity to sample some Creole dishes before taking an excursion on the well-constructed N1 to the rainforest, with its unique vegetation and beautiful waterfalls, finally arriving at La Soufrière, known affectionately as the Old Lady. In 1975, people had to be evacuated from the surrounding area when La Soufrière became active. There is not normally enough time on a cruise

Spreading out from the foot of the still-active volcano Morne Trois Pitons (1,342 m/4,403 ft), the national park that took its name, combines rich tropical forest with volcanic formations, and was established in 1975. Some fifty fumaroles, hot springs and bubbling mud pools, and five active volcanic craters ensure the smell of sulfur pervades the air. Among the jagged crags and peaks, ravines and gorges covered with dense vegetation provide a habitat for many animal and plant species. The park was designated a World Heritage Site by UNESCO in 1997.

Several natural vegetation zones can be identified in the park. Elfin woodland grows at the highest elevation (over 915 m/3,000 ft); shrubs, moss, ferns, and some palms grown here. Montane thicket is dominated by spindly trees of up to 15m (50 ft) in

Above: A small pool glows green.
Middle: Waterfall at the Emerald Pool, in the Morne Trois Pitons National Park.
Below: Iguanas have made the Lesser Antilles their home.

to make it to the top of the volcano, and the peak is often encased in mist so views are not guaranteed.

In the recent past catastrophic hurricanes have had a more devastating effect on the island than the volcano, including Hurricane Ines in 1966, David in 1979, and the tail ends of Frederic and Hugo in 1989.

⑧ Dominica The third-largest island in Lesser Antigua is a short journey away. Cruise ships anchor in the port of the island's capital city Roseau to enable their passengers to disembark and explore the island. The island is full of unspoiled natural beauty: mountainous terrain covered with untouched rainforest, and hot springs with their sulfurous vapor, and the "Boiling Lake" are evidence of the geo-thermal activity taking place just below ground. Farther on is the Morne Trois Pitons National Park (see panel, right), covering around 6,800 ha (16,803 acres), and then the

Northern Forest Reserve, home of endangered Sisserou and Jacquot parrots. The diverse flora of the rainforest includes a rare display of over fifty types of orchid and a variety of ferns. Over three hundred waterfalls and rivers are fed by heavy downpours of rain in late summer, brought about by the incessant north-east trade wind. The island's economy depends on mainly tourism and agriculture.

⑨ Martinique Like Guadaloupe, Martinique is a French island. It combines magical tropical scenery with a Creole atmosphere, and the *je ne sais quoi* of the French way of life. The island's previously peaceful volcano giant, Mont Pelée, erupted on May 8, 1902, killing the entire population of 30,000 people living in the island's former capital St Pierre, except for a single survivor who was serving time in prison. Today, Fort-de-France is the lively capital of the island. Taking a stroll through the

streets of the town, you will see colonial-style houses decorated with ornate wrought-iron work. A short excursion will take you through the capital city's suburbs, past the Sacré-Cœur church, built in the style of the original in Paris, to enjoy fine views over the town and the bay. Farther on you can see the volcanic mountain range and the town of St Pierre. Once known as the Paris of the Antilles, it is now little more than a tourist destination. A charming way to visit it is the by the Cyparis-Express tourist train, which takes in

1 Surf at Pointe des Chateaux in Guadeloupe.

2 Guadeloupe: The small colonial museum in the old town of Point-à-Pitre displays exhibits from the time when plantations formed a major part of the economy here.

3 St Pierre in Martinique was a lively colonial town until Mont Pelée erupted in 1902.

height. The trees of the Montane rainforest (above 610 m/2,000 ft) are home to mosses, lichens, orchids, and bromeliads. Mature rainforest (below 460 m/1,500 ft) has the most luxuriant vegetation, with trees averaging 30 m (100 ft) in height. Due to the thick tree canopy, there is only sparse growth at ground level. Finally, the lowest zone is characterized by trees, ariods, orchids, ferns, and a variety of vines.

Caribbean flowers

Many Caribbean islands are covered in thick rainforest. The nutrient-rich volcanic soil also provides ideal conditions to support a wide variety and density of plants. Since there is no natural downtime (no winter dormant period) trees lose their leaves at different times of the year and the forest is always green. The same applies to fruit and flowers, which ripen and bloom at different times.

The botanical garden of St Lucia shows some of the diversity of Caribbean flora.

A myriad of ferns, lichens, and mosses flourish under the thick leafy canopy. Bright orchids and bromeliads use trees as host plants. Take a walk through the forest and you can also see ginger, nutmeg, and cinnamon trees, and glowing yellow or pink mimosas.

The rainforest in Puerto Rico, part of the nature reserve of Sierra de Luquillo, is particularly recommended due to its accessibility via a network of roads and paths. But if you can't venture into the rainforest on your trip, many islands have botanical gardens that provide a good insight into the richness and diversity of the tropical forest.

all the main sights; the small Musée Vulcanologique is also worth visiting. The painter Paul Gauguin lived nearby in Anse Turin for several months. You can learn more about his stay here in the Musée Gauguin. The best beach on the island, Grande Anse des Salines, is also here. On your way out, via the Baie de Fort-de-France and the Baie des Flamands, you can tour the grounds of the 17th-century Fort-St-Louis.

🔟 **St Lucia** "The Helen of the West Indies" is how both the French and the British affectionately refer to the island of St Lucia. Both countries have contributed significantly to the island's history, as its control has passed back and forth between them least fourteen times, until the island was finally handed over to Great Britain in 1815 in the Treaty of Paris. Since 1979, St Lucia has been independent but remains a member of the Commonwealth. Bright red British telephone boxes and French place names, the Creole language, also spoken on Martinique, and of course the Creole cuisine and French architectural influences all reflect the island's cosmopolitan past.

When approaching the island and port, two prominent landmarks, the volcanoes Gros Piton and Petit Piton, surrounded by tropical green mountain forests, dominate the land-

scape. The island's capital city Castries contains little else of real interest other than the usual souvenir stores, so a trip around the island is far more worthwhile. Not far from the town of Soufrière are the two Piton volcanoes and the rainforest. If you are interested in seeing the beautiful beaches and hotel district, you can take a taxi to the north-west side of the island and visit Choc Bay and Rodney Bay.

🔟🔺 **Barbados** The next stop on your journey, Barbados, is the easternmost Caribbean island, around 4,500 km (2,796 miles) from the African coast.

It was discovered by a Portuguese sea captain, Pedro a Campos, who was caught up in a storm in 1536 and became stranded on the island. The relatively flat and sparse landscape (at least three-quarters of the land consists of a plateau of coral-reef limestone) was of little interest to the Portuguese, who moved on and left the island to be taken over by the British in 1625.

Barbados was made independent in 1966, although many reminders of the island's colonial history still remain. Except for the climate and landscape, you could easily think you were in Britain: cars drive on the left,

the government and constitution are based on the British model, people play cricket and golf, and many take tea at five in the afternoon. The origins of the island's name are unclear. It is possible, however, that the imposing bearded fig trees, with aerial roots hanging down like beards, have something to do with it.

The lively island capital, Bridgetown, with a population of over 100,000, is one of the Caribbean's major economic centers. Fishing boats and pleasurecraft are moored at the Careenage, a small, lively port with a shipyard, a variety of stores, restaurants, bars, and

Agricultural crops grown in the Caribbean include sugar cane, tobacco, cocoa, sisal, coffee, cotton, spices, citrus fruits, and also bananas (*Musa sapientium*), which were brought over from the Canary Islands by settlers. Banana plants grow almost everywhere and have become an important crop for the farmers of the French Antilles. They are sold in most markets in the Caribbean, but there is a great deal of competition in the global market, from India, Africa, Asia and South America, with trading agreements and treaties dictating export to a degree.

Banana plants generally reach a height of around 6–8 m (20–26 ft). Growing up to 3.5 m (11 ft) in length and 50 cm (1½ ft) in width, their leaves are huge. Up to 150 bananas can grow on one

⑫ St Vincent and the Grenadines The small island nation of St Vincent and the Grenadines comprising over 700 islands, coral atolls, and flat sandbanks provides a real paradise for sailors. Winds sweep steadily and constantly across these sunny Caribbean islands. Life on St Vincent, the largest island in the group, is overshadowed by the volcano Soufrière (which should not be confused with La Soufrière in Guadaloupe), which last erupted in 1979 and threatened to envelop the island inhabitants and adjacent islands in a huge cloud of ash. Fortunately due to the advance warning there were no casualties.

Those wishing to spend their vacation in the Grenadines will find a variety of luxury hotels providing all creature comforts and excellent conditions for diving. There are excursions available between the islands on the island-hopper airplanes and on various boats, or you can charter a yacht yourself.

Scenes from a banana harvest on a plantation in St Lucia.

cafés. Only a short walk away is the National Heroes Square, which was known as Trafalgar Square until only a few years ago. The parliamentary buildings constructed of coral stone are located here, as well as the statue of Lord Nelson, who was stationed on the island in his younger years. The memorial was erected here some thirty years after its famous counterpart in London.

After shopping in Broad Street, take a trip around the island in a Mini Moke, an open-top vehicle similar to a jeep, but smaller. Barbados is incidentally one of the most densely populated parts of the world with over 620 inhabitants per square kilometer (239 per square mile). The excursion will take you past sugar cane plantations and miles of banana plantations before finally arriving at the stormy east coast of the island. The Atlantic Ocean batters the coast here with huge waves, challenging those surfers who dare to ride the terrifying waves that can reach heights of 12 meters (39 ft). Make sure you include a stop at the beautiful gardens and mansions of the former plantation owners. Many island tours include the present-day luxury hotel Sam Lord's Castle, a typical mansion. Britain's Queen Elizabeth II stays here when she visits the island. It is a good spot to take a break and enjoy a refreshing rum punch.

If the experts are to be believed, the beaches on the western and southern coasts of the island are the most beautiful in the Caribbean. The nickname "Garden of Eden" does indeed suit this place: perfect sandy beaches and a turquoise-emerald green Caribbean sea glittering in the sunlight tick all the right boxes.

After splashing around in the ocean, head back to the quay to begin the final part of the journey through the vibrant Lesser Antilles.

1 The well-known landmarks of the mighty twin peaks of the Pitons on the south-west coast of St Lucia.

2 A dark volcano beach at Soufrière Bay, St Lucia.

3 A dramatic sunset framed by the palms on the west coast of Barbados.

plant, in tiers of around 12, forming the the so-called "hands" of bananas, with several hands on one stem. One stem containing several banana hands can weigh 30–50 kg (66–110 lbs). Once it has borne its fruit the plant dies, when a new plant forms from the rhizome.

13 **Mustique** The ultra-stylish island of Mustique is also part of the Grenadines. Mosquitoes gave the island its name at a time long before the jet-set arrived and built their luxury villas and the small, exclusive hotel here. It has seen its fair share of rich and famous visitors, from Mick Jagger to Princess Margaret.

14 **Grenada** The city of St George's has a picturesque setting wrapped around a fine natural anchorage. The inner part of the port, the Carenage, is the backdrop for most of the boating activity here and small fishing boats and elegant yachts bob up and down side-by-side. Grenada is the southernmost of the Leeward Islands and only 150 km (93 miles) from the South American continent. The British colony of Grenada is known as Spice Island and the island state's flag has nutmeg at its center. Spices sold in baskets of palm leaves are on on offer everywhere around the island, and in the lively local markets too of course.

With its many small alleyways, traditional houses with red-tiled roofs, and mix of 18th-century French colonial style and British influences, including examples of Georgian architecture, St George's is one of the most attractive of all the Carib-

bean cities. A tour of the town leads along Young Street to the national museum, and then to Fort George, today used as a police station, which offers fine views over the sea, then on to the Anglican and Catholic churches across from the Supreme Court.

If you have enough time, it is worth going inland to see the Grand Etang National Park in the island's volcanic mountain range. It contains ancient crater basins, one of which holds the Grand Etang lake.

Also not to be missed on this part of the cruise is a visit to the Grand Anse beach, a few miles from St George's. Its long stretch of fine white sand is world famous.

Sadly, however, this marks the end of our cruise through the beautiful Lesser Antilles.

1 The long chain of Grenadine islands runs all the way from St Vincent to Grenada offering excellent conditions for sailors. Yachts at Union Island are shown here.

2 Mustique is a well-kept secret among wealthy visitors in the Caribbean. Luxurious wooden houses and villas are located right on the beach.

3 Cruise liner in the port of Grenada's capital city St George's.

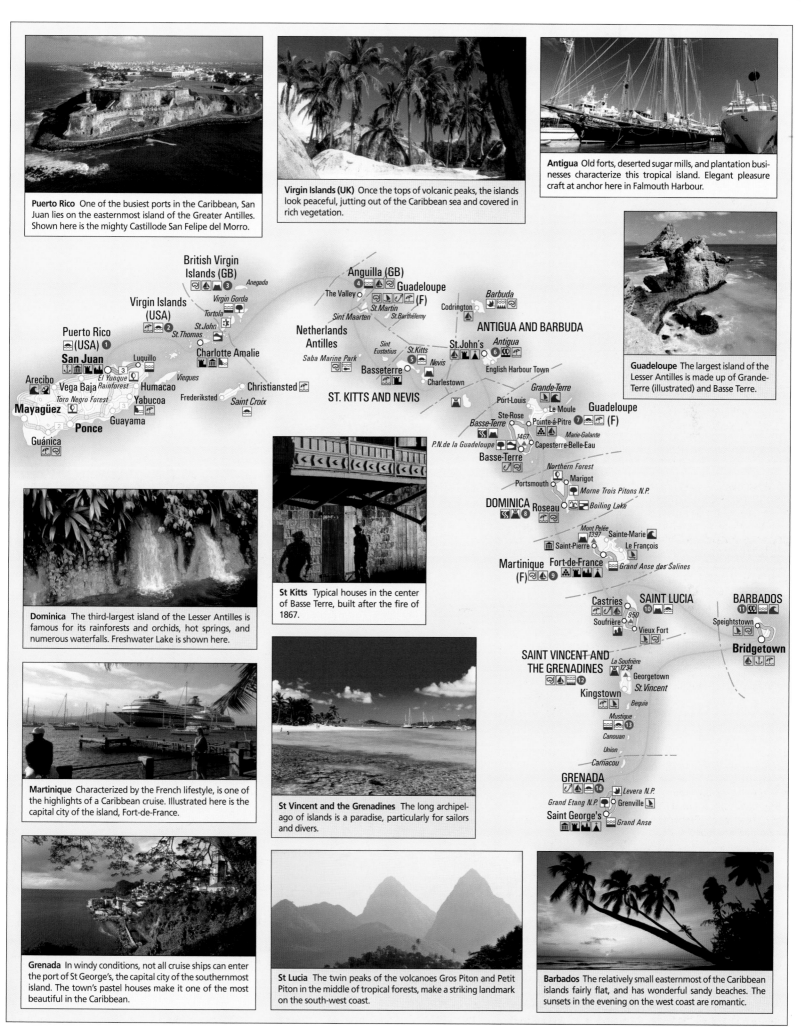

Puerto Rico One of the busiest ports in the Caribbean, San Juan lies on the easternmost island of the Greater Antilles. Shown here is the mighty Castillode San Felipe del Morro.

Virgin Islands (UK) Once the tops of volcanic peaks, the islands look peaceful, jutting out of the Caribbean sea and covered in rich vegetation.

Antigua Old forts, deserted sugar mills, and plantation businesses characterize this tropical island. Elegant pleasure craft at anchor here in Falmouth Harbour.

Guadeloupe The largest island of the Lesser Antilles is made up of Grande-Terre (illustrated) and Basse Terre.

Dominica The third-largest island of the Lesser Antilles is famous for its rainforests and orchids, hot springs, and numerous waterfalls. Freshwater Lake is shown here.

St Kitts Typical houses in the center of Basse Terre, built after the fire of 1867.

Martinique Characterized by the French lifestyle, is one of the highlights of a Caribbean cruise. Illustrated here is the capital city of the island, Fort-de-France.

St Vincent and the Grenadines The long archipelago of islands is a paradise, particularly for sailors and divers.

Grenada In windy conditions, not all cruise ships can enter the port of St George's, the capital city of the southernmost island. The town's pastel houses make it one of the most beautiful in the Caribbean.

St Lucia The twin peaks of the volcanoes Gros Piton and Petit Piton in the middle of tropical forests, make a striking landmark on the south-west coast.

Barbados The relatively small easternmost of the Caribbean islands fairly flat, and has wonderful sandy beaches. The sunsets in the evening on the west coast are romantic.

Map labels:
British Virgin Islands (GB) — Anegada, Virgin Gorda, Tortola, St.John's, St.Thomas
Virgin Islands (USA)
Puerto Rico (USA)
San Juan, Luquillo, Arecibo, Vega Baja, El Yunque Rainforest, Humacao, Toro Negro Forest, Yabucoa, Mayagüez, Guayama, Ponce, Guánica, Vieques
Charlotte Amalie, Christiansted, Frederiksted, Saint Croix
Anguilla (GB) — The Valley
Guadeloupe (F) — St.Martin, Sint Maarten, St.Barthélemy
Netherlands Antilles — Sint Eustatius, Saba Marine Park
Barbuda — Codrington
ANTIGUA AND BARBUDA — Antigua, English Harbour Town
St.Kitts, Nevis, Charlestown, Basseterre
ST. KITTS AND NEVIS
Grande-Terre, Port-Louis, Le Moule, Ste-Rose, Pointe-á-Pitre, Marie-Galante, Capesterre-Belle-Eau, Basse-Terre, P.N. de la Guadeloupe — 1467
Guadeloupe (F)
Northern Forest, Portsmouth, Marigot, Morne Trois Pitons N.P., Roseau, Boiling Lake
DOMINICA
Mont Pelée 1397, Sainte-Marie, Saint-Pierre, Le François, Fort-de-France, Grand Anse des Salines
Martinique (F)
Castries, Soufrière, 950, Vieux Fort
SAINT LUCIA
BARBADOS — Speightstown, Bridgetown
SAINT VINCENT AND THE GRENADINES — La Soufrière 1234, Georgetown, St.Vincent, Kingstown, Bequia, Mustique, Canouan, Union, Carriacou
GRENADA — Levera N.P., Grand Etang N.P., Grenville, Saint George's, Grand Anse

Antarctica

A cruise to the world's most southerly continent

This cruise to the ice world of the Antarctic sets off from the city of Ushuaia in the Argentine province of Tierra del Fuego, and heads toward the Falkland Islands. Sailing past icebergs and colonies of penguins, it continues on to the South Shetland Islands and the Antarctic Peninsula.

Norwegian explorer Roald Amundsen described the Antarctic as "more wild than any other country on earth" in his diary written in 1911. On December 14, 1911 he became the first person to reach the South Pole, after a dramatic race against the British explorer Robert Falcon Scott who, after reaching the Pole one month later tragically lost his life with several of his companions on the return. Antarctica is the fifth largest and most southerly continent in the world. The Antarctic Circle lies 66°33′ south of the equator. South of it, at the December solstice the sun never sets, and at the June

solstice it never rises. The Antarctic Convergence, better known as the Antarctic Polar Frontal Zone, is where the cold, northward-flowing Antarctic waters meet and mix with the relatively warmer waters of the sub-Antarctic.

At the center of the land mass usually referred to as the Antarctic, lies the South Pole. Most of the land is covered with ice and snow. Just one-sixth of its surface area, 12,393,000 sq km/4,783,698 sq miles (or 13,975,000 sq km/5,394,350 sq miles including the ice shelves) is free of ice. On average the ice sheet is 2,500 m (8,203 ft) thick, but in places it is more than 4,500 m

Hiding under seaweed: an elephant seal (*Mirounga leonina*) on the Falkland Islands.

The bizarre shapes of icebergs eroded by the wind and water are a familiar sight south of the Antarctic Polar Circle.

King penguins spend their entire lives in the Antarctic and breed in locations sheltered from the wind.

(14,765 ft) thick. However, the term "sheet" is misleading, as this desert of ice is often not flat, and it boasts several mountain ranges. The Transantarctic Mountain range is one of the longest in the world, stretching for over 4,800 km (2,983 miles) diagonally across the continent, from the Ross Sea to the Weddell Sea. Only the highest peaks, such as the 4,897-m (16,067-ft) high Mount Vision, break free of the huge mass of ice. The South Pole itself is some 2,804 m (9,200 ft) above sea level (including the ice).

Conditions in the Antarctic are extremely hostile. The very low temperatures (Russian researchers estimate -88°C/-126°F) are made even more extreme by ice storms carrying winds of over 350 km/h (217 miles/h). The only forms of life visible on ground that is free from ice, providing welcome glimpses of green, are mosses,

lichen, and algae. The only land-dwelling creatures here are insects and nematode worms. However, things are surprisingly different in and around the cold waters that surround the continent. Full of nutrients, they provides ideal living conditions for many sea creatures and those who forage for food in the sea: algae, seaweed, fungi, krill, sea urchins, jellyfish, seals, whales, and penguin all flourish, and albatrosses, petrels, and seagulls soar above the coastline.

The Antarctic has never really been colonized by man. Around four thousand people live here during the summer, in the continent's eighty research stations, dropping to around a thousand in winter. The largest research station, the American McMurdo Station at Hut Point on Ross Island, can accommodate up to 1,100 people during a snow-free summer.

A transatlantic yacht braves a storm in Drake Passage between Cape Horn and the Antarctic.

Penguins

If the Antarctic could be identified with just one animal, it would have to be the emperor penguin. There are seventeen species of penguin worldwide, but the emperor penguin is only found in the Antarctic. It can grow to a height of 1.2 m (4 ft) with a weight of 30 kg (66 lbs), and, like the king penguin (30 cm/12 inches smaller and 10 kg/22 lbs lighter), it is easily recognizable by the characteristic orange stripe on its neck. Emperor penguins do not build nests, but huddle together to incubate and raise their young in some of the coldest conditions on earth.

The most common penguin in the Antarctic, the Adelie penguin, is approximately 45–70 cm (18–28 in) tall and weighs about 5 kg (11 lbs). It has

Top: Young rockhopper penguins wait for food.
Middle: Rockhopper penguins have distinctive crest feathers, orange-red bills, and tiny blood red eyes.
Bottom: Breeding king penguins.

the stereotypical penguin markings of a black back and white "tuxedo" front, with a short beak, white-ringed eyes, and yellow feet. Like all the other penguins in the Antarctic, it lives in colonies, which are often quite large. Some are made up of over a million individuals. It is estimated that there are over twenty million of them in total.

The number of passengers wanting to take Antarctic cruises increases each year, but, just as for the polar explorers of a century ago, the weather and ice conditions restrict today's tourists, determining when and how far they can go. Decisions as to which islands and coves can be visited and where passengers can step ashore are normally made only shortly before departure.

1 Ushuaia Almost all of the cruises through the South Pacific and many Antarctic expeditions start in Ushuaia, which claims to be the southernmost town in the world, though there are other contenders for the title. The capital of the Argentine province of Tierra del Fuego has an impressive backdrop formed by the snow-covered Darwin Mountains and the Beagle Channel. There is an excellent view of the city from the 1,328-m (4,357-ft) high Mount Olivia and its glaciers. Cruise ships leave the Beagle Channel heading eastward to begin their journey to the Antarctic. After just a few miles, you reach Puerto Williams on the northern coast of Isla Navarino.

2 Puerto Williams This Chilean port and military base competes with Ushuaia for the title of the most southerly town in the world. If you make a stop here, you can visit the Martín Gusinde Anthropological Museum, or do

a stage of one of the trekking trips offered, if time allows. The waterfalls Cascada de la Virgen and Cascada Los Bronces are not far away. The last remaining Yamana Native Americans live in the village Villa Ukkika. A little farther on, the cruise continues past Puerto Toro with a population of around fifty. It is the southernmost settlement to be occupied permanently.

3 Beagle Channel The narrow Beagle Channel, only 5–13 km (3–8 miles) wide, divides Tierra del Fuego from Isla Navarino to the south. It is a natural waterway and provides a route from the Atlantic to the Pacific Ocean. Nowadays, Faro del Fin del Mundo marks the end of the Beagle Channel and you reach the open sea, the South Atlantic. The crossing to the Falkland Islands takes about two days.

4 Falkland Islands Known as the Islas Malvinas in Spanish, the

Travel information

Route profile
Length: approx. 2,000 km (1,243 miles)
Duration: min. 2 weeks
Start and end: Ushuaia
Itinerary (main locations): Ushuaia, Falkland Islands, Paulet Island, Deception Island, Port Lockroy, Lemaire Channel, Paradise Bay, Cape Horn, Ushuaia

When to go
Cruises operate during the southern hemisphere's summer (Nov–Feb). In November, there is still pack ice to contend with and the shores are

covered in snow. The penguin breeding season begins at this time. It is light for just four hours a day from December to January when the first penguins are born. The best time for whale-watching is February and March, when it is also possible to land and visit the Antarctic Peninsula farther south.

Tourist information
Falkland Islands:
www.falklandislands.com
www.tourism.org.fk
www.antarcticaonline.com/
antarctica/home/home.htm

Falkland Islands lie around 500 km (311 miles) off the coast of Patagonia. The two large islands called West Falkland and East Falkland, divided by the Falkland Sound, are the most well known. In addition to these, there are innumerable smaller islands. The total surface area of the archipelago is 12,173 sq km (4,699 sq miles), a rugged landscape that reminds many of the Scottish Highlands. At 705 m (2,313 ft), Mount Usborne on East Falkland is the highest point of the island group. The Falklands have belonged to Britain since 1833, but since that time Argentina has sought to regain its former power over the islands, both diplomatically and

through an unsuccessful military campaign in 1982.

The small capital city, Stanley (formerly Port Stanley), was founded in 1844, chosen for its deep anchorage for shipping. Nowadays, the population is around two thousand. The Stanley Museum provides a good insight into the islands' history. It has served as a sealing and whaling base, and a coaling station for the British Royal Navy. Today, the island's sheep still produce wool as they have done in the past and a sheep features on the islands' heraldic seal.

The wildlife is surprisingly diverse and in addition to penguins and egrets, giant petrels also nest here. You may also see colonies

of cormorants, and seals or dolphins playing at the water's edge. The cruise from here to the South Shetland Islands usually takes one and a half to two days.

5 Elephant Island This is the best-known of the South Shetland Islands, named after the southern sea elephants that live on the rocky shores of the islands. British whaler George Powell was the first to discover the island, which is just 10 km (6 miles) long and in places only 2 km (1¼ miles) wide. The island is most famous as being the place where Ernest Shackleton and his crew took refuge in 1916 after their ship *Endurance* had been lost. Nowadays, it is inhabited by

several species of animal, including gentoo penguins and seals.

6 Paulet Island The narrow Antarctic Peninsula is the most easily accessible part of the continent. Around 1,300 km (808 miles) long, it divides the Weddell Sea from the Bellingshausen Sea. Approaching from the South Atlantic, most ships cross through the Arctic Sound, which divides Dundee Island from the north point of the Antarctic Peninsula, lying to the west. Huge icebergs can often be seen here in "Iceberg Alley" as the waterway has been appropriately nicknamed. Cruise ships usually head for the circular Paulet Island with *(continued p.196)*

1 A view of Ushuaia in Tierra del Fuego, the southernmost city in the world. Mount Olivia and the Marcial Glacier rise up in the background.

2 Puerto Williams in the Beagle Channel. The waterway was named after a research ship used for the Darwin Expedition.

3 Large colonies of blue-eyed cormorants can be seen on the Falkland Islands.

4 King of the Antarctic skies: albatrosses at their breeding ground on the Falkland Islands.

5 Hundreds of thousands of Adelie penguins live together in cramped conditions on Paulet Island.

King penguins (*Aptenodytes patagonicus*) are the second-largest species of penguin and live mainly on the sub-Antarctic islands. They begin breeding when they are six years old. The egg is incubated first in the male's stomach fold, but both male and female share the incubation period, which lasts 55 days in total.

As there is not enough food during the winter months, the parents must travel long distances in order to find nourishment. They feed their chicks by regurgitating partly digested fish into the chick's mouth. The breeding cycle takes almost 14 months, so king penguins only breed twice every three years.

Antarctic Heritage Trust. Nowadays it is a museum, and an old kitchen, common room, and research laboratory give an impression of what everyday life was like at the station. The Heritage Trust staff maintain the station and also run a postal service for the Antarctic. Gentoo penguins and king cormorants nest not far from the station.

⑩ Lemaire Channel The narrow Lemaire Channel, discovered by Captain Eduard Dallmann in 1873, is one of the great natural wonders of the mountainous Antarctic Peninsula. It is 11 km (7 miles) wide at its broadest section, narrowing to just 500 m (547 yards) at one point. This is a particularly difficult navigational challenge for the cruise ships because of the drifting ice floes and icebergs. The channel entrance to the north on the mainland side is marked by the 747 m (2,450 ft) twin peaks of Cape Renard and Booth Island, providing a barrier between the channel and the sea. Tall cliffs rise up somewhat menacingly from the ocean and give the channel the feeling of a gorge. They are partially covered by snow, but in places are so steep that not even snow and ice can cling to them. Many whales cavort in the channel.

The Three Sisters, an immense rocky formation with smooth, almost vertical peaks rising straight out of the Bellinghausen Sea next to a glacier, is also a beautiful sight.

its summit crater; it is home to one of the Antarctic's largest colonies of Adelie penguins.

A stone hut was built on a hill here by the shipwrecked crew of a Swedish expedition in 1903 (led by Otto Nordenskjöld). Their expedition ship *Antarctic*, which gave the Antarctic Sound its name, sank 40 km (25 miles) off the coast of the island.

❼ Deception Island This horseshoe-shaped South Shetland island is the caldera of a volcano which last erupted in 1970. The flooded crater at the center of the island is entered via a strait named Neptune's Bellows. The big attraction here is to bathe in the warm springs of Pendulum Cove, a surreal experience when surrounded by the cold Antarctic landscape. The island's highest point is Mount Pond, at some 539 m (1,768 ft).

The British research station in Whalers Bay and a Chilean station were both damaged during the volcanic eruption in 1967,

but the British finally abandoned their station in 1969 following a second eruption. A derelict hangar and the wreck of an airplane can still be seen.

The most southerly whale-oil processing plant operated here from 1910 to 1931 in Whalers Bay, a maar (low volcanic crater) that forms a natural port. At Baily Head look out for tens of thousands of chinstrap penguins as well as a number of fur seals.

❽ Paradise Bay Islands and peninsulas of land form a picturesque bay here, bordered on one side by mountains over 1,100 m (3,609 ft) high. Towering glacial walls shelter the bay, sometimes shedding pieces of ice as fissures and cracks widen and break open. In some places, ice tongues (long narrow sheets of ice projecting from the coastline) and icebergs narrow the waterway, making negotiating this part of the route quite an exciting experience.

The Argentinean research station Almirante Brown on the Antarctic

mainland is a bright red smudge on the blue-white glacier landscape. It was set on fire in 1984 by a station doctor who could not bear the thought of another winter in such a place, but was restored in 1996. The Gonzalez Videla station, also located in the bay, can only be accessed by ship and has now been taken over by gentoo penguins. It was built by Chile to stake its claim on the Antarctic. Since the end of the 1950s, around a dozen countries have claimed the Antarctic as their own. The reason for this is simple: large amounts of natural oil, gas, coal, iron ore, gold, silver, platinum, copper, and other valuable minerals can be found here. Several countries have based their claims on geographical proximity, including Chile, Argentina, and Britain, via the Falkland Islands. Other countries referred to the role they played in discovering the continent or used other strategic arguments.

The journey continues past Anvers Island (with the US-owned

Palmer Station) and through the impressive Neumayer Channel to the old whaling station Port Lockroy.

❾ Port Lockroy Whalers and seal hunters were the first to plunder the natural resources of the Antarctic. Between 1930 and 1950, whales were slaughtered on a huge scale in the Southern Ocean with each year around 400,000 being killed. Since then, whale numbers have recovered well as a result of environmental protection in the area, but the whales are now threatened by the over-fishing of krill, their most important food source.

A British research station was built in 1944 on Goudier Island at the only anchorage point used by the whalers. Station A in the Neumayer Channel, was abandoned in 1962, but is now open to tourists and is one of the most frequently visited destinations for Antarctic cruises. After it was abandoned, it was taken over and restored by the British

The journey southward through the Lemaire Channel is often hampered by more than just icebergs. Navigation is generally difficult here, requiring special equipment such as sonar and radar. The narrowness of the passage and the rocks hidden beneath the water can make it quite dangerous. Ice conditions permitting, the ship may now chart a course for Petermann Island south of the channel.

11 Petermann Island Named after August Petermann, the German geographer, this island was discovered by a German expedition in 1873. It is one of the myriad of tiny islands that form the Wilhelm Archipelago, situated off the west coast of the Antarctic Peninsula. A large colony of Adelie penguins lives on the island and many fin and humpback whales can be spotted in the surrounding waters. A colony of blue-eyed cormorants also lives here. As the island is relatively free of ice, many crabeater seals and leopard seals have also made this their home. Drake Passage, almost 1,000 km (621 miles) wide, between the Southern Shetland Islands and the tip of South America, is

named after the English seafarer Sir Francis Drake (16th C.). Winds and treacherous currents can make this part of the cruise quite uncomfortable as the ship makes its way toward Cape Horn and then back to Ushuaia. If you are lucky, you will see whales and dolphins making their way though the nutrient-rich waters.

12 Cape Horn (Cabo de Hornos) If the weather is good enough to land using an inflatable dinghy, cruise ships drop anchor at South America's southernmost point or at least slow down for you to take photos. A lighthouse, the Chilean military station Cabo de Hornos, and the Cape Horn memorial in the shape of a huge flying albatross can be seen on a 50 m (164 ft) high plateau.

The large waves, and strong winds and currents have made the treacherous waters around Cape Horn a graveyard for shipping. Over eight hundred ships and more than ten thousand people have been claimed by the sea here. In 1945, Cape Horn and the surrounding islands were made a national park. From Cape Horn, the ship will make the return journey to Ushuaia.

1 The Antarctic mountains at Port Lockroy look like a picture-book landscape.

2 Gentoo penguins examine the skeleton of a finback whale at Port Lockroy, an old whaling station.

3 View from the Lemaire Channel of the glacial end of Booth Island.

4 On photo safari in a world of ice: a leopard seal in Paradise Bay.

5 A group of seals dozing in Paradise Bay.

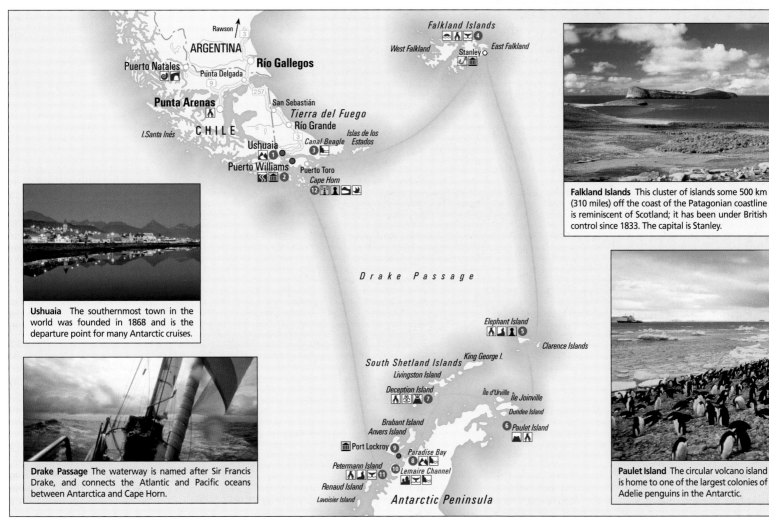

Ushuaia The southernmost town in the world was founded in 1868 and is the departure point for many Antarctic cruises.

Drake Passage The waterway is named after Sir Francis Drake, and connects the Atlantic and Pacific oceans between Antarctica and Cape Horn.

Falkland Islands This cluster of islands some 500 km (310 miles) off the coast of the Patagonian coastline is reminiscent of Scotland; it has been under British control since 1833. The capital is Stanley.

Paulet Island The circular volcano island is home to one of the largest colonies of Adelie penguins in the Antarctic.

Route 14

Indian Ocean

A cruise around the Garden of Eden

The islands of the Indian Ocean are a tropical paradise, covered with lush vegetation and edged with sun-drenched, long sandy beaches. A cruise through this still fairly unspoiled Garden of Eden provides a fascinating insight into its diverse natural world and the lively cultural mix of the people who live here.

Many islands and island groups are scattered throughout the western Indian Ocean, not far from the south-east coast of Africa and Madagascar. The islands are of three distinct types, depending on the rock from which they are formed: high, mountainous islands of granite; high volcanic islands; and flat islands and atolls formed of coral. The Inner Seychelles, the easternmost of the Seychelles, are formed of granite. The Outer Seychelles along with a few islands from the smaller groups are flat and are formed of coral limestone; while the

remaining islands are formed from volcanic rock.

The islands had a reputation for plenty: the French called them the "islands of excess" and the Dutch settlers believed that the forests of rare wood found on Mauritius could never be depleted. The islands had been left to develop undisturbed by man for millions of years. The first people to actually settle the islands were Europeans, who arrived to find themselves in a tropical paradise. Egyptian and Phoenician seafarers and traders knew of the islands' existence centuries

A young girl in Stone Town, Zanzibar.

before the Europeans' arrival, and may have used them for provisioning stops on their sea voyages. People also settled the lands near the islands: some time around the birth of Christ, Malaysian and Polynesian seafarers settled in Madagascar, and in the ninth and tenth centuries, Arabian merchants founded small bases on the eastern coast of Africa, such as Zanzibar.

The Dutch established a permanent base on Mauritius in 1598 but abandoned their settlement in 1710. They left behind an island that had been transformed. The forests of rare wood had practically disappeared and in their place new crops had been introduced: coconut palm trees, sugar cane, tobacco, cotton, pineapples, and bananas. The French took over the nearby islands of Réunion and Rodriguez in 1654 and later also

An encounter in the rich underwater world of the Adabra Atoll: divers meet a large shoal of humpback snappers.

Fishing boat in the waters off Mauritius; on the smaller islands, people earn their living from fishing and agriculture.

claimed the abandoned island of Mauritius as their own. It was used as a starting point for voyages of exploration, leading to the discovery and colonization of the Seychelles. During the French era, the physical character of the islands was changed further, also as a result of deforestation and the introduction of sugar cane, cotton, and plants used to produce the dye indigo. Today, Réunion and especially Mauritius are almost covered in sugar cane plantations. Large spice plantations were established on Réunion, Madagascar, the Seychelles, and Zanzibar.

In 1841, the Sultan of Mayotte, one of the Comoros Islands, sold the island to the French. Over the next century, the French annexed the other three islands in the Comoros. The Seychelles gained independence in 1976, and Mauritius in 1968.

Réunion and Mayotte remain under French control, while the other Comoros islands were made independent in 1974. People of many different religions, ethnic origins, and cultures live together peacefully on the islands. Languages and dialects differ accordingly. Creole is spoken in the Seychelles, and in Mauritius, Réunion, and Rodriguez, also known as the Mascarene Islands. Creole developed from the languages spoken by the French settlers and the African slaves brought to the region. Shikomore, closely related to Swahili, is spoken on the Comoros.

Visitors to the islands are fascinated by the diversity of its landscape with no island really like another. The flat, sandy coral islands, the mountainous granite islands, and the volcanic islands offer nature lovers a rich and beautiful natural wonderland to explore.

Spray splashes high in the surf on the Seychelles island of La Digue.

The island world of the Indian Ocean appeals on many levels. The conditions for water sports are excellent, and divers especially will be in heaven. Nature lovers can discover fascinating and exotic animals and plants, while visitors interested in history will be able to trace the path of the colonial powers on the islands.

① Zanzibar This exotic spice island lies directly off the coast of East Africa and is a semi-autonomous part of Tanzania. From the 17th century onward, it was used as a center for the African slave trade due to its strategically advantageous location. From the mid-19th century, Western colonial powers took an interest in Zanzibar and the island was made a British protectorate in 1890.

Stone Town, the historic old part of Zanzibar's capital, Zanzibar City, was designated a World Heritage Site in 2000 for its many fine buildings reflecting its diverse cultural heritage. Many of the houses belonging to the Arabian upper classes, built from coral limestone and with ornately carved wooden verandahs and doors, have recently been restored. The Anglican cathedral now stands where the slave market used to be located. Former slave prisons can be seen in the cellars of buildings nearby.

From Zanzibar, it is about 750 km (466 miles) in a south-easterly direction to the largest of the Comoros islands.

② Grande Comore (Ngazidja) At a height of 2,361 m (7,746 ft), Mount Karthala lies to the south and dominates the landscape of the youngest island in the archipelago. It has the largest volcanic crater on earth with a diameter of over 1.6 km (1 mile). Since 1857, it has erupted more than ten times, the last being in 1977. The effects of this volcanic activity can still be seen all over the island. The north of the island is stony and flat (La Grille) and cultivation of the land virtually impossible. The peaks of La Grille and the sides of Mount Karthala are covered in cloud forests (tropical evergreen forests characterized by low-level cloud cover). The humidity creates ideal conditions for air plants. The largest town on the island, and also the capital city of the Comoros, is Moroni, on the western coast of Grande Comore. It is a transport hub, with air and sea connections to the other Comoros Islands and the African mainland. From here, you can take a boat trip to Anjouan, which lies to the south-east.

③ Anjouan (Ndzouani) The slopes of this mountainous island emerge steeply from the sea, rising to form the two 1,500 m (4,922 ft) volcanoes, Ntingui and Trindini. The Cirque de Bambao, a basin formed from a collapsed volcanic crater, bordered by steep slopes of up to 1,000 m (3,281 ft), covers the entire central part of the island.

Travel information

Route profile
Length: approx. 5,000 km (3,100 miles)
Duration: at least 7 weeks
Start: Zanzibar
End: Réunion
Itinerary (main locations): Zanzibar, Grande Comore, Mayotte, Mahé, Praslin, Mauritius, Réunion

Travel tips
There are connecting flights between Mahé (Seychelles), Réunion, Mauritius, and Grande Comore. Mayotte can only be reached by plane from the other Comoros Islands and Réunion. Ferry services link Mauritius, Réunion, and the Seychelles.

Tourist information
Zanzibar (Tanzania):
www.tanzaniaodyssey.com
Comoro and La Réunion:
www.franceguide.com (insert country before "franceguide" e.g. us.franceguide)
Seychelles:
www.seychelles.travel
Mauritius: *www.mauritius.net*

3

4

Life below the waves

The islands of the Indian Ocean are surrounded by some of the most beautiful underwater environments in the world. Divers can discover an amazing variety of fish and countless types of cone snail here.

The harmless manta ray is one of the most impressive of the underwater inhabitants. Gliding through the water with a ghostly elegance, it can grow to 7 m (23 ft) across and weigh up to 1.8 tonnes (2 tons).

Squirrel fish are one of the most dangerous sea creatures in this region due

Top: Manta rays are an impressive sight due to their size and elegance.
Middle: Squirrel fish can be dangerous because of their poisonous gill spikes.
Bottom: The grouper grows up to 3 m (10 ft) in size and can camouflage itself well.

to their poisonous gill spikes, but since they usually hunt at night divers rarely encounter them.

Another common sight below the waves of the Indian Ocean is the grouper, which can grow to 3 m (10 ft). They are well camouflaged by their speckled, patterned skins when in pursuit of their prey comprising fish, crab, and squid,

Anjouan is also famous for its ylang-ylang plantations, which produce oil for the perfume industry. There are also many clove trees on the island; the cloves, the aromatic buds from the trees, are harvested between July and November and are spread out on the ground to dry. Small airplanes and ferries depart from Anjouan to Mayotte, around 100 km (62 miles) away, again to the south-east.

❹ Mayotte An administrative division of France, the oldest of the Comoros Islands from a geological point of view is formed of the remains of a shield volcano (a flat-domed volcano). Mayotte is surrounded by one of the most beautiful barrier reefs in the world, 140 km (87 miles) long. To the south it forms a rare double reef. Conditions for diving inside the lagoon created by the reef are superb. Deep bays, covered with mangroves have formed at the mouths of the rivers that run into the ocean. Along with the mangroves, there is a lot to see for nature lovers, including many baobab trees, whose large white blossoms give off a pleasant scent, and the endemic Mayotte lemurs that visitors enjoy feed-

ing around the hotel resorts. To the north, around 350 km (217 miles) away, are the coral-based Outer Seychelles, covering around 440,000 sq km (169,840 sq miles) and comprising around sixty small islands.

❺ Groupe d'Aldabra Part of the Republic of the Seychelles, the Aldabra Islands, a group of four islands covering an area of 135 sq km (52 sq miles), forms an atoll, an island of raised coral encircling a lagoon. Most of the land here is formed by a 125,000-m (410,125-ft) coral reef. The limestone is craggy and sharp where it has been weath-

ered by the wind and sea. The tidal range is more than 3 m (10 ft) here, virtually emptying the entire lagoon when the tide is out. The constant movement of water back and forth has eroded the underside of the reef to produce some startling rock formations that jut out over the water. Grand Terre, the main island of the atoll, has been a World Heritage Site protected by UNESCO since 1982 and is the last refuge in the Indian Ocean of the Seychelles giant tortoise.

❻ Île Desroches Part of the Amirante Islands, this coral atoll lies halfway between Aldabra

1 Today, Zanzibar is a departure point for sailing trips.

2 Moroni is the capital city of Grande Comore.

3 Erosion by the tide constantly passing back and forth has turned some of the coral in the Aldabra Atoll into mushroom-like formations.

4 Divers at Île Desroches

1

2

3

and Mahé, the principal island of the Seychelles. Its coast is bordered by 15 km (9 miles) of long fine sandy beaches. As with all the Amirante islands, Desroches is only slightly above sea level, but is protected from the sea by its surrounding reef. With its many coconut and plantations and dense tree vegetation, the island is a major supplier of copra.

7 Silhouette Around 300 km (186 miles) to the north-east is the archipelago of the Inner Seychelles, comprising twenty-nine rugged granite islands and two coral islands. The group's principal westerly island is Silhouette. It is the third-largest island in the Seychelles with a land area of around 20 sq km (8 sq miles). Silhouette's largest mountain, Mont Dauban, is 740 m (2,428 ft) high. With only 150 or so people living here, the island's hilly and forested landscape is virtually unspoiled. This is the only island other than Mahé where cloud forests can be found, and the only island where rare sandalwood trees grow. There are also tobacco,

coffee, cinnamon, and avocado plantations, and several old houses built in the Creole style.

8 Mahé The largest of the Seychelles is also its political and economic center. Around 90 percent of the Seychelles' population live here and the islands' two main ports, the international airport, and the capital city of Victoria are also located on Mahé. Victoria is one of the smallest capital cities in the world with a population of 30,000. The town's landmark is the clock tower. All kinds of

spices, fruits, vegetables, and fish are sold at the busy market named after former governor Sir Selwyn Clarke.
The island is covered with dense forest, cinnamon and tea plantations, and has more than its fair share of sandy beaches, in total there are no less than sixty-eight. The most famous is Beau Vallon on the north-west coast: 3 km (2 miles) of soft, white sand offering a variety of different water sport facilities, and bordered by hotels. Beau Vallon is ideal for waterskiing From May to November.

9 St Anne Marine National Park The entire eastern side of Mahé is bordered by an offshore coral reef. In order to protect the fragile coral, the St Anne Marine National Park was established in 1973 and was the first such park in the Indian Ocean. It lies 5 km (3 miles) to the west of the port of Victoria and covers an area of approximately 1.5 sq km (½ sq mile), including six small granite islands. The first settlers in the Seychelles lived on the largest of these islands, St Anne, possibly because the mangrove marshes surrounding Mahé made it diffi-

May to October. Around 30 km (19 miles) to the south-east, the easternmost island of the Seychelles can be reached by boat.

⑫ **Frégate (Frigate Island)** This magical tiny island is just 2 sq km (¾ sq mile) in size and is rich in vegetation. It is named after the frigate bird that can often be seen hunting off the coast. A number of endangered species live here, such as the Seychelles magpie-robin, the Seychelles giant tortoise, a giant beetle endemic to the island, and rare plants. The bare granite peaks of Mont Signale (125m/410 ft), the cliffs of the Glacis Cerf, and Au Salon Mountain (110 m/361 ft) dominate the island. The offshore coral

1 La Digue is characterized by huge blocks of granite.

2 Picturesque coves make the main island of the Seychelles, Mahé, a perfect destination for divers.

3 The small island of St Pierre near Praslin is ideal for diving and deep-sea exploration.

4 View of the Seychelles island of Silhouette from Île du Nord.

Vallée de Mai (Praslin)

This lush valley is one of the smallest national parks in the world, which includes the remainder of a prehistoric palm forest. Thanks to millions of years of isolation, many unique plant and animal species have developed in the Seychelles. The Vallée de

The Vallée de Mai is the world's largest source of the Seychelles palm nut.

Mai is the home of the endemic Seychelles palm tree. The tree's fruit, the coco de mer, can weigh up to 18 kg (40 lbs), making it the heaviest in the world. Now used as the island's symbol, in the past the coco de mer was believed to have healing and aphrodisiac qualities. The valley is also home to a rare black parrot and vanilla orchids. It was designated a UNESCO World Heritage Site in 1983.

cult to land there from a boat. Despite its relatively small size, this marine national park has a diverse underwater world. The seven most interesting areas can only be reached by glass-bottomed boat.

⑩ **Praslin** Miles of white sandy beached surround the second-largest island in the Seychelles, which lies 50 km (31 miles) to the north-east of Mahé. Several rivers flow down from of the mountainous interior of the island, forming backwater lagoons, marshes, and lowlands

covered in mangroves, creating a diverse water landscape. Almost the entire surface of Praslin is covered with a tropical rainforest. Animals and plants thrive in the heart of the Vallée de Mai, where the scent of vanilla drifts on the breeze, that wafts through the famous coco de mer palms (sea coconut), and some of the rarest birds in the world can be seen here (see panel, right). Praslin is also an ideal point from which to make excursions to the smaller islands nearby, such as St Pierre and La Digue.

⑪ **La Digue** This island is just a short journey of just 6 km (4 miles) from Praslin, and can only be reached by boat. There are no cars here, only ox-carts and bicycles. The landmarks of La Digue are the huge, smooth blocks of granite, which get their red hue from their content of feldspar. La Digue has wide, deserted beaches and beautiful forests where the rare black paradise flycatcher can be seen. Strong currents and south-easterly winds make swimming from the beaches difficult and not recommended from

Hindu festivals

Hindus are by far the largest religious group in Mauritius, making up over 50 percent of the total population. Their main festivals include the atonement festival Thai Poosam, which is celebrated at the end of January or the beginning of February. Each devotee

Statues of Hindu deities.

tries to carry the heaviest possible burdens on decorated wooden poles. The suffering that the devotees undergo is believed to purify them. After several painful hours they reach the temple, where they ask for the god Muruga's blessing amid the cheerful sounds of the vibrant festival.

reefs protect the gleaming white sandy beaches to the west. Frégate was used for centuries as a refuge for pirates.

⑬ **Port Louis, Mauritius**
Named after the French king Louis XV, Port Louis came under French control in 1735 and became the capital city and civic center of Mauritius. The town served as a contact point for ships en route between Europe and Asia, but the port became less important after the opening of the Suez Canal.
The architecture of the culturally rich Port Louis is an interesting mix of tall modern structures and historic colonial buildings. A visit to the vibrant markets is a good way to experience the particularly lively Mauritian way of life. Or take a stroll through the town to soak up some of its culture, bustle, but above all to rub shoulders with some of the friendly Mauritian people.
Port Louis is the hottest place on the island as it is sheltered from the refreshing south-easterly wind by three mountain ridges.

⑭ **Curepipe, Mauritius** Situated around 30 km (19 miles) south of Port Louis in the interior of the island, Curepipe, is the highest town in Mauritius. The climate is pleasant and many tourists enjoy shopping here, but visitors should also

not miss City Hall, an impressive colonnaded building. The main geological attraction is the Trou aux Cerfs, a huge crater in the center of Curepipe. Around 200 m (220 yards) in diameter, it serves as a reminder that Mauritius is the result of powerful volcanic activity. There is a wonderful panoramic view from the top of the rim of the crater over Curepipe, the mountainous surroundings and the picturesque volcano cone of Trois Mamelles.

⑮ **Rivière Noire, Mauritius**
From Curepipe it is only a stone's throw to the Rivière Noire National Park, 10 km (6 miles) to the south. This protected area was created in 1994

and includes a large part of the surviving Mauritius rainforest. Visitors can see spectacular landscapes and some unique species of animals and plants live here. The locals are particularly proud that the Mauritius kestrel, pink pigeon, and echo parrot populations have recovered as a result of breeding programs and by returning birds to the wild. At an altitude of 300–800 m (984–2,625 ft), the park receives around 4,000 mm (160 inches) of rainfall a year and has a total of 50 km (31 miles) of footpaths.

⑯ **Morne Brabant, Mauritius**
Morne Brabant, a peninsula that rises to a ridge 550 m (1,805 ft) high juts out into the ocean on

the south-west coast of Mauritius. Over the past few years, a series of hotels have been constructed at the base of the peninsula on a flat strip of land around 50,300 m (164,034 ft) wide between the steep rock face and the sea. Thanks to the wide, flat reef and beautiful white sand, this is safe for children, and the coast here is ideal for swimming and surfing.

(continued p.206)

1 The bizarre volcanic cones of the Trois Mamelles are a reminder of the volcanic history of the island of Mauritius.

2 Morne Brabant: the peninsula on the south-west tip of Mauritius.

Piton de la Fournaise

Piton de la Fournaise (2,632 m/ 8,636ft) is a highly active volcano in the south-east of Réunion. Since 1640, it has erupted around 150 times, the last eruption being in December 2005. Lava can frequently be seen flowing down its slopes to the sea following smaller, relatively non-threatening eruptions that attract large crowds of sightseers. Today, Piton de la Fournaise is made up of two central craters or calderas.

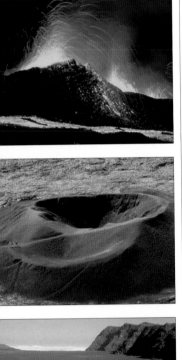

Top: The Piton de la Fournaise is one of the most active volcanoes in the world.
Middle: There are many smaller active craters on the mountain.
Bottom: The route to the volcano over the moon-like landscape of Plaine des Sables.

The clouds blown across the island by the constant south-east trade wind accumulate against the side of the volcano, resulting in large downpours of rain. The high rainful, reaching around 3,000–6,000 mm (118–236 inches) on average each year, means that this part of the coast has a reputation for being wet, while the so-called "dry coast" receives only 589 mm (23 inches) of rain per year on average.

17 Saint-Denis, Réunion The island of Réunion lies to the west of Mauritius and has the status of a French overseas département. The capital city Saint-Denis was founded in 1669 and today has a population of 130,000. It is situated to the north of the island, by the sea. A tour of the town begins with a walk along the Le Barachois, the famous shoreline promenade with buildings dating back to the time of the East India Company, and past the Préfecture the former administrative building, once guarded by city walls and canon. In the center of the town is the Jardin de l'Etat, an exotic park with fountains and palm trees; the natural history museum is also located here. Bordered by mountains on three sides, Saint-Denis also makes a good base from which to trek and explore the interior of the island. The Route de la Montagne weaves upward between lava rocks, with many breathtaking views along the way. This old road was built in the mid-19th century and was the only road between Saint-Denis and the rest of the island until 1963 when a coastal highway was built connecting the port to the main city.

18 The Cirques, Réunion The cirques are the three huge volcanic calderas that are found on the island. These massive natural amphitheatres, each with a diameter of around 10 km (6 miles),

are surrounded by dizzyingly high volcanic mountains. The Cirque de Salazie is around two hours from Saint-Denis and is most easily accessed via the village of Hell-Bourg. The best way to get a good view of the impressive ravines and peaks (including the Piton de la Fournaise, see panel, left) is by helicopter. The largest, greenest, and wettest of the three calderas, the Cirque de Salazie, lies below the Piton des Neiges, the highest peak in the Indian

Ocean. Hundreds of waterfalls, the vegetation, and the grandiose relief make this an enchanting place. The landscape in the Cirque de Cilaos is more Mediterranean in character as it is the driest of the calderas. In 1819, three hot springs were discovered here. Now a health resort of the same name offers thermal spa treatments in waters that stay between a soothing 31 and 38°C (88 and 100°F). The Cirque de Mafate, situated at the foot of the Piton Maïdo,

can only be accessed on foot or by helicopter. It seems as if time has stood still for the people living here.

1 Sunrise over Réunion.

2 A waterfall in the thick forests at Piton Maido.

3 Volcanic activity on Réunion: the lava has solidified into bizarre formations where it reaches the sea.

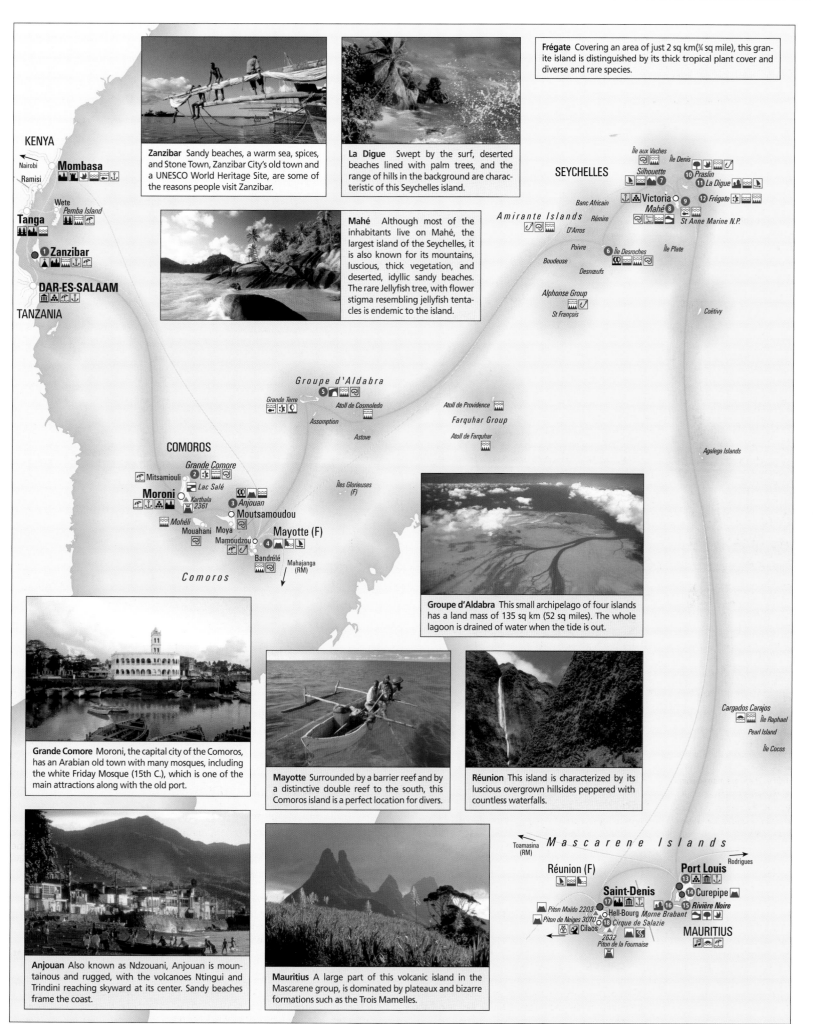

Frégate Covering an area of just 2 sq km(¾ sq mile), this granite island is distinguished by its thick tropical plant cover and diverse and rare species.

Zanzibar Sandy beaches, a warm sea, spices, and Stone Town, Zanzibar City's old town and a UNESCO World Heritage Site, are some of the reasons people visit Zanzibar.

La Digue Swept by the surf, deserted beaches lined with palm trees, and the range of hills in the background are characteristic of this Seychelles island.

Mahé Although most of the inhabitants live on Mahé, the largest island of the Seychelles, it is also known for its mountains, luscious, thick vegetation, and deserted, idyllic sandy beaches. The rare Jellyfish tree, with flower stigma resembling jellyfish tentacles is endemic to the island.

KENYA

Nairobi
Ramisi
Mombasa
Wete
Pemba Island
Tanga
❶ **Zanzibar**
DAR-ES-SALAAM
TANZANIA

SEYCHELLES
Île aux Vaches
Île Denis
Silhouette
❿ *Praslin*
⓫ *La Digue*
⓬ *Frégate*
⑨
Victoria
Mahé ⑧
❾
St Anne Marine N.P.
Amirante Islands
Banc Africain
Rémire
D'Arros
Poivre
❻ *Île Desroches*
Île Plate
Boudeuse
Desnœufs
Alphonse Group
St François
Coëtivy

Groupe d'Aldabra
❺
Grande Terre
Atoll de Cosmoledo
Assomption
Astove
Atoll de Providence
Farquhar Group
Atoll de Farquhar

Agalega Islands

COMOROS
Grande Comore
Mitsamiouli
❷
Moroni
Lac Salé
▲ *Karthala 2361*
❸ *Anjouan*
Moutsamoudou
Mohéli
Mouahani Moya
Mamoudzou
❹ **Mayotte (F)**
Bandrélé
Mahajanga (RM)
Comoros

Îles Glorieuses (F)

Groupe d'Aldabra This small archipelago of four islands has a land mass of 135 sq km (52 sq miles). The whole lagoon is drained of water when the tide is out.

Cargados Carajos
Île Raphael
Pearl Island
Île Cocos

Grande Comore Moroni, the capital city of the Comoros, has an Arabian old town with many mosques, including the white Friday Mosque (15th C.), which is one of the main attractions along with the old port.

Mayotte Surrounded by a barrier reef and by a distinctive double reef to the south, this Comoros island is a perfect location for divers.

Réunion This island is characterized by its luscious overgrown hillsides peppered with countless waterfalls.

Mascarene Islands
Toamasina (RM)
Rodrigues
Réunion (F)
Port Louis
⓭
⓮ *Curepipe*
Saint-Denis
⑰
⑯
⓯ *Rivière Noire*
Piton Maïdo 2203
Hell-Bourg *Morne Brabant*
Piton de Neiges 3070
⑱ *Cirque de Salazie*
Cilaos 2632
Piton de la Fournaise
MAURITIUS

Anjouan Also known as Ndzouani, Anjouan is mountainous and rugged, with the volcanoes Ntingui and Trindini reaching skyward at its center. Sandy beaches frame the coast.

Mauritius A large part of this volcanic island in the Mascarene group, is dominated by plateaux and bizarre formations such as the Trois Mamelles.

Hawaii

Dream beaches, tropical flowers and volcanoes: from Big Island to Kauai

Fantastic pure-white beaches, the gentle murmur of palm trees, hula dancers, and bright garlands of flowers, together with tropical rainforests, cascading waterfalls, active and dormant volcanoes, Honolulu city life, and the magic of the indigenous people: these are just some of the many faces of Hawaii. The largest island in the archipelago, and its namesake, trumps almost any other island on the planet with its magnificent and extraordinary lava landscape.

"Aloha komo mai" ("Welcome to Hawaii") will greet you on arrival at the airport. Wherever you go in these dream-like Pacific islands, you'll discover the "aloha spirit" and enjoy the islanders' infectious friendliness. The sky is a deeper blue here, the beaches wider and cleaner than anywhere else, and the wind rustles gently in the palms and along the magical cliffs on Na Pali Coast. In the language of the Polynesians, who

The Silversword grows only on Maui.

came to Hawaii around AD 500, the island's name means heaven or paradise. Every visitor is greeted with a traditional "lei" (Polynesian garland of flowers), and the warm air seems to echo with the romantic chants that rang out over the islands when kings still reigned and before Western people arrived.

The Hawaiian Islands extend some 2,436 km (1,513 miles) across the northern Pacific, meaning that travel between them is possible only by plane or boat. Island-hopping is certainly the right term for it, since the best-known islands in the archipelago are within hopping distance of each other: Kauai, Oahu, Molokai, Lanai, Maui, and Hawaii (Big Island). The islands are as varied as their names: Kauai is a surprising mix of tropical rainforests, beautiful gardens, the Waimea Canyon, and the stunning Na Pali Coast, the back-

drop to films like *King Kong* and *Jurassic Park*. On Oahu, the most developed of the islands, the main attractions are Honolulu, the legendary Waikiki Beach and the high breakers in the surfers' paradise on the North Coast. The history of Molokai is both moving and interesting, with Father Damien at its center: in the late 19th century, he cared for those suffering from leprosy on the Kalaupapa Peninsula. Lanai, one of the smallest Hawaiian Islands, is a paradise for golfers and has the most isolated beaches. Maui, the most popular haunt of American holiday-makers, boasts luxurious hotels, a tropical wilderness on both sides of the legendary Hana Road, and Haleakala, one of the largest volcanoes on earth. Big Island, the main island in the south, also has its fair share of active volcanoes and tropical flowers.

At the Akaka Falls west of Hilo on Big Island, the water pours 130 m (426 ft) down the green rock face.

A jewel of nature on Kauai: the legendary Na Pali Coast was the setting for Steven Spielberg's film *Jurassic Park*.

The turbulent past of the islands lives on in Pu'uhonua o Honaunau and a series of other villages. Before the arrival of European settlers, the larger islands were ruled by kings who reigned with absolute power over their subjects. They paraded before their people in dazzling robes, surrounded themselves with pomp and ceremony, and lived in awe of supernatural beings. Hula dance, originally reserved exclusively for men, was a Hawaiian way of worshipping the gods. Kahunas, the priests of the people, were responsible for enforcing *kapus* or rigid taboos; death was the penalty for anyone who transgressed them. Professional storytellers still tell of these turbulent times and in the cities statues are a reminder of powerful kings like Kamehameha I.

In 1778, Captain Cook discovered the islands for the Western world. A monu-ment to him at Kealakekua Bay bears the inscription, "In memory of the great cir-cumnavigator, Captian James Cook, RN, who discovered the islands on the 10th January, AD 1778 and fell near this spot on the 14th February, AD 1779". Settlers and missionaries followed and there has been a recent influx of Asian migrants. The mix of peoples on the islands has resulted in a particularly tolerant society. Hawaii became the fiftieth US state in 1959, and tourism has helped it develop into a popular and flourishing destination.

In spite of everything, the language of the islands has been preserved in Hawaii, and if there was a prize for the friendliest and most beautiful state in the USA, Hawaii would undoubtedly be up there among the top contenders. Even the relentless spread of commercialism on some islands is no match for that aloha spirit.

Mauna Loa, one of the world's largest active volcanoes, last erupted in 1984.

Pu'uhonua o Honaunau National Historic Park

The first Polynesians arrived on Hawaii around AD 500, crossing the seas in ocean-going canoes. Once on the islands, they continued to practice their belief in the supernatural. The leaders rigidly enforced the strict *kapus* and their subjects were forced to live by those laws. The term comes from the Tahitian "tapu" (also the origin of "taboo"). Anyone who

Statues of gods on Big Island.

broke a *kapu*, e.g. by standing so that his shadow fell on the king, could expect certain death. Only the temple at Pu'uhonua o Honaunau could offer fleeing offenders a place of refuge with the priests.

From Hilo, Hawaii's main port, our island journey initially crosses barren terrain, where lava still spills out of the earth. The winding roads pass through thick forests and along steep coasts, while the snow-capped peak of Mauna Kea shines like a beacon in the distance. Our route heads north-west along the curve of the islands to Kauai.

❶ Hilo, Hawaii Planes land on the east coast of Big Island in Hilo, the island's largest settlement (population: 40,000) and the southernmost city in the USA. In the mid-19th century, missionaries arrived in Hilo Bay and built churches. In 1929, a tsunami devastated the area around Hilo Bay. The town owed its expansion to the sugar plantations. When the sugar plantations closed down in the 1990s, Hilo became known as a cultural center.

❷ Hawaii Volcanoes National Park, Hawaii This National Park in the south of Big Island is a UNESCO World Heritage Site. It includes part of Mauna Loa, the active crater of Kilauea and parts of the rugged coastline. For an eye-opener of a drive, take the 16-km (10-mile) Crater Rim Drive on Kilauea and the Chain of Craters Road, past lavascapes and fern thickets to the coast, where lava flows occur every few years. Here you can get a view of the fires of Halemau-

mau, a crater cone on Kilauea. In the rainforest, lava has solidified into what is known as the Thurston Lava Tube.

❸ Kailua-Kona, Hawaii This small and bustling city, full of hotels and restaurants, lies on a sunlit coast, complete with black lava cliffs and white sand beaches. The highways lead you through a lunar landscape. Head back to Hilo via Waimea in the north. The beautiful Scenic Drive passes through the jungle along the steep coast; rising above it all is Mauna Kea, a dormant volcano.

❹ Kahului, Maui The commercial center of the island of Maui has all the conveniences

1 The peak of Mauna Kea (4,205 m/ 13,796 ft) is snow-clad, sometimes even in the summer months.

2 The Thurston Lava Tube Trail passes through the wilderness beyond the volcanic crater on Big Island.

Travel information

Route profile
Length: approx. 2,500 km/ 1,554 miles (excluding detours)
Time needed: approx. 14 days
Start and end: Hilo (Hawaii)
Itinerary (main locations): Hawaii, Maui, Lanai, Molokai, Oahu, Kauai

Travel tips
Travel between islands is simpler by air than by boat. Aloha Airlines and Hawaiian Airlines fly most days. On the islands, it is advisable to hire a car for touring.

When to go
The best time to travel to

the islands is in late spring, when you will encounter pleasantly warm temperatures, flowers in bloom and fewer tourists, since it is also before US school holidays begin (mid-June to early September). Prices rise in summer and over Christmas and the New Year.

Accommodation
Many hotels are cheaper than you might imagine; affordable accommodation is available on all the islands.

Tourist information
www.hawaii-tourism.co.uk
www.hawaiitourism.com.au

Nature at its most spectacular: what seems to be an endless flow of bubbling molten lava spurts out into the Pacific Ocean from Kilauea on Big Island. This crater next to Mauna Loa is one of the world's most active volcanoes and covers an area of around 10 sq km (4 sq miles).

Whales

Whale-watching is very popular with visitors to Hawaii. If you want a closer view of these giant mammals, you will need to head out to sea. Choose from one of the many boat trips on offer from a range of companies. You will only manage a sighting of the mighty humpback whales between December and April, when they leave the cool waters of Alaska to mate and give birth in the southern Pacific. Whale-watchers are often lucky enough to see baby whales with their mothers. The calves put on around 45 kg (100 lbs) in weight per day while they learn to swim, hunt, and breathe. Whaling was an important industry in the 19th century. Whale oil was exported all over the world as fuel for lamps and as a lubricant. The flesh,

Top: Huge as they are, humpback whales can perform out-of-the-water acrobatics.
Bottom: The humpback whale's tail fluke has a span of up to 3 m (10 ft).

blubber, baleen, and teeth or beards of whales were also put to practical use. More than five hundred whaling boats sailed between the Aleutians and Hawaii in the Pacific, spending winters in Lahaina port. The sailors who poured into the town clearly left their morals on the other side of the cape, and turned the Hawaiian coastal town into a rowdy hell hole. At least that is how the puritanical missionaries who arrived in Lahania in 1823 found it. They imposed a curfew, persuaded the governor to place a *kapu* on the whaling boats, declaring them officially forbidden, and even commissioned the construction of a fort as protection. Even when the whalers resorted to violence, the single-minded Christians pursued their mission with determination.

(and excesses) of America, including several shopping centers and the island's only movie house. Just a few miles away, in the Iao Valley State Park, the Iao Needle juts sharply out of the lush vegetation to a height of 675 m (2,214 ft) above sea level. Legend has it that the demigod Maui turned an unwanted suitor of the beautiful Iao into this stone pinnacle.

5 Lahaina, Maui This is where history and commerce come together, where business flourishes in the shade of historic buildings that date back to the whaling era. Things were much the same centuries ago, when the Hawaiian kings and nobility frequented the west coast as a

retreat. In the 19th century, Lahaina became a major whaling port. Over five hundred ships were moored in the town's bay over the winter. Post-1850, crude oil took over from whale oil and the demise of whaling hit Lahaina hard. It became a sleepy plantation town once more and did not reawaken until 1966. Part of historic Front Street was declared a National Historic Landmark and luxurious hotels and leisure centers sprang up north of Lahaina. The whales swimming offshore, once a much sought-after commodity, became a star attraction, and whale-watching is now an important feature of every visitor's itinerary. The actors Errol Flynn and Spencer Tracy both enjoyed the fabulous view

Hana Road

The road to Hana on Maui was carved out of the volcanic coastal rock in 1927. It has some 617 bends and 56 single-lane bridges and winds through forests and past waterfalls to the lava beaches in the east, clinging to steep mountainous slopes, descending into valleys, and allowing glimpses of the ocean every few yards.

from the legendary Pioneer Inn, which dates back to 1901. The massive banyan tree, planted in memory of the missionaries, goes back even further. Just behind it you will spot the old court building and jail. From Lahaina our route leads back to Kahului.

6 Haleakala, Maui Drive up to the crater of Haleakala before sunrise and you will be rewarded for your efforts with a spectacular view of the natural world. The journey up follows Routes 37 (Haleakala Highway), 377 (Upper Kula Road) and 378 (Haleakala Crater Road), a winding road popular with mountain-bikers. The islanders of Maui call Haleakala the "house of the sun" and watch with

Surfing

Surfing legend "Duke" Kahanamoku, a direct descendant of Hawaiian royalty, became a folk hero in the early 20th century when he introduced surfing to the world. It is now an extremely popular sport. In fact, surfing existed before the arrival of Europeans on the islands. Ancient Hawaiians called it

A surfer rides a perfect wave.

reverence as the fiery star seems to rise out of the crater in the morning and sink back into it at the close of day. The crater covers an area of just under 52 sq km (20 sq miles) with a perimeter of 34 km (20 miles). Add the 7,000 m (22,966 ft) lying below sea level and you have before you one of the world's biggest mountains. The volcano last erupted 200 years ago.

7 Nahiku, Maui Nahiku has the dubious distinction of being one of the wettest places on earth. Fewer than a hundred people live in this tropical little nest where ex-Beatle George Harrison once made his home. Near Wailua, Hana Road takes you to the Waikani Falls on the

Puaa Kaa State Wayside and the Waianapanapa State Park, one of nature's gems, with tropical hala trees, temples, and a wide beach of black lava sand.

The route returns to Hana and from there along the north coast and back to Kahului for the plane trip to Lanai.

8 Lanai This exclusive island is the preserve of multimillionaires on holiday. The Lodge at Koele, located in an idyllic spot in the mountains, and the Manele Bay Hotel, a luxurious beach resort boasting one of the best golf courses in the world, are two of the top hotels on the islands.

Sights worth seeing on Lanai include the Kaunolu, a huge rock massif that rises out of the

ocean around a natural port, and the Munro Trail, a steep track that is often shrouded in mist and winds its way for around 10 km (6 miles) through the tropical rainforest.

9 Hoolehua, Molokai This sleepy little place on the island of Molokai is the gateway to another world. Aloha spirit is very much alive and kicking here. The fifth-largest island in the archipelago has remained virtually untouched by tourism. There are no skyscrapers, no gourmet restaurants, and not even a set of traffic lights. Instead, the island boasts wide expanses of beach and is imbued with the essence of Hawaii as it once was.

10 Kalaupapa, Molokai Visitors can only reach this infamous peninsula by helicopter or on the back of a mule. Kalaupapa is (continued p.216)

1 Nature's drama: sunrise over Haleakala on Maui.

2 Beyond Hana Road at Wailua the Waikani Falls cascade 70 m (230 ft) into the depths below.

3 Cooler and more refreshing than the Pacific is a dip in the waterfalls.

4 The only place in the world where the Silversword grows is on Suu Kukui and the crater of Haleakala on Maui.

5 Craters in Haleakala National Park.

"he'enalu" or wave-sliding. "To have a neat floatboard, well-kept, and dried, is to a Sandwich islander what a tilbury or cabriolet, or whatever light carriage may be in fashion is to a young English man", wrote Captain the Rt Hon. Lord Byron (cousin of the poet) as HMS *Blonde* lay at anchor off the Hawaiian coast in 1820. Back then Hawaiians used wooden boards strong enough for the powerful waves. Modern fiberglass boards take surfers on spectacular rides through the "Pipelines" off the North Coast of Oahu.

Sometimes the waves on the North Coast of the Hawaiian Islands swell to a dangerous height. On these occasions, and particularly in winter, people indulge in two kinds of surfing. Windsurfing originated in New Zealand and the USA and is more akin to sailing than surfing. Hookipa Beach on Maui is a popular meeting

place for windsurfers, who traverse the waves on their sailboards at speeds of up to 40 km/h (25 mph). Hawaiian wave-riding needs less equipment. Simply lie on a board, paddle out to the crest of a breaking wave, stand up, and ride the wave as it rushes towards the shore. It's that easy…

Honululu and Waikiki

Honolulu, a busy metropolis (around 380,000 inhabitants) in the Pacific, is the only big city on the islands. Formerly the seat of the Hawaiian kings, it is now the center of government and the hub of all social and political life. Honolulu was once a major port and an important supply base for the American troops during World War II. Nowadays the city makes its living from trade with Asia and from tourism.

The very heart of the city can be found on King Street, a bustling area right in the middle of Honolulu. A statue commemorating King Kamehameha I stands here.

Nestled among parkland boasting palms and tropical trees, the Iolani

Top: Waikiki beach.
Bottom: Honolulu skyline.

Palace is the US's only royal palace. The US flag was raised here on August 12, 1898. Opposite the Iolani Palace are the Kawaiahao Church and the Mission Houses. This was the first Christian church on the island. Built between 1836 and 1842 by the Reverend Hiram Bingham, it is made of 14,000 slabs of coral rock. The three houses next door are a reminder of the missionary years and various attempts to bring the Polynesians into the Christian fold. Waikiki is one of the best-known beachside cities in the world. This Honolulu neighborhood is bordered in the north by the Ala Wai Canal and in the south by the Pacific. Plush luxury hotels, eateries, and shops line Kalakaua Avenue and Kuhio Avenue. After extensive renovation, the beach resort has resumed its reputation as a top location.

isolated from the outside world by high cliffs and rough seas. For almost a century it served as a detention center for more than eight thousand lepers.

The next stop on our route is Honolulu on the island of Oahu.

⓫ Honolulu, Oahu See side panel, left.

⓬ Pearl Harbor, Oahu See side panel, right.

⓭ Haleiwa, Oahu Haleiwa, the former mission station at the mouth of the Anahulu River, has become a mecca for aging hippies, New Age followers, North Coast surfers, and others in search of an alternative lifestyle. The surfing beaches along the

legendary North Shore are less than 100 m (109 yds) from the two-lane road that leads to the ocean in Haleiwa and ends on the surfers' beaches.

Just a few miles further up the road is Banzai Pipeline, which ranks among the most famous surfing beaches in the world. It was the location for the 1950s film *Surf Safari*, which attained cult status and brought worldwide fame to the tunnel-shaped breakers on the North Coast. Only the most experienced surfers brave the "Pipeline" wave that is thrown up by a flat tabletop reef.

Next door is Sunset Beach with its long (3 km/2 mile) stretch of sand, packed with surfers' cars during the winter. According to

surfing pros, this is where you'll find the best waves. Beginners should look for calmer waters before trying their hand at the sport, however. The breakers here are extremely dangerous and should be braved only by skilled surfers with years of experience.

⓮ Polynesian Cultural Center, Oahu Students admitted to the Mormon Brigham Young University in Laie swear that they will never grow a beard and promise to lead a wholly moral life, free of alcohol and drugs. They earn their pocket money in the nearby Polynesian Cultural Center, an informative pleasure park with a touch of Disneyland about it in the early

evening. Later in the evening the park explodes into a kitschy but spectacular and opulent show, in which Polynesian musicians, singers, and dancers perform the history and myths of the South Seas. Volcanoes spewing fire, rushing waterfalls and palm-roofed huts are the backdrop to a spectacle that not even the IMAX Polynesia Theater's big screen can rival.

The Polynesian Cultural Center was built in 1963 and many people expected it to flop. Few believed that tourists would travel from Waikiki to Laie to visit a cultural park. They thought that people visiting Hawaii would want to do little else but lie on the sand and swim in the sea. How wrong they

Pearl Harbor

On December 7, 1941, Japanese bombers, torpedo jets, and fighter-planes attacked the US naval base of Pearl Harbor. It was one of the great defining moments in world history. The Americans were taken utterly by surprise, even though intelligence services had cracked the Japanese secret code months before. Some people still maintain that the US President withheld his knowledge of the forthcoming attack to pave the way for his country's entry into war following the catastrophe. The US Pacific Fleet was unprepared: seven of its battleships lay anchored like open targets in Battleship Row. Japanese planes appeared over Pearl Harbor at 7.55am and launched their

Top: The Arizona Memorial was erected in remembrance of the dead.
Bottom: The USS *Arizona*.

were. The "PCC" as most locals call it, has become a real tourist magnet. Profits go to Brigham Young University and the Latter-day Saints.
The Center's seven villages represent the cultures of Samoa, New Zealand, Fiji, Hawaii, the Marquesas, Tahiti, and Tonga. Polynesian students, mainly from the same islands, sing traditional songs, play historical instruments, cook their native dishes, and relate the stories and legends of their home. Their houses are situated on the banks of a man-made river and lectures and concerts are held in the public square.

15 Valley of the Temples, Oahu The Valley of the Temples, a non-denominational place of worship, is set against the dramatic backdrop of the verdant mountain slopes of Oahu's Windward Coast, which are usually covered in cloud. It offers magnificent views over the coastline.
The Byodo-In Temple is a faithful replica of the 900-year-old Byodo-In in Uji, Japan. It was built in 1968 to commemorate the centenary of the arrival of the first Japanese immigrants to Hawaii. Kiichi Sano, a famous landscape architect from Kyoto, designed the tranquil garden refuge at a distance from the hustle and bustle of Honolulu. The sound of a 3-ton brass bell spreads the word of Amidha Buddha and calls people to

meditation while peacocks fan out their bright tail feathers along the pathways.

16 Kailua, Oahu The journey along the Windward Coast heads south and through the old part of Kailua, past the beach homes of the rich and famous. Kailua Beach Park, a wide expanse of sandy beach with perfect conditions for surfing, is the meeting place for Hawaii's bravest and most experienced surfers. The only place you will see brighter sails is on the North Coast of Maui. Windsurfing is relatively rare on the islands, since any surfer worth his salt would prefer to take to the waves aboard a "proper" surfboard.
Sparse woodland separates the white strip of sand from the inland area and provides some extremely welcome shade during the midday heat. The beach is relatively quiet, in fact by Oahu's standards it is virtually deserted, and particularly popular with families. Kailua Beach is one of the safest beaches on Oahu, since it shelves further out to sea and there is no strong current; the only danger is at the weekend, when the bay is packed with surfers and you might get hit by the sharp end of a surfboard.

Further south is Lanikai Beach, which slopes even more gently into the sea and is not widely known. The place has managed to hold out against the spread of commercialism. Its key attractions include soft sand and clear blue water, making it the perfect spot for a picnic.
As you head back to Honolulu, just some 20 minutes away on the Pali Highway, it is worth making a slight detour along the coast via Kahala. This is Honolulu's smart suburb, filled with luxurious villas.

17 Lihue, Kauai Our tour of Kauai begins in Lihue, the island's capital, and as a result of the impassable cliffs on the north-west coast the route is best described as fork-shaped. Lihue has a busy shopping area and many commercial outlets.
(continued p.218)

1 Stormy weather on Oahu's Windward Coast.

2 Molokai remains relatively untouched by civilization.

3 A young Hawaiian woman greets the sunrise.

4 Lush nature and a dramatic crater in the Oahu interior.

deadly attack. At 8.10am the USS *Arizona* was hit by a huge bomb. The massive vessel sank in less than nine minutes, with 1,177 crew on board. The USS *Oklahoma* was hit in the side and rolled over, trapping 400 men inside. The USS *Utah* also keeled over in the water and other ships were seriously damaged. The Japanese ceasefire came at 10am, leaving a scene of devastation and destruction in its wake. In total, 2,395 soldiers were lost, 164 planes destroyed, and the proud ships of the Pacific Fleet lay sunk or severely damaged. The USS *Arizona* Memorial marks the spot where the battleship went down and is a reminder of this horrific event in history. The white, open-air shrine displays the names of all the men lost on the *Arizona* and remains one of Hawaii's most visited historic sites.

The Kauai Museum provides information on the island's past. Kalapaki Beach and the palm-flanked Kauai Lagoon are just a few miles away.

18 Kapaa, Kauai The route to Na Pali Coast takes us via Kapaa, a small town with an attractive shopping area. The "Sleeping Giant" is a gigantic rock in the mountains that lies just inland. Legend has it that the giant once helped to build a temple and ate so much during the ensuing festivities that he fell asleep, never to wake again. One of the must-dos in this region is a boat trip on the Wailua River to Fern Grotto, a romantic cavern covered in ferns. The Wailua Falls are not far from here.

19 Hanalei, Kauai This sleepy fishing village serves as a base camp for trips to Na Pali Coast. Several artists have settled here and there's a lively nightlife in the few local pubs and bars. A luxury hotel is situated on nearby Hanalei Bay, and Hanalei Lookout offers fantastic views over the ocean and the lush tropical landscape.

20 Na Pali Coast, Kauai The rugged mountain slopes on this legendary coast are one of the world's most amazing natural wonders. The sun creates bizarre images on the furrowed rock face that rises high above the ocean and casts a long shadow. Most of Na Pali Coast is a conservation area. Above the coastline, the Kalalau Trail passes through forests and over ridges to the Kalalau Valley. The trail ends at Kalalau Beach.

21 Poipu Beach, Kauai The route initially heads south via Lihue and then west to the most popular beach on Kauai. A massive reef protects the sandy beach against the raging waves. This is where half of the island's inhabitants meet at the weekend. A bumpy sand track leads to nearby Mahaulepu, the collective name given to Gillin's Beach, Kawailoa Bay, and Haula Beach, all of which are usually peaceful and deserted.

22 Waimea Canyon, Kauai Waimea means "red water" and the glistening red river of the same name lies embedded here in the volcanic earth. Above the river, the winding Waimea Canyon Drive heads up into the mountains. With its luscious vegetation and emerald-green forests, highlighted oasis-like against the red, brown, and purple rock, the Waimea Canyon is the largest in the Pacific and is a dramatic, awe-inspiring sight. It is the Pacific's answer to the Grand Canyon and, although smaller, it is just as spectacular. There are numerous lookouts offering fabulous panoramic views. The canyon brings our journey to a spectacular close.

1 The wildly romantic Na Pali Coast in the north of Kauai.

2 The Wailua Falls, not far from Kapaa, cascade 30 m (99 ft) down the rock face.

3 The dramatic shades of the Waimea Canyon.

Na Pali Coast (Kauai) Fabulous sandy beaches line the rugged slopes, most of which are conservation areas, in the north of Kauai.

Molokai Just 8,000 people live on the fifth-largest Hawaiian island. The absence of tourist facilities has helped to keep the whole island relatively unspoilt.

Maui The north of the island features excellent conditions for surfers. Winter months are best for stunning views of huge breakers rolling onto the shore.

Pearl Harbor (Oahu) Since December 7, 1941, Pearl Harbor on the island of Oahu has been remembered for a traumatic event in modern US history. Japanese planes bombarded the battleships anchored there, leaving a scene of devastation behind them. Today the port is still a US deep-water naval base and includes a memorial to those who died.

Haleakala National Park (Maui) A walking trail winds up the side of the crater of Haleakala, a massive volcano that covers three-quarters of Maui.

Waikiki Beach (Oahu) The world-famous city shoreline in the south of Oahu is a suburb of Honolulu. Many restaurants, hotels, boutiques, and bars vie for tourist trade.

Mauna Kea (Hawaii) Few views can beat the one over Hawaii from this peak, named "white mountain" in Hawaiian for the snow that usually covers its summit.

Pu'uhonua o Honaunau Historical Park (Hawaii) The Ku-Kaili and Ku-Ki'i-Akua statues belong to the temple gardens in the park where breakers of *kapu* once sought sanctuary.

Hilo (Hawaii) This bustling city lies at the most southerly point of the USA and is the main settlement on Big Island, as the largest island in the archipelago is also known. The sugar-cane industry that made Hilo its fortune has now all but vanished, but with its Caribbean ambience and houses of bright hues, the city is now a center for arts and culture. It also has a number of dockyards and tourists come here to enjoy its great variety of tropical flowers.

Hawaii Volcanoes National Park This park, located in the south of Hawaii, has been designated a UNESCO World Heritage Site, as are parts of Mauna Loa, Kilauea, and the coast. Molten lava can often be found flowing through the dark and primeval-looking scree landscape. A journey along the 16-km (10-mile) Crater Rim Drive on Kilauea is an extraordinary experience.

Galápagos Islands
Noah's Ark in the Pacific

When Hermann Melville, the author of *Moby Dick*, visited the Galápagos in 1841 he described them as "enchanted islands" that were unlike any-where else in the world in terms of their surreal appearance. Piles of vol-canic ash cover the landscape, which appears as the earth might look after a terrible, global fire.

The Galápagos Islands are a surreal and rather inhospitable place, with hills and mountains of lava and sparse forests instead of sandy beaches and palm groves, not to mention the cold water that sur-rounds them. The average sea tempera-ture in August is a chilly 19°C (66°F), only rising by another 10 degrees or so in March and April, so this is no tourist's dream trop-ical destination. However, the islands form a truly unique natural paradise for animal and plant life, with species that do not exist anywhere else on earth, including sea lions, reptiles, and water birds. The animals

and birds are also unique in that they have no natural enemies on the islands, and, having no fear of humans either, they do not automatically run or fly away when humans approach them.

It is vitally important that this natural world be protected, but inevitably the large numbers of people who now visit the islands represent a threat to its extraordinary wild life. In an effort to preserve the islands, the Ecuadorian government declared them a national park in 1959, and in 1978, the Parque Nacional y Reserva Marina Galápagos

A land tortoise on the island of Santa Cruz.

became the first area to be designated a UNESCO World Heritage Site.

The islands are located almost 1,000 km (620 miles) from the coast of Ecuador between 90 and 92°W longitude and 1.4°N and 1.3°S latitude. The group com-prises thirteen main islands and around fifty smaller ones. The largest island is Isabela, with a surface area of 4,855 sq km (1,874 sq miles). The volcano of Cerro Azul (1,689 m/5,542 ft), the highest mountain in the island group, is a dis-tinctive landmark. The north-westerly islands of Fernandina and Isabela, the youngest islands geologically-speaking, have the most active volcanoes.

The islands were formed as a result of volcanic activity. They lie on a hotspot, a zone beneath the earth's crust where there is known volcanic activity, with magma rising up from the earth's inner

The Sally Lightfoot crab is the most striking of the three types of crab that live on the islands. In contrast to the mature crabs, the young are gray-black.

A glowing sunset sky over Puerto Villamil on the island of Isabela.

core. Due to continental drift, part of the the earth's crust, in this case the Nazca plate, is moving slowly to the south-east toward the South American continent. The islands were formed around nine million years ago and were initially an empty wasteland, but today they are famous for their animal and plant life. So how did plants and animals reach these islands so far from the mainland? The majority of the plants were brought here in the form of seeds and spores on the wind, while birds such as albatrosses and terns, and some insects could naturally fly here. Seals, penguins, and sea tortoises could reach the islands by sea, assisted by strong ocean currents. Driftwood and clumps of vegetation floating on the sea may have served as a means of transportation for animals from South America, including the land-dwelling tortoises and lizards. However, only animals that can survive for a long period of time without food and water have been able to survive on the archipelago, explaining why some species are common on the island and others are rare. There are, for example, many sea birds, sea mammals, and reptiles, but no land mammals except for two species of bat (and also rats and goats, introduced by man). For many people the islands are inextricably linked with just one man, Charles Darwin, the English naturalist who, after visiting them in 1835 while on his five-year voyage aboard the *Beagle*, proposed his theory of evolution. In his seminal work *On the Origin of the Species* (1859), Darwin proposed that through a process of natural selection all species of life have evolved over time from one or a few common ancestors.

A wide variety of tropical fish live in the sea around the islands: a shoal of yellowfin surgeonfish.

To make the most of a visit to the Galápagos Islands, you really need to spend several days cruising the islands. Not all of them can be visited, however, the national park administration has set up numerous official visitor sites that are open to the public and can be explored with a guide. As a province of Ecuador, the official names of the islands are Spanish (as used here), but they also have English names: Albemarle for Isabela, Narborough for Fernandina, Indefatigable for Santa Cruz, Charles for Floreana, etc.

❶ Santa Cruz Almost all the cruises start on Santa Cruz. It is the second largest island in the archipelago and has not only the most diverse vegetation and the largest town, Puerto Ayora, but is also the location of the Charles Darwin Research Station, the islands' center for scientific research. The creation and evolution of life on the islands is explained at the museum there. The largest tortoise in the world, the Galápagos giant tortoise, endemic to several of the islands, is one of the main attractions here. The station has established a breeding program in an effort to preserve the breed and increase its numbers. As soon as the tortoises have reached a cer-

tain size, they are released into the wild, many into the tortoise reserves near Santa Rosa and Santa Cruz, where they lie in the meadows, motionless like large rocks.

In the north of the island is the Caleta Tortuga Negra, a cove with mangroves where a large number of pelicans nest and sea turtles, small whitetip sharks, and rays can be seen in the water.

❷ Islas Plaza Sur To the east of Santa Cruz are the two Plaza islands, though tourists are only allowed to visit Plaza Sur. Several rare species live here so it is one of the early highlights of the cruise. Sea birds such as the

red-billed tropic bird and the swallow-tailed gull nest on ledges along the steep coast and sea lions slide off the rocks to frolic in the water. The Galápagos sea lion, one of the six mammal species that live on the islands, is a subspecies of the Californian sea lion. They live in colonies of around twenty to thirty females to one bull. The males are considerably larger and can weigh up to 250 kg (550 lbs). They have a strong skull and a massive, thick neck. Usually playful and curious, young sea lions are often encountered in the water by divers.

Under the *Opuntia* (fig cacti), seemingly lethargic iguana sit in a motionless state. They are small, dragon-like lizards, typically with an orange-yellow back and a red-brown stomach and a ridge of spines running down the neck and back. However, do not be fooled by their apparently quiet demeanor; male land iguanas will defend their territory and females against rivals very aggressively. The only natural enemy of adult land iguanas, which grow to

Travel information

Route profile
Length: approx. 1,000 km (620 miles)
Duration: at least 1 week
Start and end: Puerto Ayora (Santa Cruz)
Itinerary (main locations): Santa Cruz, Islas Plaza Sur, Floreana, Española, Isabela, Fernandina, Santiago, Bartolomé, Genovesa, Santa Cruz

Travel tips
The cruise ships travel at

night and visit the islands during the day when passengers are taken to the islands for excursions. All boats have at least one guide on board. Tourists on package deals who book in Europe or Ecuador are met by the organizer at the airport. Cruises can also be booked in Puerto Ayora on Santa Cruz.

Tourist information
www.visitecuador.de
www.darwinfoundation.org

around 1 m (3 ft) in length and weigh around 13 kg (29 lb), are their own kind.

❸ Floreana One of the few inhabited islands in the archipelago is Floreana. The first European to set foot on the Galápagos was the Spaniard Tomás de Berlanga. Having failed to find fresh water there he thought them worthless, just a pile of rock inhabited by strange animals. Until the early 1800s the islands were mostly used by English pirates who ambushed Spanish galleons on their way from South America

to Spain. Then whalers arrived around 1790 and used the islands as a base from which to hunt not only whales but tortoises until around 1870. They sometimes took live tortoises on board ship with them to ensure a fresh supply of food. On some of the islands, the tortoises were completely wiped out. Floreana has an interesting history. The first person to settle here permanently was an Irishman called Patrick Watkins. Stranded on the island in 1807, he made a cave near Post Office Bay his home for several years.

He grew vegetables and traded them for rum from passing whalers, but eventually had his

fill of the solitary life, stole a dinghy and persuaded five sailors to take him to the main-

land. After Ecuador annexed the islands in 1832, Floreana was initially used as a penal colony. In the 1930s, a group of German and Austrian bohemians arrived, dreaming of a life lived close to nature. However, disputes arose and some of the group died in mysterious circumstances, leading to much speculation in the press at the time. In World War II, Ecuador

1 This land iguana on the island of Plaza Sur looks like a strange prehistoric creature.

2 Mist shrouds the peaks of the volcanoes on the island of Santa Cruz.

3 Curious sea lions are not afraid to swim close to visitors under the water.

4 A brown pelican's nest, protected by mangroves.

5 The fruits of the fig cactus are popular with land iguanas.

6 A marine iguana warms itself in the sun after a swim.

Darwin's finches

Charles Darwin visited the Galápagos archipelago in 1835, but it wasn't the giant tortoises or strange iguanas that sparked the insight that would eventually lead to his famous theory of evolution, but rather the humble Galápagos finches. There are thirteen different species of finch on the islands, each

Top: Small-beaked Darwin finch.
Bottom: Medium ground-finch.

with a different beak shape, varying from a narrow beak suited to catching insects, to a thick beak to crack open seeds, or one that enables the bird to use cactus spikes to dig maggots out of the bark of trees.

Darwin initially thought the birds were descendants of different types of bird, until biologists told him that they were all related. Darwin theorized that the finches had changed and evolved over the course of many years in order to adapt to their respective environments, and that the specific characteristics they developed would eventually be inherited.

granted the US navy permission to establish a base on the islands to guard the approaches to the Panama Canal.

Today, only Santa Cruz, San Cristóbal, Floreana, and the south of Isabela are inhabited, but now tourists are arriving in numbers, bringing money to the islands and boosting their economy which otherwise relies on agriculture and fishing.

One of the visitor sites on Floreana is Punta Cormorán to the north of the island, where flamingos can often be seen in the lagoon. At nearby Post Office Bay you can see a ragtag of mailboxes marking the spot where English whalers first set up a post box in the 18th century. Sailors passing back and forth would stop off to leave mail here to be taken by ships on their way home, or collect post that had been brought out. Today it is the tourists who use the mailboxes however.

④ **Española** The southernmost island of the archipelago has several beautiful visitor sites. On the coast at Bahía Gardner in the north-east of Española, you can see a large group of sea lions, while at Punta Suárez in the north-west, you can follow a circular trekking path (around 2 km/11/4 miles), which takes you past colonies of blue-footed and masked boobies. The birds will often remain quite happily in their nests on the ground as tourist pass by just a few feet away. Elegant in flight but awkward on the ground, albatrosses also nest here, while marine iguanas inhabit the cliffs.

⑤ **Isabela** This is the largest of the Galápagos Islands but one of the least populated. Its capital city, Puerto Villamil, is in the south-east of the island, with around two thousand inhabitants. Nearby, a short walk away through mangrove forests, is the Laguna de Villamil, a popular feeding-ground for flamingos. Puerto Villamil also has the most beautiful beaches of the islands and a breeding station for Galápagos tortoises. You can see them around the crater of the volcano Alcedo (1,097 m/3,599 ft). On a trek up to the peak from the eastern side of the island, you will pass through several different vegetation zones before arriving at the top from where you can see down into the huge caldera (around 7 km/4 miles in diameter). These almost circular, very deep craters are a typical feature of the islands' volcanic landscape. They are formed when the magma chamber beneath the cone empties, causing the rock above the now hollow chamber to collapse.

As on the other islands, there are six different vegetation zones on Isabela, determined by the height above sea level. In the coastal zone, almost all the plants, such as mangroves, are resistant to salt and strong ocean winds. The arid lowland zone extends from the coastal zone to an elevation of around 100 m (328 ft) and is dominated mainly by cacti and palosanto trees, which have no leaves for most of the year. Thanks to more frequent rainfall, evergreen plants flourish in the next

(continued p.228)

1 Flamingos search for food in the shallows of the lagoon on Floreana.

2 Marine iguana in the surf.

Despite being all around the same size, the different types of Darwin finches on the island have all developed different shapes and sizes of beak, to suit their different feeding habits. The cactus finch, shown here, feeds mainly on pollen and the fruit of the *Opuntia* (fig cactus).

Covering an area of 4,855 sq km (1,874 sq m), Isabela is the largest of the Galápagos islands and is more volcanically active than most of the others. Situated slightly east of the Galápagos Hotspot, thought to be near Fernandina, Isabela has five active volcanoes. Arranged roughly from north to south these are:

zone, the transitional, which extends to around 200 m (656 ft). Next is the Scalesia zone, which rises to 400 m (1,312 ft) above sea level. It is named after the *Scalesia* plant, a member of the daisy family endemic to the Galápagos Islands. Some species of *Scalesia* grow so tall they can be classed as trees. The next level is the Miconia zone (up to 500 m/1,640 ft), named after the *Miconia*, a type of shrub also endemic to the islands that grows up to 4 m (13 ft) in height and often forms an impenetrable tangle of vegetation with other plants. Beyond the Miconia zone, the Pampa zone is the highest and wettest. There are virtually no trees or shrubs growing here, just ferns, grasses, and sedges.

The Pampa zone is also the preferred habitat of the Galápagos tortoise, which can be seen here in large numbers. There were originally fourteen different tortoise subspecies on the island, but today only eleven remain, living on different islands. In 1835, when Charles Darwin visited the islands, he met the English governor of Floreana, Nicholas Lawson, who told Darwin he could identify from which island any tortoise had been brought by the shape of its shell. Larger and heavier

tortoises have evenly formed and dome-shaped shells, while the slightly smaller tortoises have a saddle-shaped shell. The saddle-back tortoises gave the islands their name as *galápago* means tortoise in Spanish. While the larger subspecies of tortoise eats mainly grass, the saddle-back tortoise feeds on slightly taller vegetation, low-growing leaves, and twigs. This is why their shell is arched high at the neck and their legs and necks are slightly longer.

Land tortoises mate during the rainy season, which on the Galápagos is January to June. Then, at the beginning of the dry season, the female tortoise lays two to sixteen eggs in a hole in the ground around 30 cm (12 in) deep, which she digs with her back legs. After four months, the baby tortoises emerge from their shells. Their gender is determined mainly by the temperature at which they are incubated; males develop when the temperature is low and females when it is high. The very young tortoises are at risk from predators such as buzzards, but once their shells start to harden they are better protected. If attacked, their defensive strategy is normally passive. Expelling air from their bodies with a hiss, they with-

draw their head and legs into their shell.

In addition to the tortoises, there are twenty-two other species of interesting reptiles on the islands, twenty of which

are endemic. Reptiles are cold-blooded vertebrates that are unable to regulate their body temperature, but are resistant to extreme changes in temperature. They may sit motionless in

the sun to warm themselves up after a cold night or after a spell in cold water, while in very hot weather they spend their time keeping cool in water or in the shade.

The marine iguana is unique to the islands; it is the only iguana that swims and forages in saltwater. "A hideous-looking creature, of a dirty black color, stupid, and sluggish in its movements" is how Darwin described it in disgust. It lives on land, but finds most of its food in the ocean, grazing on algae at depths of up to 15 m (50 ft), and can even survive underwater for up to an hour. Marine iguanas store oxygen in their tissues, which they then consume when underwater, and can also reduce their heart rate from its normal forty-five beats per minute to only eight to twelve beats, and can sometimes stop it altogether. They are excellent swimmers, holding their legs close to their bodies and propelling themselves forward with their long tails. Untroubled by strong currents, they can cling securely to rocks underwater with their strong claws. The marine iguana has no natural predators on land, but while in the ocean it can fall prey to hungry sharks.

After a spell in the water, the iguanas lie close to each other on rocks in the sun to warm themselves up. They expel the salt that they have taken in with their food by spraying it out through a gland in the head.

6 Fernandina The third-largest island of the Galápagos is the youngest and also the most volcanically active, situated almost exactly above the hotspot that created the island group. Fernandina's first major eruption did not take place until 1988, which is why the lava formations are different here. The layers of lava are very thin, causing fresh lava to flow out of the crater rather than erupt explosively, and it solidifies very slowly. Two types of lava are characteristic here: pahoehoe, or skeleton lava, which has a lumpy or ropy surpface, and aa lava, which is rougher and more rubbly in appearance, composed of clinker.

At Punta Espinosa, you can see the flightless cormorant, which is endemic to the islands. Since it has no natural predators, but has a plentiful supply of food available on land, it has lost the ability to fly. The largest colony of Galápagos penguins also lives here, which is incidentally the only species of penguin that lives north of the equator.

Brown penguins are also found on Fernandina. They build their nests in low-lying bushes on the coast or in mangrove trees, of which there are also many on the island. The females lay two to three eggs and both male and female share first the incubation of the eggs and then the feeding of the young.

7 Santiago The fourth-largest Galápagos island has a desert-like volcanic landscape. There are a number of official visitor sites on the island. At Sullivan Bay to the east of the island, you can see a fresh lava field that is barely eroded, though fresh in volcanic terms means it is around two hundred years old. You can see the different types of lava here and some of the first pioneer plants (species that colonize previously uncolonized land) such as the lava cactus, though plant life develops very slowly here.

Southern fur seals live at Puerto Egas, on the west of the island, and many varieties of long-legged wading birds can also be sighted along the coast, searching for food in shallow water or marshes. Some of the most striking are flamingos and red-billed American oystercatchers. Great white egrets, cayenne night-herons, and lava herons also live here.

(continued p.232)

1 Giant tortoises relaxing in the pampa vegetation zone of the Alcedo volcano on Isabela.

2 Close to some red Sally Lightfoot crabs, a group of marine iguanas, warm themselves up after swimming in the cold water.

3 Impressive volcanic activity on the island of Fernandina.

4 Wild flowers manage to grow on slopes overlooking a volcanic crater lake.

There are two types of iguana on the Galápagos Islands. As its name suggests, the Galápagos land iguana lives almost exclusively on land, the usual habitat of iguanas, while its cousin, the marine iguana, has developed quite a taste for the sea. As a result of the small area of food to be found on land, it forages in

the ocean, where temperatures can sometimes fall to below 18°C (64°F). The marine iguana can stay underwater for up to an hour, an unusual length of time for a cold-blooded animal. During the mating season, it changes its appearance and the skin of the males turns various shades of green and copper.

The bird island of Genovesa

Genovesa (Tower Island) is a paradise for birds. Bird watchers wanting to see some of this tranquil island's amazing bird life should take one of the two paths that lead from the Playa de Bahía Darwin into the island's interior. They can see three types of booby: blue-footed boobies, which also live in large colonies on Española and Seymour; the rare red-footed boobies

Top: Albatross courtship.
Middle: A red-footed booby landing.
Bottom: Short-eared owl.

with their blue bills and red feet, which dive spectacularly into the ocean in search of fish; and masked boobies, which are easy to recognize thanks to the dark grey mask on their face, against a coat of feathers that is completely white. Unlike other types of booby, which lay their eggs on the ground, red-footed boobies build their nests in bushes and small trees. Colonies of frigate birds can also be seen here, along with storm petrels and swallow-tail gulls.

Punta Espumilla is a good place for snorkeling and exploring underwater, but it can often be quite difficult to identify the different fish; there are around three hundred different types to be seen in these waters. You can also see larger marine creatures such as rays and sharks. Of all the different types of ray, only stingrays are dangerous, but even so they are not likely to attack in aggression. They like to hide on the sea bed, burrowing into the sand. They may sting in a reflex action if stepped on, or if attacked by a predator. Gold rays and the eagle ray (easily identifiable as it is black with white spots) are both far more vibrant in appearance than the stingray. A diverse range of sharks also live here, some are harmless, such as the gigantic whale shark, which can grow up to 15 m (49 ft) in length and which is seldom glimpsed by divers, while others should be given a wide berth. Oceanic whitetip sharks are fairly common here and can be aggressive; hammerhead sharks are also aggressive and are easy to identify from their odd hammer-shaped head; and large tiger sharks, which are very dangerous predators, can also be seen. Feral pigs and goats were introduced to Santiago by humans but caused a great deal of harm to the endemic species. They are likely to have been introduced fairly shortly after Charles Darwin's visit in 1835. The pig population was reported to be

numerous as early as 1875. As pigs are omnivores they eat both native plants and animals, including green turtles, lava lizards, petrels, and the eggs and hatchlings of tortoises. Since their presence was clearly threatening the survival of these species it was decided that drastic action would have to be taken. An eradication program was launched in 1968, and the island was finally cleared of pigs in 2000, while the goat population is now virtually zero too.

8 Bartolomé The landscape on the tiny island of Bartolomé looks desert-like in places, but its two sandy beaches, sepa-rated by a narrow isthmus, are perfect for swimming and snorkeling. Climb up Bartolomé's volcanic cone, its highest peak, passing cinder cones and lava tunnels on the way, for some beautiful views over Isla Santiago and the Pináculo (Pinnacle Rock), a volcanic rock formation that that rises out of the sea like an enormous shark fin. Divers venturing into the cold water might come across sea lions and, if they are lucky, and if the water is cold enough, penguins. The sandy beaches are also the stomping ground of ghost crabs (also called sand crabs), with their eyes on stalks they have an excellent field of vision.

9 Genovesa This small, horseshoe-shaped "bird island" (see panel, left) north of the equator is the all that is left of a submerged volcano. It covers just 14 sq km (5 sq miles) and its highest point, a volcanic peak, is just 76 m (249 ft) above sea level.

1 The two beautiful beaches of Bartolomé are separated by a narrow isthmus. On the right is the Pináculo rock formation. The island of Santiago is in the background.

2 Storm-battered cliffs on the coast of Santiago are a perfect habitat for cliff-dwelling birds such as white-faced shearwaters and storm petrels.

Cerro Azul (Isabela) At 1,689 m (5,542 ft), this is the highest volcano on Isabela and has a round crater lake. As the island is only just east of the Galápagos volcanic Hotspot, earth tremors are quite common.

Alcedo (Isabela) Giant tortoises inhabit the pampa zone on this volcano (1,097 m/3,590 ft), where they feed on grass. The giant tortoise can live for as long as 200 years.

Santiago Vegetation is sparse here, but it is a good diving location; sharks and rays can be seen as well as marine iguanas who brave the cold waters in search of food.

Bartolomé This small island is characterized by its rugged rocky cliffs and isolated beaches. The Pináculo rock rises up in the distance to the right.

Santa Cruz The second-largest Galápagos Island is the starting point for many of the islands' tours, It is known for its diverse vegetation and its land tortoise reserve.

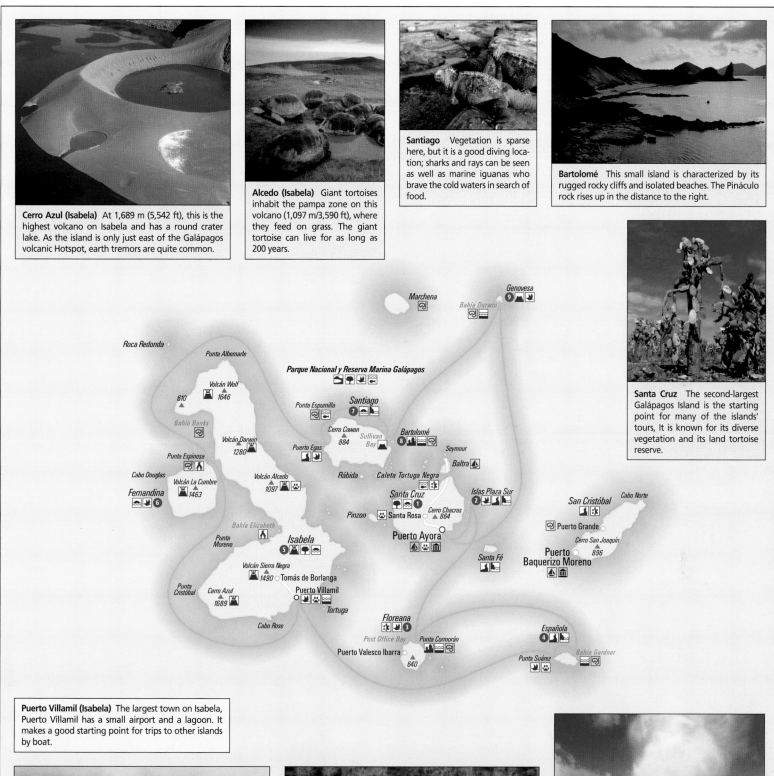

Marchena

Genovesa 9
Bahía Darwin

Roca Redonda

Punta Albemarle

Parque Nacional y Reserva Marina Galápagos

Volcán Wolf
610   1646

Punta Espumilla

Santiago 7

Bahía Banks

Cerro Cowan 884   Sullivan Bay

Volcán Darwin 1280

Puerto Egas

Bartolomé 8

Punta Espinosa

Seymour

Cabo Douglas

Volcán La Cumbre

Fernandina 6

Volcán Alcedo 1097

Rábida

Baltra

Caleta Tortuga Negra

Santa Cruz 1

Islas Plaza Sur 2

Pinzon   Santa Rosa

Cerro Chacras 864

San Cristóbal
Cabo Norte

Bahía Elizabeth

Punta Moreno

Isabela 5

Puerto Ayora

Santa Fé

Puerto Grande

Cerro San Joaquín 896

Puerto Baquerizo Moreno

Volcán Sierra Negra 1490   Tomás de Borlanga

Punta Cristóbal

Cerro Azul 1689   Puerto Villamil

Tortuga

Cabo Rose

Floreana 3

Post Office Bay   Punta Cormorán

Puerto Valesco Ibarra   640

Española 4

Punta Suárez   Bahía Gardner

Puerto Villamil (Isabela) The largest town on Isabela, Puerto Villamil has a small airport and a lagoon. It makes a good starting point for trips to other islands by boat.

Fernandina The youngest and most volcanically active of the Galápagos Islands experienced its last major eruption in 1988. This is a good place to see several of the different types of lava.

Floreana Though now almost deserted, you can still see traces of human activity here, the legacy of early settlers, whalers, and pirates. Flamingos inhabit a lagoon to the north of the island.

Española This island is worth visiting for its rich wildlife, including lava lizards and marine iguanas, and birds such as albatrosses, finches, and boobies.

Fiji, Tonga, and Samoa
Island-hopping in Western Polynesia

The island states of Fiji, Tonga, and Samoa are made up of a number of islands and beaches spread over a wide expanse of sea. Mountain ranges criss-cross volcanic islands covered in virgin forests, and in contrast there are also many flat coral islands and atolls. The cultural diversity of Western Polynesia is equally fascinating.

On average, the Pacific Ocean seabed lies at a depth of 4,000 m (13,124 ft). This unimaginably vast expanse is punctuated by numerous volcanic islands, coral reefs, and atolls; these island chains were formed by movement of the earth's tectonic plates. The Pacific Plate slowly slid toward the Australian and Philippine Plates and, where these plates met, the Pacific Plate was submerged, creating deep sea rifts, such as the Tonga Rift: these are among the lowest points of the earth's crust. The submerged rock then melted deep down in the earth's mantle, ex-

panded again and, through powerful volcanic eruptions, was thrown back up to the surface, creating the volcanic islands that make up the "Pacific Ring of Fire" as they are also known. These volcanic islands can reach considerable altitudes. By contrast, the coral reefs and atolls are often only a few feet above sea level.

The first settlers to the islands came from Australia and New Guinea. They arrived in Fiji around 1500 BC, reaching Tonga and Samoa a little later. Their vast knowledge of wind and weather conditions, ocean currents, stars, and bird migration routes

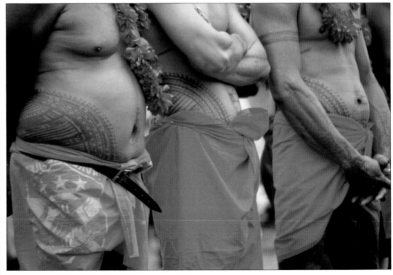

Tattooed male hips and stomachs are a cultural tradition in Samoa.

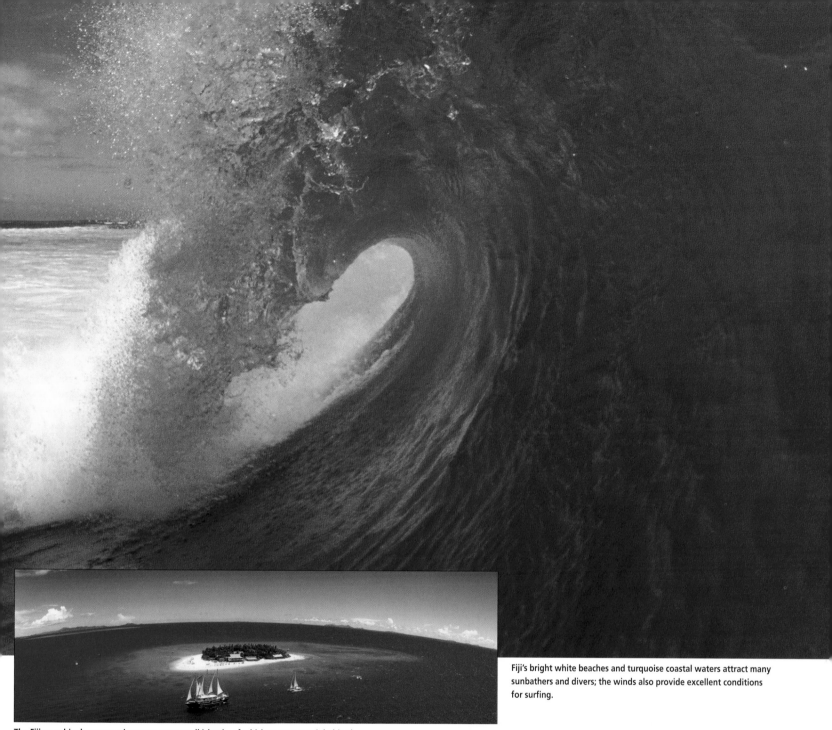

Fiji's bright white beaches and turquoise coastal waters attract many sunbathers and divers; the winds also provide excellent conditions for surfing.

The Fijian archipelago comprises numerous small islands, of which many are uninhabited.

enabled Polynesians to undertake extensive voyages of discovery through which they gradually established settlements on most of the Polynesian islands.

Fiji comprises around three hundred islands, although only one hundred or so are permanently inhabited. Its scenic diversity sets Fiji apart from other South Sea islands. Fijians are very traditional and set great store on maintaining their cultural values. They see themselves as ambassadors of the Pacific way of life, embodying the essence of what makes their political and cultural lifestyle different from that of the West. However, there is also a large population of Fiji Indians, who were originally imported as plantation workers by the islands' British colonial rulers.

Roughly 500 km (310 miles) to the east, the kingdom of Tonga is Fiji's neighbor. Tongans are hospitable people, polite and reserved. Proud of their traditions, they enjoy a laid-back lifestyle. Tonga is made up of some 150 islands, mostly strung out at quite some distance from each other. Its gems can be found in the north: the islands of the Vava'u group are among the most beautiful in the South Seas.

In Samoa, the Polynesian way of life has been preserved in its purest form. "Fa'a Samoa" (meaning "the Samoan Way"), a traditional system of behavior and responsibilities, is still a strong influence and Samoans have so far succeeded in defending it against Western incursions. It manages to fulfill most tourists' romantic expectations of life in the South Seas. As a result of former colonial days, Samoa is now divided into Western Samoa and American Samoa to the east. Culturally, however, the islands continue to form a unified whole.

Barracudas armed with frightening sets of teeth dart through the coastal waters of Polynesia.

Wildlife of the Fiji islands

Fiji's reptiles include not only crocodiles but two remarkable iguanas: the banded iguana and the larger Fijian crested iguana, which can grow up to 1 m (over 3 ft) long. Birds include sunbirds, kingfishers, several species of parrot and dove, as well as many native birds, including the Fiji goshawk and the Fiji bar-winged rail, which are threatened with extinction

Top: The collared lory (*Phygis solitarius*) is one of Fiji's parrot species.
Bottom: Banded iguanas (*Brachylophus fasciatus*) live in the temperate forests of the Fiji archipelago.

or may already be extinct. Red-tailed nightingales and Indian myna were introduced to Fiji in 1890 in order to combat coconut pests, but they have proliferated considerably and are now considered to be pests in their own right because of their noise and numbers.

Our South Seas route takes us through the western part of the Polynesian islands, starting out in Viti Levu, Fiji's main island, site of the capital, Suva. Via Vanua Levu (Fiji), we travel eastward to Tonga and then continue to the north. After around 2,300 km (1,430 miles), our journey ends in Samoa.

1 Suva (Viti Levu) Its population of around 150,000 inhabitants makes Suva the largest city in the South Pacific. It has been Fiji's capital since 1877, and it is also home to the University of the South Pacific, which is jointly maintained by eleven Pacific island states. From Suva's central market, head south on foot to a road junction known as The Triangle. This marks the beginning of Victoria Parade, Suva's main street. At its southern end, you will find the Fiji Museum, which houses a large collection of Fijian historical artefacts.

2 Colo-i-Suva Forestry Reserve (Viti Levu) Leave Suva on the northbound Princess Road; after about 12 km (8 miles), you will reach this small rainforest reserve. Its altitude (120–200 m/ 400–650 ft above sea level) makes it a refreshingly cool spot. Further to the north, our route passes the Tomaniivi

range, Fiji's highest mountains. At Rakiraki, you reach Viti Levu's northernmost point. Here, the road heads west, arriving after another 50 km (31 miles) at Latuoka, the island's second largest town.

3 Koroyanitu National Heritage Park (Viti Levu) This nature and culture park in the Koroyanitu mountain range behind Latuoka is accessible via a number of hiking trails. Local guides can take you to the mountain gardens of this wild, rocky landscape where once bloody tribal feuds were fought. The way to the park is not signposted and is relatively hard to find, so it is advisable to book a guided tour from Latuoka. Back in town, it is only 20 km (12 miles) to Nadi on the southbound island road.

4 Nadi (Viti Levu) Located in the drier western part of the

Travel information

Route profile
Length: approx. 2,300 km/ 1,430 miles (excluding detours)
Duration: min. 3 weeks
Start: Suva (Fidschi)
End: Aganoa Beach (Samoa)
Itinerary (main locations): Suva, Savusavu, Nuku'alofa, Vava'u, Apia

Travel information
Some roads may become impassable after heavy rains. A national or international driving licence is required. On Fiji and Tonga, you drive on the left, on Samoa on the right. Cargo boats and

passenger ships are the islander's main method of transport and are relatively cheap. Boats also go to some of the more remote islands on a regular basis.

Tourist information
Fiji:
www.bulafiji.com

Tonga:
www.tongaholiday.com
www.vacations.tvb.gov.to

Samoa:
www.visitsamoa.ws

Life on the reef

The magnificent shapes and hues of diverse marine life are one of the key attractions of the Pacific islands. Most impressive are the countless coral reefs that provide a habitat for a huge variety of species and represent the most complex ecosystem on earth. The tropical rainforests come a close second.

Among the many reef dwellers are turtles, rays, sharks, swordfish, and tuna. Snorkeling and diving give splendid opportunities for observing the sheer size and beauty of these coral gardens and their astonishing

Red lionfish are not at all shy but they are venomous.

biodiversity. Admire the intricate patterns of the many fish, including doctor fish, triangle butterflies, angel fish, parrotfish, clownfish, cuttlefish, pipefish, sweetlips, trigger fish, and moray eels. You may also see sea urchins and starfish, seashells, snails, octopuses, sea anemones, and punkfish. Last but by no means least, feast your eyes on the coral. Larger fish that you may encounter close to the coast include rays and some harmless reef sharks. Some sea creatures, however, may sting; these include coelenterates such as some corals, sea anemones, and jellyfish, as well as some cone shells, sea urchins, and starfish.

⑤ Sigatoka Sand Dunes National Park (Viti Levu) Travel a further 35 km (22 miles) along Viti Levu's southern coastline, known as the Coral Coast, to the charming town of Sigatoka, on the shores of a river of the same name. Just outside Sigatoka are some giant sand dunes, not immediately recognizable as such because they are covered in grass. The area, which is also of archeological significance, reaches right down to the coast and became the island's first National Park in 1989. After around 100 km (62 miles), the Queen's Road ends in Suva. From here, there are regular ferries to Vanua Levu.

⑥ Savusavu (Vanua Levu) Without doubt, Vanua Levu's second largest town is one of the

1 The clear waters off Fiji's beaches are a wonderful way to discover the underwater world of the South Seas.

2 Fish sellers are a common sight offering their wares on many beaches on the Fiji Islands.

3 Viti Levu is Fiji's main island. Its mountainous interior with steep volcanic slopes and its narrow coastal stretches are typical of many islands in the group.

4 Many islands in Fiji are volcanic in origin. They are often protected by offshore coral reefs.

5 Vanua Levu is Fiji's second largest island. It is sparsely populated and its natural delights remain almost unspoilt.

island, Nadi is close to Fiji's main international airport, through which the majority of visitors arrive. The town has a population of around 30,000, with a large Indian presence, hence the predominance of Indian markets and restaurants. Nadi is also the starting point of the Queen's

Road, the coastal road back to Suva that takes you through some extremely varied scenery. About 35 km (22 miles) south of Nadi, the small Maro Road takes you to one of the most beautiful beaches of the island. Recently, Natadola Beach has become a popular surfing spot.

The volcanic island of Tofua

Covering 56 sq km (22 sq miles), Tofua is the largest island in the Tongan archipelago of Ha'apai. The Lofia volcano at its center is 500 m (1,640 ft) high and visible from great distances. Since it is an active volcano, a cloud of

The volcanic island of Tofua was the scene of the famous mutiny by the crew of the *Bounty*.

smoke constantly rises from it. Tofua's caldera (a large, circular depression at the summit of the volcano) is 4 km (2½ miles) across and the crater lake is 230 m (755 ft) deep. It made history in 1789, when mutinous sailors on the *Bounty*, among them Fletcher Christian, abandoned William Bligh, their captain, and a number of crew members in a small boat in the waters just off the island.

most attractive spots in Fiji. This small town, situated on the beautiful Savusavu Bay, has around five thousand inhabitants. Savusavu is famous for its hot springs, of which there are more than twenty on this island. From here, it's 150 km (93 miles) by boat to Fiji's third largest island, Taveuni.

❼ Bouma National Park, Taveuni Because of its luxuriant vegetation, Taveuni is also known as the Garden Island. Its mountain ranges, which reach altitudes of up to 1,000 m (3,280 ft), are covered in jungle-like rainforests. In addition, there are coconut plantations that reach all the way down to sea level. Bouma National Park has picturesque waterfalls, some of them cascading from heights of up to 24 m (78 ft). Heading south-eastward and crossing the international dateline, you will reach the adjacent island state of Tonga.

❽ Nuku'alofa (Tongatapu) In Tonga's early history, the "place of love" (as Nuku'alofa, Tonga's capital, literally translates) was a fortified settlement from which Tongan kings ruled the surrounding islands. These days, the town still looks like a 19th-century colonial settlement, with largely wooden buildings. The

principal landmark is the Royal Palace, built in 1867 from prefabricated wooden elements made in New Zealand. Nuku'alofa makes an ideal starting point for a tour around Tongatapu. The coastal road takes you to the most attractive beaches and key sights of Tonga's main island.

❾ Ha'amonga Trilithon (Tongatapu) This massive stone archway stands at roughly 32 km (20 miles) from the capital, near Niutoua and at Tongatapu's most northerly point. Legend has it that the Polynesian demi-god

Maui carried this monument on his shoulders all the way to Tonga from the island of Wallis. This also explains the name of the trilithon, known as Ha'amonga'a Maui (Maui's burden). It consists of three huge rectangular stones, weighing more than 110 tonnes (100 tons) in total. It is thought that it served as a solar calendar for astronomical calculations. On 21 June, the shortest day of the year in the southern hemisphere, the sunrise is in direct alignment with the trilithon. Our route now takes you past the Haveluliku dripstone caves and

the Tongan Wildlife Centre (featuring the Aviary and Botanical Gardens) to Houma in the west of Tongatapu.

❿ Houma (Tongatapu) Along the rocky coast of Houma with its terraced slopes, sea spray is forced through hundreds of rock holes, spouting up to 20 m (66 ft) in the air. When viewed at high tide in particular, it soon becomes clear why in Tonga these blowholes are called Mapu'a a Vaca (King's Pipes). The high pressure generated by the water makes a truly

3

4

shoreline. They were created by a series of eruptions from Mount Matavanu (433 m/1,421 ft) that took place between 1905 and 1911. Several legends recount how the lava flow miraculously divided and then rejoined around the grave of a Samoan nun. This "virgin's grave" is still visible at the base of a rectangular depression in the lava flow. The coastal road takes you back to Salelologa, from where you can take the ferry to the island of 'Upolu, arriving after 45 km (28 miles) at Apia, capital of this island state.

(continued p.242)

1 The Vava'u islands, Tonga's most beautiful island group, are breathtaking, even when viewed from the air. The thirteen inhabited islands and twenty-one uninhabited islands are a paradise for swimmers and divers.

2 The scenic attractions of the Vava'u islands include their rocky coastline with its many caves.

3 Savai'i boasts wonderful waterfalls, including Mu Pagoa, and lava fields from nearby volcanoes.

4 Savai'i also has the most amazing blowholes. When high waves crash against the shoreline, water is forced through holes in the rock and spurts skyward like a fountain.

deafening noise. After 15 km (9 miles) east on the coastal road, you make your way back to the capital of Nuku'aluofa, where you can catch a ferry to the Vava'u islands, about 275 km (170 miles) away.

11 Vava'u islands The Vava'u group consists of thirteen inhabited islands and twenty-one uninhabited ones, all of them densely forested. Extensive coconut and vanilla plantations blanket the hills of Vava'u, the main island, which covers an area 90 sq km (35 sq miles) in size. The

main town of Neiafu with its numerous colonial wooden buildings is Tonga's second largest settlement, with a population of five thousand. A walk up Mount Talau (Mo'unga), 131 m (430 ft) high, offers the best views of Neiafu's port and the surrounding islands. From here, you can also see the island of Pangaimotu, which is some 9 sq km (3½ sq miles) in size.

Around 750 km (465 miles) to the north of the Vava'u islands lies the island state of Samoa; its largest island is Savai'i, formed from a massive volcano.

12 Mu Pagoa Falls (Savai'i) The ferries dock at Salelologa, and it is not far from the airport, making it an ideal starting point for a tour around the island. Since the interior of Savai'i is inaccessible, the best way to see the island is along the coastal road. Around 10 km (6 miles) west of the town, you reach the prehistoric Pulemelei pyramid near Vailoa. This large stone mound, some 61 m (200 ft) in diameter and 50 m (164 ft) wide, reaches a height of 12 m (39½ ft). You can then visit the nearby Mu Pagoa waterfalls and their idyllic natural pool.

13 Taga (Savai'i) Near Taga, about 25 km (16 miles) farther west along the coastal road, you will encounter more blowholes, where sea is forced through narrow openings in the coral rocks and spurts upward like a fountain. These blowholes really are a spectacular sight, especially at high tide and in high winds. The coastal area is a popular surfing spot, in particular between May and October.

14 Safotu (Savai'i) The island's north coast is notable for its huge lava fields that reach down to the

Most South Sea islands are surrounded by fringing or barrier reefs, lying respectively just a few yards from the coast or at several miles offshore.

... and yellow leaf corals shown above. When stimulated, individual corals light up like fluorescent lamps. Corals can live at depths of 10–40 m (33–130 ft), but they grow best at around 10 m (33 ft) below the surface. They need clear water at a temperature of 27°C (80° F) in order to survive.

1

2

3

Excursion

American Samoa

This US outpost in the South Pacific comprises five main islands of volcanic origin and two low coral atolls. Rainforests cover more than two-thirds of the land mass. One of

Rugged rock faces are typical of the southern coast of Tutuila. Its northern coast is even more inhospitable.

the attractions of American Samoa is the town of Pago Pago, located on Tutuila at the base of Mount Pioa. Due to the mountain winds, the bay here receives up to 7000 mm (270 in) of rainfall per year.

⑮ **Apia ('Upolu)** Around a quarter of the Samoan population lives in the state capital on 'Upolu's northern coast. Apia is made up of several individual villages. You can admire some typical wooden buildings dating from colonial times, such as the Palace of Justice and the Congregational Christian Church. Samoa was a German colony from 1900 to 1914, when New Zealand took administrative control until independence in January 1962. A pyramid-shaped monument on the Mulunu'u peninsula marks the spot where the colony was declared in 1900. South of the island, along Falealili Road you will reach the

estate of Robert Louis Stevenson, author of *Treasure Island*. The summit of Mount Vaea (475 m/ 1,558 ft) provides a splendid view over the island's north coast. From Apia, you can take an excursion to American Samoa (see panel, left).

⑯ **Sopoaga Falls ('Upolu)** All island tours start in Apia and travel around 'Upolu in a clockwise direction. First up are the beaches beloved by surfers on account of their wonderful high waves. At Falefa, the road heads into the interior of the island and to the Lemafa Pass. This takes you to the Sopoaga Falls, located in the midst of magnifi-

cent tropical vegetation. Following the southern coastal road to the west, you then have to take a track running north of the waterfalls, if you want to make your way to Siuniu. This track is suitable for all-terrain vehicles only. One picturesque village follows another all along the south coast.

⑰ **Aganoa Beach ('Upolu)** The southern coast of 'Upolu is noted for its immaculate beaches where you can enjoy a swim and a chance to relax. This is also where the Samoan National Park of O Le Pupu Pu'e is located. A walk on the O Le Pupu Trail gives an excellent overview of the vari-

ety of local flora. The main road takes you back to the north coast and to Apia, the capital.

1 The beaches of Savai'i, Samoa's largest island, are fringed with palm trees. Its mountainous interior is mostly inaccessible.

2 Between 'Upolu and Savai'i lie a number of tiny islands and islets; their beaches are protected by coral reefs.

3 'Upolu, Samoa's second largest island, has many idyllic beaches, and also some picturesque waterfalls, such as the Sapoaga Falls, in the interior.

Viti Levu This island boasts a huge range of different scenery: wild, volcanic mountain landscapes alternate with narrow coastal strips with beautiful sandy beaches.

Savai'i The attractions of Samoa's largest island include Mu Pagoa Falls, a climb up Mount Matavanu, and the blowholes with their dramatic seawater fountains.

'Upolu Samoa's second largest island is overlooked by gentle volcanic hills up to 1,000 m (3,200 ft) high. The beautiful beaches in its south are renowned.

Suva Since 1877, the South Pacific's largest town, with a population of 150,000, has been the capital of the Republic of Fiji. It is located on Viti Levu, the archipelago's main island. It is also of cultural significance as the University of the South Pacific is also based here. The Fiji Museum and the Orchid Island Cultural Centre will give you a good overview of Fiji's many traditions and cultural practices.

Tutuila This island forms part of American Samoa and has some truly impressive scenery to offer. Highlights include tropical rainforests with their luscious vegetation, white sandy beaches and the American Samoa National Park in the north. You can enjoy wonderful panoramic views from several places on this mountainous island.

Apia Samoa's capital, located in the north of 'Upolu, developed from a large number of small villages and has a population of 40,000. Numerous colonial-style wooden buildings have given way to more modern architecture. Among the architectural sights in this lively city are the Palace of Justice and the Congregational Christian Church. Robert Louis Stevenson spent the last years of his life here and is buried on Mount Vaea.

Sigatoka Sand Dunes National Park Sigatoka is a good starting point for a trip along the Sigatoka River, which is bordered by high, overgrown sand dunes. The region has been a National Park since 1989.

Vava'u The paradise islands of Vava'u, Tonga's most beautiful archipelago, according to some, comprises thirteen inhabited and twenty-one uninhabited islands. Extensive coconut and vanilla plantations flourish on the hills of its densely forested main island, which covers 90 sq km (35 sq miles).

Taveuni Fiji's "Garden Island" (covering 420 sq km/162 sq miles) is rich in luscious vegetation. At the heart of the island lies the crater lake of Tagimaucia.

The kingdom of Tonga These "Friendly Islands" (thanks to the friendly reception received by Captain Cook) form the only state in the South Pacific never to have been colonized. However, it is part of the British Commonwealth, and is governed by a dynasty of kings who have been in power since 1845. The current ruler is King George Tupou V, who will be officially crowned in 2008. His wooden palace, built in 1867, is located in Nuku'alofa, the capital.

Tongatapu In contrast to the archipelago's smaller islands, Tonga's larger ones, including Tongatapu, are coral islands that have surfaced from the sea and are sheltered by the coral-laden barrier reefs that form a protective barrier against the high waves. Apart from the ubiquitous coconut palms, agricultural crops account for most of the vegetation on the main island.

Route 18

Polynesia
From the Marquesas to the Cook Islands

Fabulous tales of the South Seas have been told since the first explorers returned with reports of a lost paradise rediscovered. The myth has been perpetuated by many a writer. Descriptions abound of hospitable islanders, endless sunshine, blue lagoons, white beaches, and a relaxed, carefree lifestyle.

Within the continental grouping known as Oceania, Polynesia ("many islands") is the largest group of small island nations, followed by Melanesia and Micronesia. Geologically, there are two very distinct types of island in the area: those of volcanic origin and flat coral ones. The existing islands are in fact simply the summits of mountains from a continent that was submerged in prehistoric times. Atolls represent a very distinct type of island, formed when a coral reef grows around a volcanic island that later subsides into the

ocean, leaving only a circular reef above sea level. A chain of sandbanks and overgrown islets then develops, known in the Polynesian language as *motus*. These islets enclose the lagoon of an atoll.

The climate in the southern Pacific is tropical and heavily influenced by the sea and the trade winds. There is every kind of island you could imagine, from flat, hot, and dry coral islands to humid, warm, mountainous, and densely forested ones. The trade winds blow endlessly from a south-easterly direction, bringing wel-

Traditional Polynesian flower garlands.

come freshness. Each island has its own ecosystem, with its particular combination of flora and fauna. Native species of plants and animals have developed on most islands, some of them unique to the environment in which they flourish.

Our route through the island world of eastern Polynesia starts on the Marquesas Islands, approximately 1,200 km (745 miles) north-east of Tahiti. These are the first islands in French Polynesia and were populated around 300 BC by Polynesians from Samoa and Tonga. In 1595 the Spaniard Alvaro de Mendana was the first European to discover them. He named them after the Marqués de Cañete, then viceroy of Peru.

Captain Cook arrived some two hundred years later and after him came the whale hunters and slave traders, bringing with them diseases that reduced the native

Volcanic and mountainous Huahine, one of the Society Islands, is 680 m (2,230 ft) high and wholly enclosed by a reef.

The main attraction of Bora-Bora is its lagoon with crystal-clear waters and fascinating marine life.

population from 50,000 to around 1,000. Today, around 7,000 people live on the islands, the largest of which are Nuku Hiva and Hiva Oa. Both have rocky, partly inaccessible coasts unprotected by reefs. The Marquesas are a popular stopover for yachts en route from the west coast of America to Tahiti.

From the Marquesas Islands, the route takes you south to the Society Islands and to Tahiti, the main island in the group. Tahiti epitomizes all our romantic dreams of the South Seas. The concept of an earthly paradise originated with the fabulous accounts of early explorers and was perpetuated by the Hollywood versions of *Mutiny on the* Bounty.

Today, Tahiti still has much to offer: picturesque volcanic islands with steep slopes, flat atolls with turquoise lagoons, wonderful scuba-diving sites, and sailing resorts, along with delightful Polynesian dance and song. It is a unique mix that puts French Polynesia in a different league to other island groups in the South Seas. Heading west, the route finally takes you to the Cook Islands, in effect a miniature version of Polynesia. The Cook Islands comprise eight larger volcanic islands and numerous small coral atolls; many of the *motus* (islets) are uninhabited. Rarotonga is the main island, and with its volcanic, jagged mountain tops it is a smaller version of Tahiti, whereas Aiutaki, a mixture of atoll and volcanic island, is more like Bora-Bora.

Cruising around the Polynesian islands is a dream journey, but most of these very beautiful islands have not remained untouched by the trappings of modern life. You will still find paradise, but it is a modern-day version.

Paul Gaugin's *Mountains of Tahiti* (1893) is now in the Minneapolis Institute of Art.

Most of our South Seas journey, from the Marquesas via the Tuamotu Archipelago and the Society Islands, takes us through the wide, seemingly endless island world of Polynesia. After some 3,500 km (2,175 miles) we at last reach the Cook Islands, which are linked with New Zealand.

1 Taiohae (Nuku Hiva) The largest island in the northern archipelago, Nuku Hiva, is also home to the Marquesas Island's administrative and economic center, Taiohae, a small town located at the foot of Mount Muake (864 m/2,835 ft). Nuku Hiva covers 330 sq km (127 sq miles) and has a population of 2,100, making it the largest island in the archipelago. The port in Taiohae Bay is protected by two small islands often used as a stopover by long-distance sailors. The church of Notre Dame, built in 1974 and now the seat of a Catholic archbishop, was constructed with multi-hued stones from six different islands in the Marquesas group. The sculptures inside this church demonstrate the great skill of woodcarvers from the archipelago. On a headland at the eastern end of Taiohae Bay, the remains of Fort Collets testify to the occupation of the island by French soldiers, following its annexation in 1842.

2 Hakaui-Tal (Nuku Hiva) After heading south-west along the coastal road from Taiohae for about 15 km (9 miles), you reach the Hakaui Valley, where you will see some traditional houses and ceremonial platforms. The valley is famous for its waterfall, which is 350 m (1,150 ft) high. The western side of the gorge is flanked by 1,000-m (3,200-ft) high vertical cliffs rising dramatically from the river edge. On the next part of our journey we head north, through the rocky, dry terrain of the western part of Nuku Hiva, passing the fertile Plateau de Toovii in the middle of the island.

3 Hatiheu Bay (Nuku Hiva) A number of important, partly restored cultural sites are located near Hatiheu Bay, on the northern coast of the island. This was a much-loved spot of the famous Scottish writer, Robert Louis Stevenson, and it is one of the prettiest parts of the Mar-

quesas Islands. On a basalt peak, some 300 m (984 ft) above the bay, stands a statue of the Virgin Mary. The coastal road now takes us along the eastern coast, which is rocky and inaccessible in places. Back in Taiohae, we take the ferry across to the island of Ua Pou, located around 50 km (31 miles) to the south.

4 Ua Pou The name means "two pillars" and refers to the spectacular backdrop of its dramatic sugarloaf mountain peaks, which look like church spires. Ua Pou inspired the Belgian songwriter Jacques Brel to compose one of his songs ("La Cathèdrale"). Its highest mountain is Oave at 1,232 m (4,042 ft) and the main town is Haka Hau in the north-west. The island has around 1,200 inhabitants. The most notable building in this pretty settlement, with its many flowering trees and shrubs, is the church of St Stephen, designed in traditional Polynesian style. It contains some very impressive wood carvings. The island's interior is covered in dense rainforests and is only partly accessible by road and path. In several valleys, there are abandoned settlements, which you can recognize by their over-

Travel information

Route profile
Length: 3,500 km/2,175 miles (including sea crossings)
Time needed: at least 4 weeks
Start: Nuku Hiva (Marquesas Islands)
End: Aitutaki (Cook Islands)
Itinerary (main locations):
Nuku Hiva, Bora-Bora, Tahiti, Rarotonga, Aitutaki

Traffic information
In French Polynesia, cars drive on the right and seatbelts are compulsory; on the Cook Islands cars drive on the left. The speed limit is 40 km/h

(25 mph) inside towns, 60 km/h (31 mph) outside towns and 80 km/h (50 mph) on multi-lane highways. There are regular sea and air connections between the larger islands.

Information
www.tahiti-tourisme.co.nz
www.tahiti-tourisme.com
www.tahitinow.com.au
www.cook-islands.com
http://au.franceguide.com/
what-to-do/overseas-france/
destinations

Tikis: ancestral images

Tikis are sculptures that depict the islanders' ancestors; they are usually carved in palm-wood, but sometimes also hewn from stone. In some South Seas cultures, ancestors are worshipped like gods. The term "tiki" comes from the Marquesas language; it is also used by the Maori, the Polynesian first settlers in New Zealand, and it has been suggested that "hei-tiki" are fertility charms representing the human embryo. Hei-tiki are often carved out of pounamu (greenstone or New Zealand nephrite jade) and worn on a string around the neck as talismans. After World War II, during which many American and Japanese soldiers encountered the Pacific way of life while serving in the South Sea islands, tiki became known in the West, first mainly on the west coast of the USA, and subsequently throughout the world. Following a general rise in interest in the South Seas and in

Tiki at the Gauguin Museum, Papeari, Tahiti.

exotic fashions, tiki became a term for all sorts of primitive likenesses of gods, and also for imitations, either produced in the Islands specifically for Western tourists or made by Western artists, sometimes bearing only a tenuous resemblance to South Seas art.

The acceptance of tikis in western popular culture was fostered by modern art when, in the early 20th century, artists like Pablo Picasso and Georges Braque discovered the art of so-called "primitive" peoples and Impressionism merged into Primitivism. The term gained world-wide currency in 1947 thanks to the Norwegian explorer Thor Heyerdahl, who journeyed from Ecuador to the Polynesian islands of Tuamotu by wooden raft in order to prove that the South Seas could have been settled from South America. The diary of his expedition, *Kon-Tiki*, was a world-wide bestseller.

grown "paepae" or house platforms. Very little has been excavated or restored in any way. The site of Te Menaha Takaoa in the Hakamoui Valley is worth visiting. This compound has many house and ceremonial platforms and is almost entirely overgrown. It covers a large area of a wild, romantic valley where coconut palms, giant banyan trees, mango, and pandanus grow. From Haka Hau, it is around 100 km (62 miles) by ferry to Atuona, the main town on the island of Hiva Oa.

5 Hiva Oa This island covers 320 sq km (124 sq miles), making it the largest and most important island in the southern Marquesas archipelago. It features a jagged mountain range that runs from south-west to north-east, some peaks being up to 1,100 m (3,600 ft) high. Hiva Ova has a population of 1,800 and the largest settlement is the village of Atuona on the southern coast. Its sheltered bay allows medium-sized vessels to call at the island, which became famous thanks to the French painter Paul Gauguin. On his second sojourn in the South Seas, the artist fled to Hiva Oa after unhappy experiences in

Tahiti. Following a long illness, he died on May 8, 1903 and now lies buried in Calvary Cemetery, in the north of Atuona.
Archeological digs have led to the reconstruction of an ancient village in the Upeke Valley, one of many excavation sites on Hiva Oa. Near the village of Puamau on the northern coast, amid tropical rainforest, is Marae Takii, the largest ceremonial site in the Marquesas Islands. Its eleven expressive stone figures stand on carefully constructed stepped stone platforms and are up to 2 m (6½ ft) high.

1 A typical jagged coastline at Nuku Hiva (Marquesas Islands).

2 The island of Hiva Oa (Marquesas Islands) has many ceremonial sites, including the MeAe Oipona temple.

3 On most of the islands in the Marquesas group (such as Nuku Hiva) you will find ancient ceremonial sites with tikis and a variety of sculptures.

4 The rocky shore of Hiva Oa is broken up by many small bays; it is partly inaccessible.

1

Marae Taputapuatea

Ancient Polynesian culture involved ceremonies that entailed sacrifices to the gods, such as food, animals, and sometimes even humans. These rites were enacted on stone platforms called *marae*. These sacred sites also documented the property rights and

Temple ruins on Raiatea, one of the Society Islands.

social standing of families. Today, the remains of these *marae* can mainly be found in eastern Polynesia, although they are generally no more than a few centuries old. The largest *marae* in Polynesia, Marae Taputapuatea, is located on the remote island of Raiatea, around 250 km (155 miles) to the north-east of Tahiti and around 100 km (62 miles) south of Bora-Bora.

6 Fatu Hiva This island covers an area of around 80 sq km (31 sq miles) and has a population of 500. Located around 60 km (37 miles) south of Hiva Oa, it is the southernmost island in the archipelago and receives more rain than any of the other islands in the Marquesas group. The explorer and archeologist Thor Heyerdahl was inspired to write his famous work, *Fatu Hiva*, describing his stay of several months here in the 1930s. The Hanavave Valley and the village of the same name in the Bay of Virgins are famous for their tropical beauty. Tapa, a type of cloth made from the bark of the paper mulberry tree, is today produced only on Fatu Hiva. From the Marquesas Islands, the northernmost archipelago in French Polynesia, it is around 1,000 km (620 miles) south-west to the Society Islands.

7 Rangiroa On the 1,000-km (620-mile) voyage from the Marquesas to the Society Islands, you will pass the Rangiroa atoll, which forms part of the Tuamotu Islands. Its lagoon, at just under 80 km (50 miles) long and up to 25 km (16 miles) wide, makes Rangiroa the world's largest fully enclosed atoll. There are three inhabited *motus* at the northern ring of the lagoon but

2

most of the population lives in the two pretty villages of Avatoru and Tiputa.

8 Bora-Bora The "Pearl of the Pacific" Bora-Bora is one of the most famous of the Society Islands. Its mountains rise in pinnacles above the deep blue and sunlit turquoise waters of the lagoon. The mountains are the remnants of a volcanic crater, as are the two hilly islets off the island's west coast. A long chain of sandy *motus* surrounds the reef to the north and the east. In World War II, Bora-Bora served as a supply station for the American navy and air force. Its military airport later served to open up the island to tourists. This beautiful South Sea island has often been used as a loca-

tion by film directors. With the exception of Anau to the east of the island, most villages and hotels are located along its western coast and on the southern tip of Bora-Bora. From Vaitape, you can take a challengingly steep hiking trail across forested slopes up to Mount Pahia, but beware as the starting point for this hike of several hours' duration is almost impossible to find without a guide.

9 Huahine Around 200 km (124 miles) south-east of Bora-Bora, and halfway to Tahiti, you will come to the island of Huahine, which, until now, has largely been spared the mixed blessings of mass tourism. Like most of the Society Islands, Huahine is completely enclosed

by a reef, encircling a lagoon as well as several *motus*. Excavations have unearthed the Society Islands' most ancient relics to date. In 1972, the ruins of an entire village were discovered north of Fare. These indicate that the island was populated around AD 650–850 by voyagers from the Marquesas Islands. The Maeva temples are most impressive in documenting the original cultural significance of the island. From Huahine, it is around 100 km (62 miles) to the southeast to Tahiti, the island that epitomizes everyone's idea of the South Seas.

10 Papeete (Tahiti) When Captain Cook landed on Tahiti, Papeete was nothing more than a sparsely populated, boggy

Exotic flowers

Flowers have always played a big part in the culture of the South Seas islands. They are given to guests when they arrive and when they leave. Flower arrangements and palm fronds are used for decoration at festivities. Polynesians use flowers to decorate their bodies and hair, and wear them around their necks for fragrance. Bright flowers generally signify hospitality and *joie de vivre*, and have thus become a trademark of the South Seas.

Most flowers used for decoration grow throughout the year on trees and shrubs, such as gardenias (Polynesian: *tiare*), hibiscus, or frangipani (*tipani*). Hibiscus, which probably

Top: The pink-and-white cup-shaped frangipani flowers have a powerful fragrance.
Bottom: Many scented plants such as hibiscus, heliconias and bird-of-paradise are native to the Society Islands.

and three-quarters of the island's population lives in and around the town.

The tourist information office at Boulevard Pomare is a good starting point for a tour of Papeete. This building is notable for its characteristic traditional Polynesian style, rarely found in Tahiti these days.

⑪ **Pointe Venus (Tahiti)** In 1769 Captain Cook chose the island's northernmost point, some 10 km (6 miles) east of Papeete, to carry out the astronomical observations that were the main reason for his journey to the Pacific. He wanted to observe and measure the transit of Venus through the sun, hoping that it would help calculate the earth's distance from the sun.

Pointe Venus is a popular excursion destination. To reach it, turn left off the main road in Mahina. Back on the island road, drive south past the Fa'arumai waterfalls and the fountains at the cliffs of Pointe d'Arahoho to

1 Bora-Bora lagoon: the quintessential South Seas fantasy.

2 Turquoise waters and tropical vegetation on Bora-Bora.

3 Huahine's beautiful scenery is easy to explore by bicycle or boat.

4 The Rangiroa atoll (Tuamotu Islands) is one of the world's largest.

5 The Kia Ora Village Hotel on Rangiroa is an oasis of tranquillity.

originated in China, and of which there are many hybrids in different shapes and shades, is among the best-known decorative plants of the tropics. Frangipani are easily recognized by their strong scent and striking white, yellow, pink, or red flowers. The red flame tree or flamboyant, an unmistakable part of the island scenery, flowers only from December through to March. It provides useful shade and is therefore planted along many of the roads and pathways. Heliconias and bird-of-paradise (*Strelitzia reginae*) are some of the other beautiful flowers of the South Seas.

stretch of land. Its sheltered bay contributed to its development and in 1842, the town became the capital of the French protectorate.

Today, houses and apartments increasingly encroach on the surrounding hills. Papeete is both the economical and political center of French Polynesia,

Polynesian dance festivals

Above all, dance is an expression of the Polynesian way of life and the joy of living. As legs and hips twirl, hands and faces tell entire stories. They are all variations on a theme: gods and legends, Tane and Wahine (Man and Woman), love, separation, longing, flowers and birds, voyages, fishing, and adventures, as well as stars, wind, and waves. Both men and women dance in groups, either together or taking turns. The dancers form lines, each dancing individually but with every man and woman moving in perfect harmony with everyone else. The women's basic movement is a rhythmical swaying of the hips, the men's a scissor-like opening and closing of the knees. Upper bodies hardly move, arms and hands make gesture-like movements.

Top: Polynesian dancers tell a story with their body language.
Bottom: Fire dancers on Moorea.

The obvious sexual connotations of many dances led missionaries to banish them from Polynesian life. Only in the last few decades have they been revived, thanks partly to tourism. The art of dancing is taken very seriously, mainly on the Cook Islands and in French Polynesia, and is much more than a tourist magnet. Children learn basic dance movements at school and there are nationwide contests to find the best groups and individual dancers.

1

reach Taravao, and from there the Tahiti Iti peninsula.

12 Tahiti Iti (Tahiti) This peninsula is linked to the main island via a very narrow stretch of land and has less remarkable mountains than its bigger sister, but boasts some impressive scenery. The Plateau de Taravo is one of the most beautiful viewpoints. To the east, a small road winds its way up to the plateau from Afaahiti through farmland and scrub. Fresh mountain air and a fantastic view of Tahiti Nui await visitors, as well as magnificent gardens and picturesque villages along the road to the remote area of Vairao. Just before you reach the village from the north, you'll see a large footprint on the reef, which, according to legend, was left by the Polynesian demi-god Maui.
In the south-east of the peninsula, the cliffs of Te-Pari rise dramatically from the water and are considered the highlight of the local scenery.

13 Papeari (Tahiti) From Taravao, the coastal road takes us back towards Papeete. The area around Papeari is particularly attractive due to its vibrant gar-

2

dens and the many fruit and vegetable stalls lining the road. Back in Papeete, you take a ferry to Moorea, only 40 km (25 miles) to the north-west.

14 Moorea The jagged mountain range and the deep, picturesque bays to the north make the scenery of this island particu-

larly attractive. Mount Rotui (900 m/2,953 ft) sits on the peninsula separating the two bays. Its proximity to Papeete makes Moorea a popular tourist destination alongside Tahiti and Bora-Bora. Tourists mainly visit Paopao in Cook's Bay and the north-west coast with its choice of sandy beaches.

White milestones shaped like the outline of Moorea itself indicate the sealed road around the island, which is 60 km (37 miles) long. Halfway between Temae and Cook's Bay, near Maharapa, is Maison Blanche. Located at the foot of verdant hills, this well-maintained, colonial-style building from the early 20th

Paul Gauguin arrived in Tahiti on June 9, 1891, at a time when Polynesian culture had already vanished almost entirely. In Papeete in particular, the capital of the French colony, life ticked on just as it would in any small town in Europe. Gauguin had set off in search of the "noble savage" but instead found men decorously wrapped in loincloths while women wore the frilly dresses introduced by the missionaries.

So Gauguin soon decided to move to the country. In Mataiea on Tahiti's southern coast he found a home and also the company of a Tahitian woman. But even here, little Polynesian culture remained.

Paul Gauguin: *Ea Haere ia Oe*, Where are you going? (1893).

After two years, financial problems and poor health forced Gauguin to return to Paris. His last European years (1893–1895) convinced him that his place was no longer in the Old World, so he boarded another ship to Tahiti. In order to escape the vagaries of life in the colonies, he decided in 1901 to relocate to the mythical Marquesas Islands. His time on Hiva Oa, however, was anything but paradisiacal. Worn out by disease, he managed to create some outstanding works of art before, alone and bitter, he died on May 8, 1903.

nets laid out to dry underline the laid-back, idyllic atmosphere.

15 Tetiaroa This atoll, located around 40 km (25 miles) east of Moorea, comprises thirteen *motus*, the largest of which is 3.2 km (2 miles) long. Tetiaroa used to be a summer retreat for the royal family of Pomare. On the Rimatuu *motu*, a giant tuu tree still marks the royal picnic spot. The tree is so large that it creates a patch of shade 1 ha (2½ acres) wide. Female members of noble families were brought here and, according to Polynesian tradition, fattened up before their weddings.

16 Manuae This is the most westerly island of the Society Islands group also known as the Leeward Islands ("islands under the wind"). Manuae is located 550 km (342 miles) west of Tahiti and 350 km (217 miles) west of Bora-Bora. The atoll measures some 11 km (7 miles) across, and its area of dry land is under 4 sq km (1½ sq miles). If you want to visit Manuae, you need to have your own boat or charter one. These days the atoll is not inhabited year-round, but fishermen from Raiatea call here on a regu-

lar basis. There are many species of turtle on Manuae that return to the beaches every year to lay their eggs.

17 Motu One This atoll, also called Bellinghausen, is located 150 km (93 miles) north of Manuae. The German explorer Otto von Kotzebue named the atoll in memory of the Russian explorer Fabian Gottlieb von Bellinghausen. It consists of four islands with an area of 2.3 sq km (0.9 sq miles) and makes a good starting point for exploring the underwater world of the South Seas.

18 Rarotonga From the western group of the Society Islands to the main island of the Cook (continued p.254)

1 Moorea's serene bays set against a jagged backdrop are a popular stopover point for ocean-going yachts.

2 Moorea's interior is wild and mountainous, but its bays are peaceful and quiet.

3 Tahiti: On the way from Papeari to Papeete, it is worth visiting Vaipahi Gardens, which has tropical plants and a small waterfall.

century was owned by a plantation farmer. Such farmers used to make a fortune from growing vanilla. Past the hotels and restaurants on the eastern shore of Cook's Bay, you will come to Paopao, situated at the end of the bay. Further inland is a fertile plain with fields of taro, tapioca, and pineapple. The road then

makes a few hairpin bends on the way up to the Belvedere viewpoint, Moorea's most visited panoramic spot. About 3 km (2 miles) south of Hauru, you will reach Tiki Théâtre-Village, a reconstructed Polynesian village. Further along the southern and eastern coast, small villages, tropical gardens, and fishing

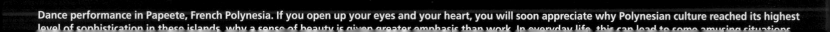

Dance performance in Papeete, French Polynesia. If you open up your eyes and your heart, you will soon appreciate why Polynesian culture reached its highest level of sophistication in these islands, why a sense of beauty is given greater emphasis than work. In everyday life, this can lead to some amusing situations.

when, for example, a young Tahitian spontaneously stops delivering breakfasts to the guest bungalows in a honeymoon resort because he is so enthralled by

Traditional fishing

Alongside tourism, fishing is one of the South Seas islands' most important economies. For millennia the fish-laden waters have contributed to the islanders' diet. Even now, traditional fishing methods are used. For

Top: Tahitian fish traps.
Bottom: Parrot fish in the market at Papeete.

example, in the lagoons, intricate canal systems weighed down by stones are created, so that fish cannot find their way out. Such fish traps have been constructed for centuries.

Islands is a distance of 1,000 km (620 miles). The fertile narrow coastal strip of Rarotonga ("the island of flowers") is planted with many different kinds of tropical crops, with the result that it looks like a large garden. The steep mountains in the interior are covered in dense vegetation. There are two main roads on the island: you can circle it on a sealed coastal road, around 32 km (20 miles) long, or take an inland route along a road, built more than a thousand years ago and hewn directly from the coral rock. Along the latter, you will find remains of several *marae*, sacred places destroyed when the island was Christianized.

The lagoon near the picturesque village of Titikaveka offers some excellent snorkeling opportunities. Muri Beach is the island's most beautiful beach with some spectacular views of the lagoon and its *motus*. Some of the Polynesian stone buildings on the island are up to 800 years old, the most sacred places being the *marae* of Arai-te-Tonga. To this day, the Ariki, the highest-ranking local chieftains, are enthroned on this *marae*.

⑲ Aitutaki This island lies 225 km (140 miles) north of Rarotonga. Aiutaki is surrounded by what many consider to be the Pacific's most beautiful lagoon and has some wonderful white beaches on the twelve uninhabited *motus* in the east and south. There are many activities to choose from when staying on Aitutaki: boat trips to the

motus, reef hikes, a bicycle tour around the island, which is around 7 km (4½ miles) long, or a walk up Mount Maungapu, 124 m (407 ft) high.

1 A key factor in the abundant vegetation on the Cook Islands is the high average temperature of 26°C (79°F); even in winter the temperature rarely drops below 22°C (72°F).

2 The Cook Islands comprise eight larger volcanic islands and numerous small coral atolls; many *motus* (islets) are uninhabited.

Nuku Hiva The largest of the volcanic Marquesas Islands (330 sq km/127 sq miles) has around 2,100 inhabitants. The highest mountain on the island is Mount Muake (864 m/2,835 ft).

Hiva Oa This mountainous island in the Marquesas is famous for its sacred sites. Here, the stone temple of MeAe Oipona, with tikis. Painter Paul Gauguin died in Atuona on Hiva Oa.

Fatu Hiva With its densely overgrown rainforests and abundant vegetation, Fatu Hiva in the south of the archipelago is the wettest of the Marquesas Islands.

Society Islands The majority of the population of French Polynesia lives on this group of islands. The islands and islets are mostly of volcanic origin. The turquoise lagoons are wonderful for diving. The Society Islands are divided into the Windward Islands ("islands of the wind") and the Leeward Islands ("islands under the wind"). The capital, Papeete, is located on Tahiti, the main island. The islands and their diverse fauna and flora were first discovered and charted in 1768. Most of the population lives on the coastal strips of these volcanic islands. The climate is tropical and hot and also very humid.

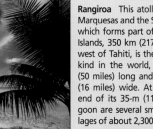

Rangiroa This atoll between the Marquesas and the Society Islands, which forms part of the Tuamotu Islands, 350 km (217 miles) northwest of Tahiti, is the largest of its kind in the world, being 80 km (50 miles) long and up to 25 km (16 miles) wide. At the northern end of its 35-m (115-ft) deep lagoon are several small fishing villages of about 2,300 inhabitants.

Rarotonga The main and most populous of the Cook Islands, Rarotonga is characterized by flat, fertile coastal plains. The interior, by contrast, is made up of steep mountains which are densely forested. The island is surrounded by a lagoon hemmed in by a reef. It is wonderful for snorkeling and diving, particularly near the village of Titikaveka.

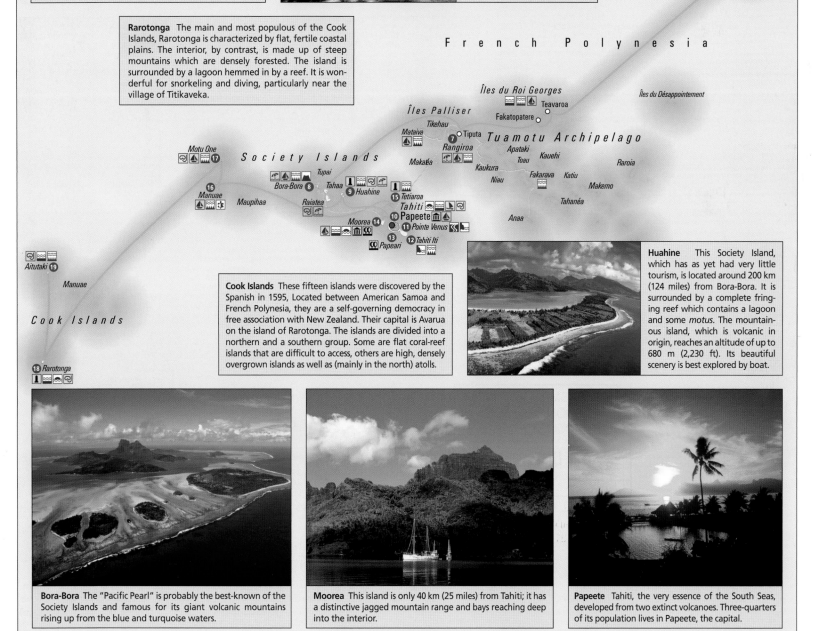

Cook Islands These fifteen islands were discovered by the Spanish in 1595, Located between American Samoa and French Polynesia, they are a self-governing democracy in free association with New Zealand. Their capital is Avarua on the island of Rarotonga. The islands are divided into a northern and a southern group. Some are flat coral-reef islands that are difficult to access, others are high, densely overgrown islands as well as (mainly in the north) atolls.

Huahine This Society Island, which has as yet had very little tourism, is located around 200 km (124 miles) from Bora-Bora. It is surrounded by a complete fringing reef which contains a lagoon and some *motus*. The mountainous island, which is volcanic in origin, reaches an altitude of up to 680 m (2,230 ft). Its beautiful scenery is best explored by boat.

Bora-Bora The "Pacific Pearl" is probably the best-known of the Society Islands and famous for its giant volcanic mountains rising up from the blue and turquoise waters.

Moorea This island is only 40 km (25 miles) from Tahiti; it has a distinctive jagged mountain range and bays reaching deep into the interior.

Papeete Tahiti, the very essence of the South Seas, developed from two extinct volcanoes. Three-quarters of its population lives in Papeete, the capital.

This edition is published on behalf of APA Publications GmbH & Co. Verlag KG, Singapore Branch, Singapore by Verlag Wolfgang Kunth GmbH & Co KG, Munich

Distributed in the United States by:

Langenscheidt Publishers, Inc.
36-36 33rd Street
Long Island City, NY 11106
Phone: 1-800-432-6277
www.Langenscheidt.com

ISBN 9-789812-58858-6

Original edition:
© 2007 Verlag Wolfgang Kunth GmbH & Co. KG, Munich
Königinstr. 11
80539 Munich
Ph: +49.89.45 80 20-0
Fax: +49.89.45 80 20-21
www.kunth-verlag.de

English edition:
Copyright © 2008 Verlag Wolfgang Kunth GmbH & Co. KG
© Cartography: GeoGraphic Publishers GmbH & Co. KG
Topographical Imaging MHM ® Copyright © Digital Wisdom, Inc.

Text: Gerhard Beer, Gerhard Bruschke, Christiane Gsänger, Thomas Jeier, Dr. Sebastian Kinder, Barbara Kreißl, Carlo Lauer, Michael Neumann, Peter Schröder, Dr. Heinz Vestner, Walter M. Weiss, Günther Wessel
Translation: JMS Books LLP (Jackie@moseleystrachan.com)

Printed in Slovakia

The information and facts presented in the book have been extensively researched and edited for accuracy. The publishers, authors, and editors, cannot, however, guarantee that all of the information in the book is entirely accurate or up to date at the time of publication. The publishers are grateful for any suggestions or corrections that would improve the content of this work.